1928

beyond craft:
the art fabric

beyond craft:
the art fabric

Mildred Constantine / Jack Lenor Larsen

VNR VAN NOSTRAND REINHOLD COMPANY
NEW YORK   CINCINNATI   TORONTO   LONDON   MELBOURNE

Van Nostrand Reinhold Company Regional Offices:
New York   Cincinnati   Chicago   Millbrae   Dallas

Van Nostrand Reinhold Company International Offices:
London   Toronto   Melbourne

Library of Congress Catalog Card Number 72-9706
ISBN 0-442-21634-3

Designed by Lorraine Hohman

Printed in Japan

Printed and bound by Toppan Printing Co. Ltd.,
Tokyo, Japan

Published by Van Nostrand Reinhold Company
A Division of Litton Educational Publishing, Inc.
450 West 33rd Street, New York, N.Y. 10001

Published simultaneously in Canada by
Van Nostrand Reinhold Limited

16 15 14 13 12 11 10 9 8 7 6 5 4 3 2 1

Frontispiece:
Sheila Hicks
L'EPOUSE PREFEREE OCCUPE SES NUITS (detail)   1972
See page 192 for complete piece.

Contents

introduction

The Art Fabric is one of the robust, vital arts of our time. Although the development of Art Fabrics is so recent and so varied that they defy classification into the accepted disciplines, it can be claimed with assurance that these are works of art. The artists who create with fiber have united creativity and intuition, principles and skills to form an aesthetic entity. They have molded and extended the meaning of their medium and transcended technique and materials; they have liberated their work from tradition and thus heightened their recognition by critics and public. The great works that have been produced in the fiber medium during the last decade have validated the whole movement. These achievements by a relatively small group of women and men of genius and talent have changed our visual concepts and comprehension. Their works have gained status throughout the world, and while this art form may be in search of nomenclature, it demands and deserves autonomy.

The Art Fabric shares with modern tapestry a common tradition, a common vocabulary, tools and materials. Both relate to modern painting, however differently. The modern tapestry is the result of methods and attitudes following a tradition of centuries, produced by artisans working from the cartoons of others. The brilliant colors and simple composition of the modern painter are merely substituted for the woven pictures of pageantry, allegory, and history of the past.

The Art Fabric is a construction, individually created by an artist. It may be woven *on* the loom or *free* of the loom or may be produced by knotting, knitting, crochet, or other techniques. An Art Fabric is conceived and created by one artist whose personal involvements and expressive potentials are integrated with his skillful use of techniques and chosen materials. The metamorphosis of the Art Fabric in recent years is parallel with that of other visual arts. They share the same artistic currents and cross-currents, employ technological ingenuity, and enjoy experimentation and manipulation of materials that have stimulated new concepts in all arts of the twentieth century.

In the Art Fabric there has been perhaps the strongest transformation. Today's artist who works with natural fibers or synthetic yarns uses his materials to produce works possessing form and space, with surface and mass interchangeable. His work clearly expresses the pure design qualities inherent in his technique, structure, processes, and materials, as well as his experience and his inspirations.

The rigid line distinguishing the fine and the so-called decorative arts has become uncertain and in fact seems to have disappeared. Painting is no longer limited to the application of pigment to canvas or wood; sculpture is no longer limited to stone or wood carving, modeling, or casting. The sculptor uses iron, steel, plastic; he welds and he blasts. Barbara Rose, the eminent art critic, recently said, "Such distinctions separating the 'minor' arts of photography, film, graphics, and the various crafts from the 'major' arts of architecture, painting, and sculpture are status distinctions imposed at the end of the Middle Ages when the guilds disappeared to be replaced by the Renaissance academies . . . these prejudicial distinctions continued until the present day. If we dispense with the distinction between the major and minor arts, and think in terms of quality alone, we see that the *quality* of American photography, film, graphics, crafts is at least as good as American paintings today and certainly better and more innovative than the collapsing sculptural tradition. . . But the minor arts are in an upsurge, as we rediscover the importance of craft, the human body, and the natural and man-made world around us." (*New York Magazine,* March 6, 1972)

The artists of the fiber medium have found new freedom—freedom from the loom, and, perhaps more important, or at least more universal, a transformation of purpose—the freedom to choose an aesthetic over a utilitarian need. This involves an enormous input of skill, discipline, even physical effort, but more importantly it involves the intensity with which the creative and aesthetic factors operate, which are basic to any work of art. Factors such as these become the only legislative authority by which these works are evaluated. The Art Fabric exists in a most protean state; its definition is neither rigid nor finite, but belongs to the rich and complex phenomenon that is art which goes beyond craft.

In the catalog for the 1972 exhibition of the work of Olga de Amaral, Galaor Carbonell, the eminent Colombian critic, wrote what is applicable to all these artists: ". . . do not think of weaving as a means whereby fabrics are made. Do not think of handicraft or industrial activities exercised in order to produce a useful object to be bought or sold. Do not think of a mechanical activity through which, in an unconscious fashion, things go on being done through inertia, nor . . . as the elaboration of luxurious or decorative objects.

"One of the most fallacious of the critical judgments of our culture has been that of classifying and establishing hierarchies based on the presence of basic materials and the technical methods applied to those materials . . . the majority of the public regard the work of Olga de Amaral as handicraft, which is appealing because it is made by hand and entails a great deal of work. For this public the work in question is handicraft because with threads, needles, and looms, it is only possible to weave. This attitude means categorically that weaving is the inevitable result of the presence of certain materials and techniques.

"Olga de Amaral makes weavings, but not because of the presence of materials and techniques, but because of the presence of complex and rich ideas which force her to the act of weaving. In short, she seeks in the threads, needles, and looms the necessary elements with which to make her statement. . . . She weaves because, like living organisms, or man's ideas, she must. The difference between the weaving of Olga de Amaral and those of craftsmen consists in the different localization of the idea of weaving in each of the two concepts. In handicrafts, weaving is the inevitable result of the use of hands, tools, and materials. But, for Olga de Amaral, the hands, tools, and materials are subjected to the will of the weaver, a concept which acts as a dynamic force completing the action of the hands."

Eloquently yet directly stated, these ruminations are akin to those of critics and scholars who have long recognized that the quality of art lies in concept and quality of insight, not in materials or tools.

Art Fabrics can be most readily divided into several categories. The most obvious one is that which completely dominated the scene during the 1960s—wall hangings, a category that has considerable range. These are objects with presence both in size—often they are monumental—and character.

A wall hanging is meant to be hung in front of a supporting wall; a work conceived for non-utilitarian purposes, it extends the formal possibilities of fabric. Hangings such as those of Scholten (p. 247) have a thickness and depth of weave, achieving a three-dimensional relief quality; others, such as those of Landis (p. 204), involve a two-dimensionality, with perhaps a visual play of light and surface detail to articulate the forms.

Wall hangings are also walls that exist independently in space—fully in the round—free-hanging or two-sided like the woven walls of Olga de Amaral (p. 98), Moik Schiele (p. 244), and Rousseau-Vermette. Or, like bricks, they may replace or cover walls, as do the highly original thread constructions of Sheila Hicks (p. 182). In each of these areas the requirements of being more or less impervious to the ravages of handling and soil are elementary.

For most of their time span, both Western and Eastern art have attempted detachment. Both the picture plane in painting and the proscenium arch in theater were boundaries to separate art from reality. By mid-twentieth century this precept was rapidly losing ground. The old ideal of appealing to the refinements of a gentle audience seems less valid than the solid contact of gut reaction.

The artists of American popular culture have created environments using as subject matter identifiable images in unfamiliar contexts, transformed by scale, such as the work of Claes Oldenburg, or familiar scenes without narrative frozen in time, such as George Segal's *Drug Store.*

Frederick Kiesler developed sculpture and architectural models to embrace and surround the participants. John Cage in music, and the members of the Living Theater also thought in these terms. During the 1960s, about the same time environment entered the vocabulary of architecture and ecology, there developed, internationally and simultaneously, a keen awareness of the possibilities of environmental art. Although the concept has taken on several meanings, chief among them is the idea of the heightened emotional involvement of an art to be *in*—not to look *at*. In addition to such logical considerations, the environmental approach borders on mysticism and the surreal and is identified with bowers and lairs, the shrine and the womb. Although the environmental concept was early considered by weavers, and attempted by a number including Lenore Tawney, none was able to successfully realize this vision until Elsi Giaque showed *Spatial Elements* in Amsterdam and the startling exhibition of Magdalena Abakanowicz was presented in Sweden (p. 90).

In the cultures of the past, basketry, body coverings, masks of ritual and dance were woven in Africa; shirts, mantles, and dolls come from the ancient cultures of the Andes. Today, some of our artists are producing such conventional objects for unconventional purposes—for instance, the baskets of Ed Rossbach that are studies of pure research. These are not art, at least in the monumental sense, but purposefully abstract. So too are the *Ceremonial Blanket* by Geraldine Scalone, the body coverings by Debra Rapoport (p. 213), and the gigantic dolls by Barbara Shawcroft (p. 60).

A revolution in the last five decades has liberated the Art Fabric from the tapestry tradition. To understand the nature of the revolution and the evolution that followed it, to arrive at the present summit that the Art Fabric represents, we must consider the significance of particular earlier events, prophetic and searching.

While indeed there may be still other categories of Art Fabrics, in this book the authors are not concerned with works created with such decorative techniques as embroidery or appliqué or printing. The concern is for the structural and aesthetic characteristics of the Art Fabric as an art form.

Mariette Rousseau-Vermette
(Canadian, born 1926)
NUMBER 165   1967
8' x 26' turned 90°
tapestry
wool, brushed after weaving; red, yellow, black
Collection: Banque Canadienne Nationale,
Place d'Armes, Montreal (installed in Boardroom)

In filling her commissions for interior architecture, Rousseau-Vermette almost invariably treats her pieces as walls—not hangings against a wall. In this sense she adheres to the dictums of Jean Lurçat and Le Corbusier that Art Fabrics be murals, not "pictures." Her quiet architectonic image and the strong, structured color is appropriate to the sparsely furnished interior spaces her work visually dominates.

Frederick Kiesler
(American, born in Austria, 1892–1965)
GALAXY 1951
12' high; dimensions around base 13' x 11',
6'' x 10', 10'' x 7'
wood construction
Collection: Nelson Aldrich Rockefeller, New York

Elsi Giaque (Swiss, born 1900)
PURE SPATIAL ELEMENT 1968–69
with Kathi Wenger and Festi Ligerz
13' x 13' x 13'
silk and synthetic fibers; polychrome
Shown here as installed in
"Perspectief in Textiel,"
Stedelijk Museum, Amsterdam, 1969

Colored yarns are wrapped vertically and diagonally on metal frames. The images are tapestry-
woven on these sparse warps. The individual elements, hung in a three-dimensional composition,
create an enviroment into and around which one
can move. The overlapping planes of multicolored
transparency are cumulative in effect and extend
the space.

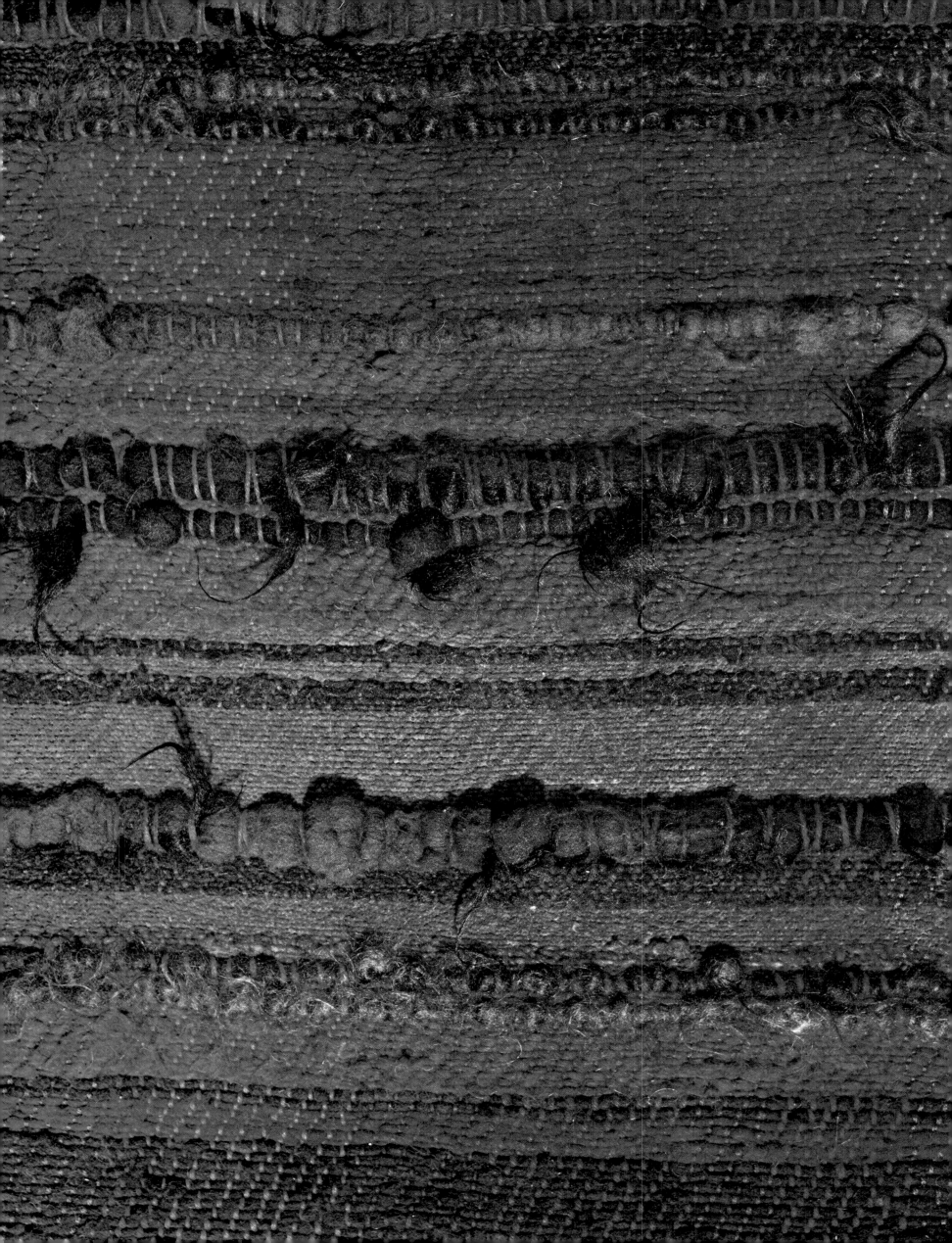

With accolades from some, derision and criticism from others, Thomas Paxton's Crystal Palace in London, an exposition hall entirely of iron and glass, celebrated the Industrial Age in the first Great International Exhibition (1851).

From most accounts, both the British exhibit and those of the other nations represented were the most appalling assemblage of taste, especially in the areas of crafts and industrial art. The outrage of English critics John Ruskin and Edward Burne-Jones was surely justified. On the continent the significance of this exhibition was perhaps best expressed by the reaction of German architect and theoretician, Gottfried Semper, writing in 1852. He demanded honesty of materials and genuineness of workmanship and the reunification of arts in building.

It would appear that in the field of textiles at this time the Industrial Revolution had made no essential contribution to the process of weaving but only to the amount produced and the speed of production. Aesthetic qualities were submerged by the ostentatious vulgarity that the manufacturers were feeding a new consumer class.

The disparity between the contents of the exhibition and the radical architectural qualities of the Crystal Palace itself gave great impetus to the Arts and Crafts movements in England and throughout Europe.

Among the artists and artisans the overwhelming energies of commercial power, the machine, and the stress of art as a career produced distrust of and discontent with the Industrial Age. William Morris, the English painter, poet, craftsman, lecturer, and militant pamphleteer, fought against standards lowered by cheap mass-produced goods and called for rebellion against a tyranny compounded of utilitarianism and dilettantism. (Arts and Crafts Circular Letter, published by Longmans & Company, London, 1898.) Morris was most clamorous in his demand for a unification of all the arts and crafts so as to bring about important reforms in architecture. Similarly, Arthur Mackmurdo, who founded the Century Guild in 1880–81, emphasized the indivisible unity of the arts and crafts, as did the Art Workers' Guild, established by Walter Crane and Lewis Day. The Arts and Crafts Exhibition Society, founded in 1888, brought a comprehensive program to the attention of a wide public by means of its exhibitions, lectures, and demonstrations.

Morris's theories, derived mostly from Ruskin, were both aesthetic and social. He blamed industry as a conditioner of life; he deplored the use of art for the few; he turned the attention of young painters and architects toward craft and design to enrich the everyday environment.

The importance of Morris to the generations that followed was not in his style, which tended toward nostalgic revivalism, but his insistent campaign for honesty

Geraldine Scalone (American)
TO J.L.L. (detail) 1969
9' x 5'
sateen weave
hand-spun wool and mohair; red, blue, and violet
Collection: Jack Lenor Larsen, New York

This work was woven as a ceremonial blanket—not a hanging or a bedcover, but an object and a medium of expression through the most abstract means of texture and color. Both are optimum. The texture is maximized by the great range in size and irregularity of the hand-spun yarns and rovings. The color of the dominant weft bands is given variety by an underlying warp stripe.

and simplicity. What he admired in Tudor masonry and timber work was a vigorous expression of materials and of construction, not plastered over with classic ornament. Its rustic simplicity befitted a hardworking, democratic society. Thus, while Morris may be best remembered for his revivalist ornamentation, he is most significant for stating the values for a pan-craft movement. In his furniture and the idealized cottages are the roots of his functionalism. He also served as a catalyst for the stylistic movement called Art Nouveau.

From the mid-1890s through 1905 occurred the germination and flowering of a unified style heralded all over the western world; a movement that encompassed all branches of artistic endeavor, from architecture to the minute details of daily life. This movement, known as *Art Nouveau* in England and *Modern Style* in France, *Stile Liberty* in Italy, *Jugendstil* in Germany and Austria, had already signified a general acceptance of the machine as a tool for the designer and this point of view became the liberating factor that set the stage for the developments of the twentieth century. The specific formal characteristics of this style were also not so influential as the theories underlying them, and both were to have strong effect on the Wiener Werkstätte; on all of Scandinavian art, architecture, and design, as well as on such American adherents as Louis Comfort Tiffany.

Although the artists admired the quality of such machines as locomotives and ships, most of their designs were not meant for machine production. When they were produced, as in the case of Hector Guimard's Paris *Metropolitain* entrance gate, the designer still used the tools of the craftsman.

The miracle of a new century was felt in many ways and the first decade of the twentieth century brought with it a whole new outlook on life. Among the intellectuals there was a continuing search for the new, a faith in progress and newness, an almost complete break with Victorian eclecticism. From the 1860s through the time of Art Nouveau, Japanese art had affected the individual styles of Western art. At the beginning of the twentieth century the search for the new opened minds and eyes to other non-European cultures as well, and these exotic influences were brought into the mainstream of artistic consciousness. The impact of African sculpture and objects brought in by adventurous dealers was inestimable in providing sources of new visual inspiration. These were readily accessible to the French artists and public in the ethnographic collections of such institutions as the Trocadéro. The effect of this introduction of African arts to the School of Paris is perhaps best exemplified by the work of Pablo Picasso—particularly in his famous *Les Demoiselles d'Avignon,* completed in 1907, which introduced structural innovations heralding the advent of Cubism.

The Fauves' radical departures in color and form also marked a complete break with the past. By 1910 Sigmund Freud had begun to make his world-shaking contributions in psychoanalysis. The reign of architecture as a social art was in full swing on the continent of Europe. It seemed impossible not to have a reconciliation between art and industry.

In *Pioneers of Modern Design* Nikolaus Pevsner wrote: "In 1907, Hermann Muthesius, then Superintendent of the Prussian Board of Trade for the Schools of Arts and Crafts, had delivered a public lecture in which, in a very outspoken manner, he warned German crafts and industries against continuing with the imitation of the hackneyed forms of bygone times . . . before the end of the year, a number of adventurous manufacturers together with some architects, artists, and writers, had made up their minds to found a new association called *Werkbund,* with the aim . . . of combining all efforts towards high quality in industrial work, and of forming a rallying point for all those who were able and willing to work for high quality."

Henry van de Velde, the Belgian architect, painter, and designer who was a participant in the founding of the Deutsche Werkbund, insisted that crafts were the great creative reservoir for the future—an idea that he carried with him into the Weimar School of Applied Art.

Pevsner said, further: "Morris had started the movement by reviving handicraft as an art worthy of the best men's effort; the pioneers of the turn of the century had gone farther by discovering the immense untried possibilities of machine art. The synthesis, in creation as well as in theory, is the work of Walter Gropius. . . At the end of 1914, he began preparing his plans for the reorganization of the Weimar Art School. . . The opening of the new school, combining an academy of art and a school of arts and crafts, took place in 1919. Its name was *Staatliches Bauhaus* and it was to become the paramount center of creative energy in Europe. It was at the same time a laboratory for handicraft and for standardization; a school and a workshop. It comprised, in an admirable community spirit, architects, master craftsmen, abstract painters, all working for a new spirit in building."

It is important in this context to read again the words of Walter Gropius in 1919 in the Bauhaus Proclamation: "Architects, painters, and sculptors, we must all turn to the crafts. Then there will be no 'professional art.' There is no essential difference between the artist and the craftsman; the artist is a craftsman raised to a higher power."

The first fabrics produced in the Bauhaus weaving workshop had been "pictorial weavings" or tapestries woven under the influence of painter Paul Klee. It was not long, however, before the architectural concepts of Gropius became pervasive. Emphasis was more and more on materials and construction. Color was neutralized so as to reflect architecture and machine art. Subject matter became first abstract, then concrete. In this spirit wall hangings of tremendous beauty were produced by, among others, Anni Albers, Otti Berger, and Gunta Stölzl. The same artists were encouraged to design for special commissions and to be involved in experiments for utilitarian fabrics. Gunta Stölzl, who was a student in the Bauhaus in Weimar from 1919 to 1925, became teacher and master of the weaving workshop at the Bauhaus in Dessau. She and other weavers at first put more stress on craftsmanship and intuitive aspects.

There was by no means complete agreement on the principles and practices of the weaving workshop in the Bauhaus. George Muche, when director of the workshop, emphasized the importance of grappling with the problem of mechanization. Decorative and even aesthetic function was all but dismissed, especially in the later years. The weaving workshop at the Bauhaus became active in exploring new synthetic materials such as cellophane and rayon. More than this, for both masters and

Otti Berger (German)
RUG woven at the Bauhaus, Dessau, about 1927
tapestry weave with unspun wool
Smyrna wool and hemp;
white, black, brilliant blues, red, yellow

The wavy relief was produced by laying handfuls of silky Smyrna wool into an open shed. The interstices are filled solidly with eccentric tapestry. At the selvage the tapestry element becomes a lively arcade.

The restraint and the palette of primary colors are peculiarly Bauhaus. The organic vigor of the handcraft expression is atypical: the Bauhaus workshop was at this time preoccupied with the formalized asymmetry of the International Style and with researches into new materials and textures for production techniques.

Gunta Stadler-Stölzl (German, born 1897)
COVER woven at the Bauhaus, Weimar, 1923
72" x 47"
tapestry with brocade
wool, cotton, silk, rayon; gray, white, and violet
Collection: Kunstgewerbemuseum, Basel

Here the machine aesthetic, new at the Bauhaus, is combined with a painterly composition. As the artist is executing her own work in an admittedly industrial age, the length of time given to execution has become an important factor. The three decorative devices here are all labor-saving: the stripes which "come free"; the brocade which is loom-controlled; and the tapestry which is limited to one join across the entire width. The contrast of dull and shiny textures caused by admixing fibers is certainly modern.

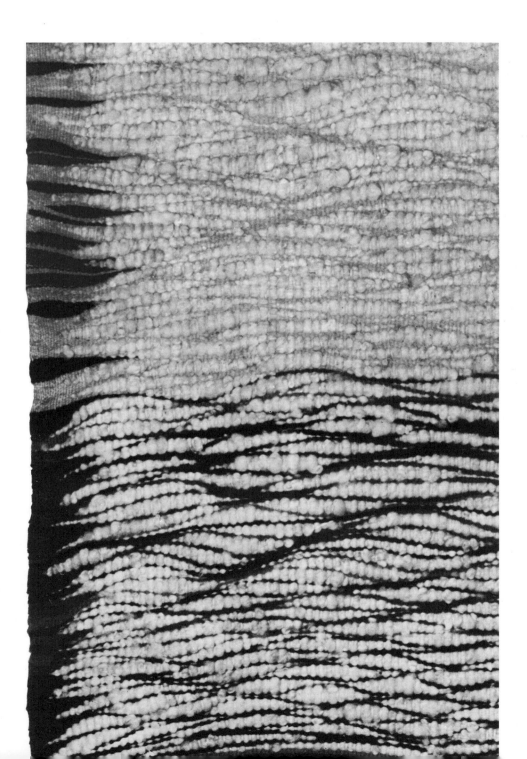

students, it became a laboratory for experimentation in the potentials of the machine to produce forthright, anonymous designs for a broadening market. The focus was toward probing the practical aspects of machine production but perhaps more importantly the stylistic dictums of a machine aesthetic.

When Bauhaus emphasis passed from fine art and handcraft to the social and technological requirements of twentieth-century architecture and industrial design, a new style was embraced. As ethical and intellectual commitments were made and new materials and processes embraced, visceral and emotional aspects diminished. However, the most basic element remained in the (now) glorified expression of materials and of structure in Bauhaus design. At least as influential as the work itself have been the well-structured philosophies stating the aims and limitations of modern fabric. Not only was the Bauhaus primary to the rediscovery of the importance of expressing texture, structure, and broken color and in finding new aspects of pattern with the vertical-horizontal format of woven cloth, but through the teaching and—more importantly—the writings of Anni Albers, Gunta Stölzl and others, the influence has been universal.

Writing in 1926 in the journal *Buch-und Webekunst,* Leipzig, No. 7, Gunta Stölzl said, ". . . woven fabric constitutes an aesthetic entity, a composition of form, color and material as a whole.

"Today in all fields of design there is a quest for law and order. Thus, we in the weaving workshop have also set ourselves the task of investigating the basic elements of our particular field. For example, while at the beginning of our Bauhaus work we started with image precepts—a fabric was, so to speak, a picture made of wool—today we know that a fabric is always an object of use and is predicated equally upon its end use and its origins.

"The factors affecting the production are:
   The loosely knit structure, which can only be made into a definite surface by
      the arrangement to which it is subjected
   A multiplicity of interlocking threads, which produce a "sculptured" surface
   The color, which is intensified or toned down by being glossy or dull
   The material, whose characteristics limit us in its use

"The fabric has to meet further requirements: It has to be a surface and always has to have the effect of a surface. This does not imply that elements of a static, dynamic, sculptured, functional, constructional, and spatial nature are excluded from consideration. These elements count, in as far as they are means of designing the surface and are subject to the laws of plane geometry. . .

"Since today mechanical weaving has not yet been developed to the point of incorporating all the possibilities of hand weaving, and since the developing creative person needs to know all these possibilities, we concern ourselves primarily with hand-loom weaving. Only work at the hand loom allows the kind of latitude for an idea to be developed. . ."

Anni Albers (American, born in Germany, 1899)
PICTORAL WEAVING   1959
32" x 18"
wool; natural, black, yellow, blue, and red
Collection: Mr. and Mrs. Ralph W. Bettelheim,
New York

Against a furrow of a rep-woven ground, Albers has achieved a lively arrangement of multicolored knots. The technique, and therefore the piece, is unique. The freedom is, for Albers, new found. Within the freedom are three controlling disciplines: the continuity of the woven technique and of materials; the similar size of the knots; and, as an integrating force, the use of the same colors in the wefts and the knots.

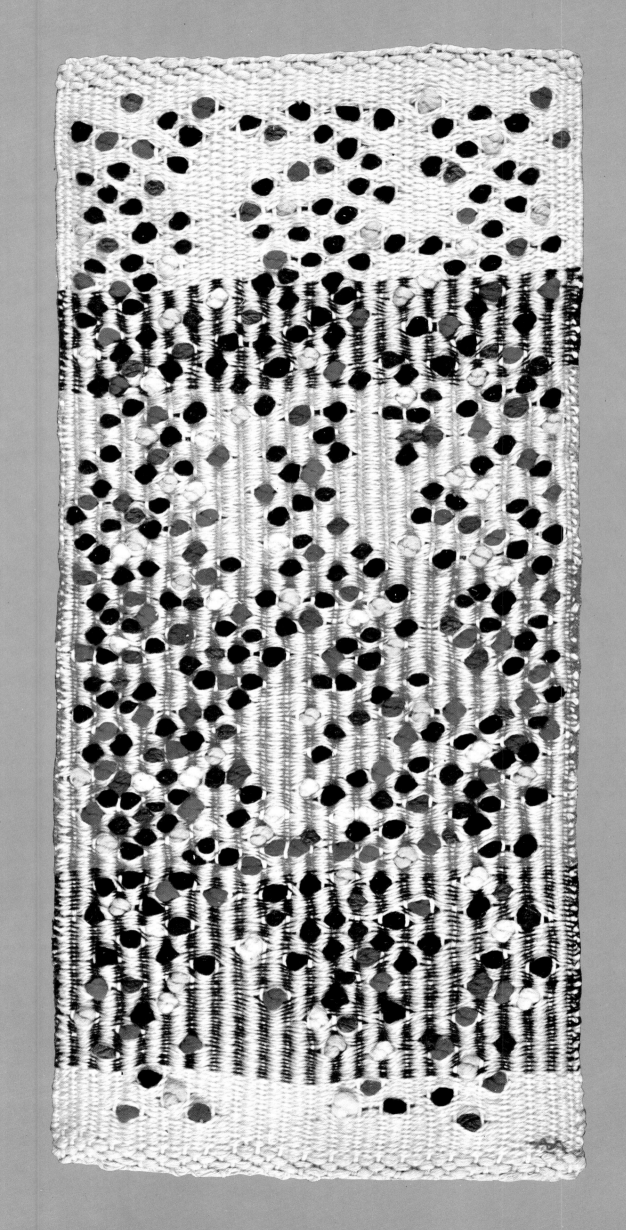

Anni Albers
WALLHANGING III 1964
(originally designed in 1927)
58″ x 48″
double weave
silk; black and white
Collection: The Museum of Modern Art, New York

This piece is typical of a series designed by Albers during the Bauhaus years. The problem she has set herself is to achieve the interest characteristic of a "pictorial weaving" but woven within the laws of the loom, so that labor-consuming free weaving would be eliminated or reduced to a minimum. Two factors are at play here: one, that in the accelerated pace of the post-industrial era time itself is a design element; two, that even within a structural system such as multiple-harness weaving there are underlying mysteries. The discovery and expression of these is a valid pursuit and an art form suitable for the period.

To a weaver the piece seems at first too impossibly complex not to employ either tapestry or a Jacquard attachment. Albers's solution was conditioned by using only black and white yarns. Because the cloth is unbalanced, with more warp yarns per inch than weft, areas of two shades of gray result.

On twelve harnesses she has arranged three pattern units in a (left to right) threading sequence of A, B, C, A, B, A, C, B, A, C, which allows for horizontal blocks 1, 2, 3, or 4 units wide. The bottom-to-top weaving sequence is 1, 2, 3, 4, 5, 2, 3, 4, 5, 2, 3, 6, 1, 2, 5. By multiplying the horizontal and vertical sequences, the maximum number of variables is achieved. Further variation occurs in the horizontal and vertical lines centered within the black and white squares.

This is a cerebral art predicated on a beauty existing within the discipline of hard, clean thought.

The piece was woven at the workshop of Gunta Stadler-Stölzl in Switzerland in 1964 from a small watercolor drawing (one of a large series) in the collection of The Museum of Modern Art, New York.

Anni Albers
LA LUZ I   1945
18¾″ x 31¼″
sateen weave with discontinuous brocade
linen and metal gimp; multicolor
Collection: Richard Lippold, New York

In major contrast to Wallhanging III, this small work is relatively free and organically random especially in the weft pattern sequence. The random pattern and the irregularity of the slubby yarns are exaggerated by occasional pattern change within the ground.

Unlike Wallhanging III, in which there was rigid adherence to loom control, here the diagonals are achieved with free weaving. Only the vertical and horizontal changes are threaded into the loom.

By the time the Bauhaus doors were closed, the notion of the Art Fabric was completely subordinated to the design for production. Because of the wide dispersion of Bauhaus doctrine and because of the credence given it, for three decades (1930–60) the utilitarian form all but eclipsed any major focus on fabric without function —the Art Fabric—which is the concern of this book.

However, for the development of the Art Fabric, the Bauhaus was of major importance. Although many works were irrevocably lost during Germany's military period, the great body of work that remains intact or recorded in photographs in such institutions as the Busch-Reisinger Museum in Cambridge, Massachusetts, The Museum of Modern Art in New York, and the Bauhaus Archives in Darmstadt has been of inestimable influence on succeeding generations of students and designers.

The Bauhaus had drawn teachers and students not only from Germany and Austria but from Holland, Switzerland, and Eastern Europe as well. Even before the Bauhaus was closed in 1933, there were strong advocates for an International Style. The outward movement was greatly accelerated by the scattering of the Bauhaus masters and students in the thirties. Some went—if only temporarily—to Eastern Europe, Switzerland, France, and England. However, a great many ended up in the western hemisphere, scattered over South America or concentrated in centers such as Montreal, Los Angeles, Chicago, New York, and Cambridge.

One of the Bauhaus masters came to Black Mountain College in North Carolina in 1933. Josef Albers was the pathfinder and rebel, a painter and educator who revolutionized approaches to aesthetics and creativity. His philosophies were to shape the direction of the new generation of teachers, artists, and designers throughout the United States. From Black Mountain, his wife, Anni Albers, wrote and lectured, conducted workshops and methodically developed concepts for production fabrics.

As it had that of other Europeans working in America, the new country affected the nature of Anni Albers's work. The accelerated sense of time, the limited size and complexity of looms, the absence of apprentices or artisan assistants, the isolation and the lack of support or patronage all served to make her Art Fabrics smaller and less formal. Indeed, few such works appeared until the years after the Second World War. And although she had influenced and indeed goaded two generations of American weavers with her seminal concepts, structural rather than decorative approaches, with rationalism, with an openness to Peruvian ingenuity and to the consideration of research and expression through the Art Fabric medium, she has had, curiously enough, no disciples working in her unique style. Anni Albers, working in her studio in New Haven, has said, "I think of my wall hangings as an attempt to arrive at art, that is, giving the material used for their realization a sense beyond itself. . . Breathing does not express anything; one's work should be like breathing, essential to just being."

Sweden began to re-examine the national character of her arts as she moved from the influences of the Morris era, Art Nouveau, and the radical ideas of the Vienna Secessionists who were successors to the Austrian Art Nouveau movement. The English Arts and Crafts movement had found fertile ground in Sweden because, unlike England and Germany in the Industrial Revolution, she had not broken her ties with the traditional folk arts.

The Swedish textile tradition reaches back over a thousand years. From still-preserved tapestries dating back to the twelfth and thirteenth centuries, there runs an unbroken line leading to today's home craft movement and free-weaving artist-craftsmen. The wall hanging especially has retained its popularity. While Sweden, like other Scandinavian countries, does not boast an exceptional academy of fine arts, her many artist-craftsmen are so celebrated as to be known by the average citizen.

Sweden's most significant contribution to Art Fabrics came from Marta Maas Fjetterstrom, who created a weaverly modern tapestry inspired by peasant traditions, Persian carpets, and Swedish landscapes. Although she had already made her debut by the turn of this century and was to make her most important contribution during the twenties and thirties, her influence carries on to the present.

By the end of the last century, Finland was making long strides toward entering the modern era. In the new cities and especially in Helsinki, a far-northern Art Nouveau flourished in architecture and with it a vital arts and crafts movement. From these roots, and from a reawakened interest in folk art fanned by Finnish nationalism, grew the architectural style of Eliel Saarinen. His buildings embraced all the arts. Not only were craftsmen commissioned to enrich his buildings with their work, but there were also close professional and friendship ties between him and the artist-craftsmen.

Family ties too provided the atmosphere for this development. His wife, Loja Saarinen, was a major force in the fabric area. From the beginning of the century she wove carpets and wall hangings in the long knotted pile of the Finnish rya technique. For her husband's architecture she created a new tapestry style that was flat and architectonic with strong emphasis on expression of materials and the order of their interlacing. Because color tended to be low key and light in value and the weaving open rather than heavy and dense, the textural contrast of wool, silk, and especially linen yarns was most important. Frequently the ground was so sheer as to carry the eye through the piece. Some work was not tapestry-woven but of discontinuous brocade woven over a slubby linen gauze.

HVITTRASK   built in 1903
Eliel and Loja Saarinen's house (now a museum)
outside Helsinki

Against a romantic background of admixed Art
Nouveau and modern elements, old Finnish ryas
are the major visual elements. A rya by Axel
Gallen-Kallela is molded to the planes of wall,
bench, and floor.

Beyond the importance of the Saarinens' own work was their enormous influence as teachers and supporters of craftsmen both in Finland and, later, in America. Saarinen's work led him to the United States, where he moved permanently in 1925. In Bloomfield Hills, outside Detroit, Saarinen was engaged by the Booth family to work on a series of buildings that were to become Cranbrook Boys Academy. He offered commissions to the sculptors, potters, and weavers who came with him from Finland and Sweden.

When the Cranbrook Academy of Art was founded in 1926, one of America's most important arts and crafts centers auspiciously began. Since that time this small school has had enormous influence; a contributing factor certainly was the founder's encouragement of the cross-fertilization of the various visual disciplines with a dominant architectural bias.

From 1929, while Loja Saarinen directed the weaving studios, both Art Fabrics and rugs continued to be produced, particularly for the Saarinen buildings. When in 1937 Marianne Strengel took over the direction of the studio, the emphasis, as at the Bauhaus, shifted to designing prototypes for production. From this base, Cranbrook alumni have filled key positions in the design and art fields or become influential teachers—among them are Ed Rossbach, Tashiko Takaezu, Mary Jane Leland, Walter Nottingham, Sherri Smith.

Loja and Eliel Saarinen
(American, born in Finland)
TAPESTRY for main dining room,
Kingswood School, Cranbrook, 1935
18' x 16' turned 90°
discontinuous brocade
linen, wool, and silk

Within a pervasive architectural format the figures
are rendered two-dimensionally, as a frieze. The
tapestry style, which was developed in Finland by
Loja Saarinen in the first decades of this century,
was employed in a large suite of hangings for the
various Cranbrook institutions. The weaving is not
tapestry but brocading over a heavy sheer ground
of hand-spun linen. The rich formalism is Art
Deco, making this a period piece. The strong,
direct expression of technique and materials and
of opacity and translucency are prophetic of later
work by Tawney and others.

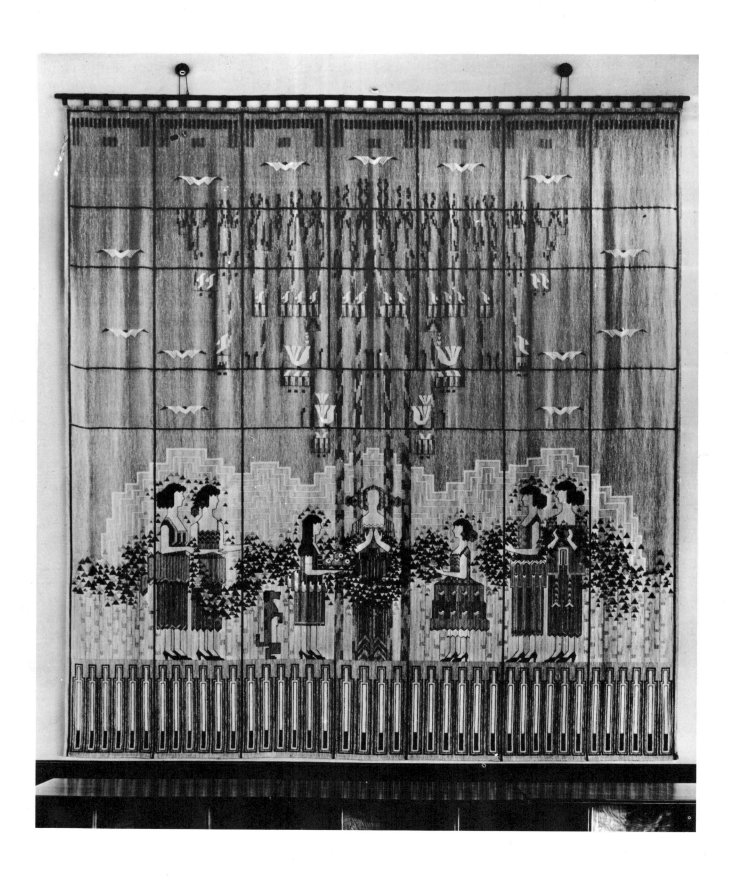

Now the twisting of the varied currents that emerged from Europe even before the influx of the continental masters in the middle and late 1930s became the core of divergent achievements in the United States. Two parallel developments merit attention.

Since the time of Bernard M. Maybeck and Charles and Henry Greene (1910–20), the West Coast had fostered an organic, humanistic architecture provocatively independent of the *beaux-arts* tradition. This was spurred by the arrival from Austria of architects Rudolph Schindler and Richard Neutra, who settled in Los Angeles in 1926. Neutra, whose work was widely published, was especially helpful in providing a hospitable climate for the craftsmen.

In the Northwest John Yeon and Pietro Belluschi had, by the end of the thirties, established an organic style expressed in the use of natural wood for residential architecture. They and their clients provided both inspiration and patronage for the craftsmen. The East, with its industry and class-structured industrial wealth, seemed far away indeed. In the small western communities, intellectuals, architects, patrons, artists, and craftsmen shared their cultural isolation. This was a milieu in which contemporary craftsmen found support and encouragement.

Remote from the mainstreams of American art and architecture, western regional art was personal, providing a poetic vision to which craftsmen could easily respond. Painters such as Mark Tobey, Morris Graves, C. S. Price, and later (in the early 1940s) Clifford Still and the recently arrived Hans Hoffman were to show works that were intensely individual and strange to the accepted categories of American art. Then too the West Coast museums placed at least as much emphasis on the decorative arts of the Orient and American Indian crafts as on European painting.

From the 1930s on there were centers for craftsmen such as the Oregon Ceramic Studio in Portland, later to become the Contemporary Crafts Association. In San Francisco, Gumps, V. C. Morris, and the City of Paris featured the work of craftsmen. From Europe came famous potters such as Gertrude and Otto Natzler, and Marguerite and Frans Wildenhain, who in the early forties founded the school at Pond Farm, north of San Francisco.

None of the newcomers enjoyed the magic and fanfare of native Californian Dorothy Liebes, who in the thirties and forties combined extraordinary materials in clashing "Chinatown" colors. Her success stimulated the market for special hand weaves, and more importantly, on an expanded scale, the serious pursuit of weaving as a profession.

Although the whole West Coast was involved in the craft revolution—as were, to some extent, other American centers, especially the Great Lakes area under the impetus of Cranbrook Academy in Michigan and the Institute of Design in Chicago —it was the San Francisco Bay Area that nurtured the new American Art Fabric.

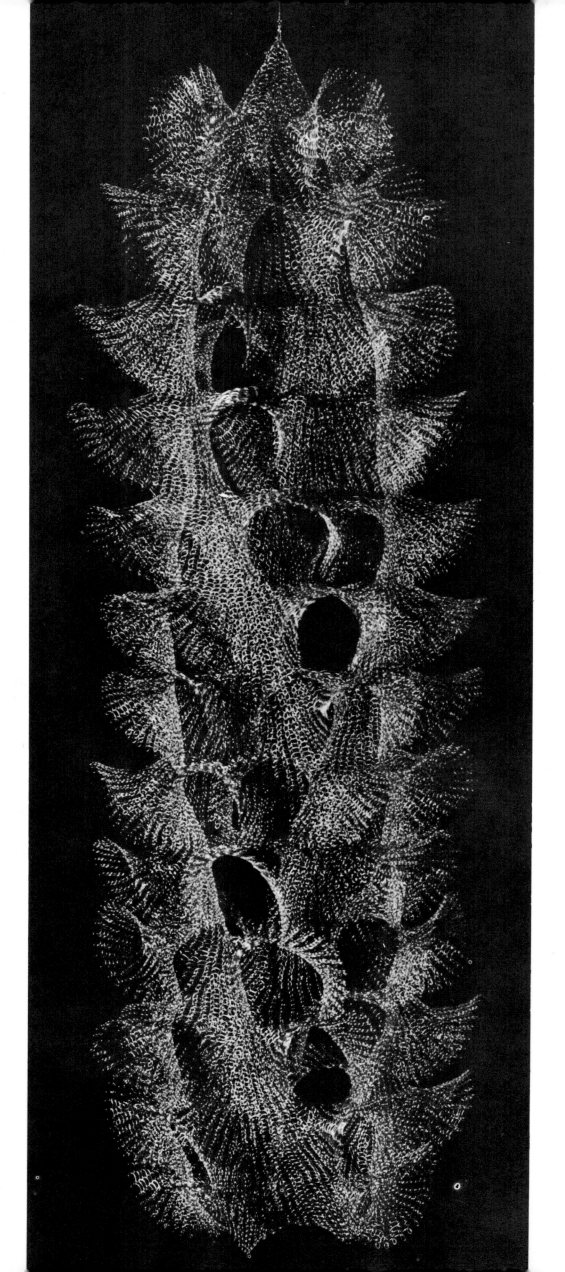

Ruth Asawa (American)
UNTITLED   1958–59
height 9', diameter 2'
tubular knit
Monel
Collection: The artist

For years the University of California at Berkeley had boasted one of the great departments for physical anthropology. It was natural for that department's researches in American Indian and pre-Columbian basketry and fabrics to spill over into the Department of Decorative Art. The weaving director, Lea Van Pembrock Miller, spent years exploring ramifications of Peruvian gauze weave. Through her department, in the forties, Berkeley was the only university offering a Master of Fine Arts degree in weaving. The department was reinforced when Ed Rossbach joined it in 1952. He had already started his long series of researches into non-production, non-utilitarian fabric.

In the mid-1940s Trude Guermonprez found her way from Europe via Black Mountain College to Pond Farm. She taught weaving first there and later in the California College of Arts and Crafts. Like her student Kay Sekimachi, Guermonprez has mostly concentrated on the technical and aesthetic considerations of Art Fabric. So did her contemporaries, among them Lyn Alexander, who displayed a short-lived brilliance in the early 1950s but returned to production handweaving for others because of financial pressures.

There was in San Francisco a lone pioneer, Ruth Asawa, who much earlier utilized an Art Fabric medium without precedent and even today without peer. Her material was wire, her technique tubular knitting, often in layers, with one floating inside the other like a series of carved Chinese ivories. With this technique she was able to create large volumes of shadow-producing filigree in a material that is durable and soil-free. These, America's first monumental Art Fabrics, are an unequivocal success.

While the West Coast was developing its own tradition of artist-craftsmen within the cultural climate of the native and the newly arrived, a different process, parallel in time, was evolving in Chicago.

The renowned Chicago school of architecture under such masters as Louis Sullivan and Frank Lloyd Wright had early laid the groundwork for an international revolution of design disciplines. In the 1930s, Chicago was the perfect host city for the creation of the New Bauhaus, later to become the School of Design. In this ambiance, Lenore Tawney, among others, studied sculpture with Alexander Archipenko and weaving with Marli Ehrman.

Trude Guermonprez (American, born in Austria)
UNTITLED (detail) 1954
84" x 16"
double cloth
walnut slats, wool yarns; black, natural
Collection: Win Anderson, New York

For a small hanging, Guermonprez has made an interesting variation on the hand-woven blinds popular in California in the mid-fifties. Whereas those were invariably plain-woven with half of the warp over the rigid weft, Guermonprez has used a double-cloth technique. The slat is either exposed or covered with warp and weft. The weft yarns are discontinuous—they do not weave across the narrow band but only half of it.

Lyn Alexander (American)
SPACE HANGING 1953
about 9' x 3'4"
cotton and rayon; black and bronze
Collection: Estate of George Mason, Philadelphia

This piece is hardly weaving at all, as most of the warp is not interlaced with weft but only stretched taut by rods at top and bottom. The several scales of linear pattern were created by hemstitching on the loom each horizontal band in even modules of one, two, four, or eight warp ends. In the second and fourth sections from the top a different module is used for the upper and lower hemstitch. Within this technique Alexander achieved a quiet perfection. The concept is original; the technique that serves so well is masterly; the proportions seem inevitable, the work durable. The handling of solidity and translucence works well whether the piece is hung in space or in front of a wall so as to cast shadows upon it. Unheralded, little known, Alexander may have been the first to use the unfettered warp (see Weitzman, p. 280, and Giaque, p. 13), to use gravity as a major element, and to so thoroughly exploit translucency as well.

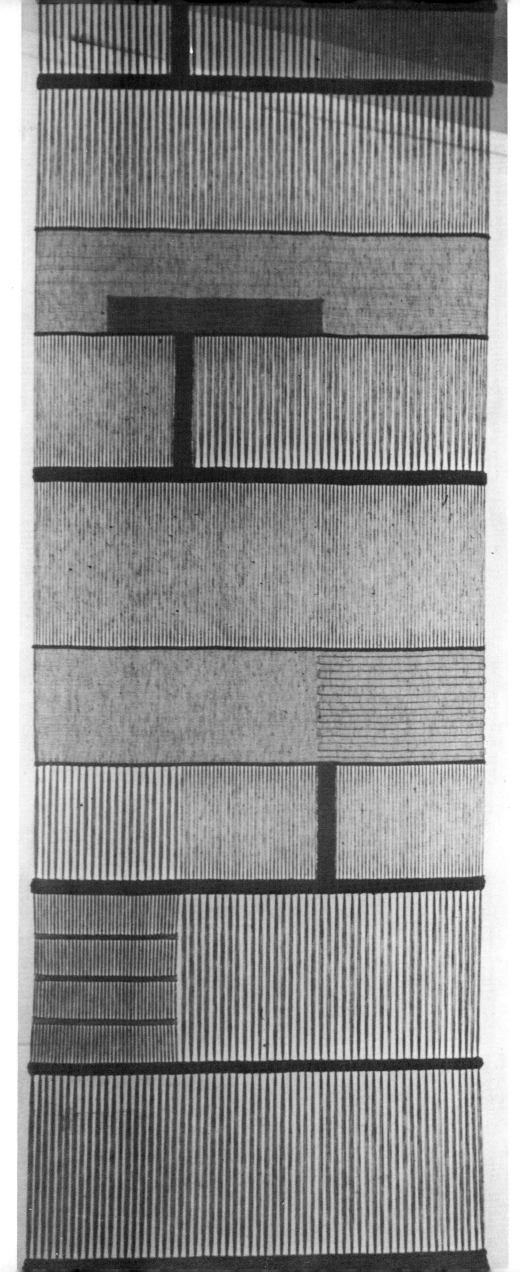

In northern and eastern Europe, in the late 1950s, the Art Fabric brought some fresh air into an over-precious and over-refined modern tradition. Finland came out of a long isolation with new fabric statements that included the glowing color of much-simplified art ryas. Dora Jung worked within the complexities of the draw loom to create first free-woven double cloths called Finn weave, then damasks such as *Doves.* In three consecutive Milan Triennales these were awarded gold medals. The modern Finnish tapestry idiom established much earlier by Loja Saarinen and others had produced more personal statements, smaller and less abstract. Under Eva Anttila and Marta Taipale, brilliant clear colors were introduced in a broad range of fiber.

In Sweden craftsmen such as Ulla Tulluf broke with the heavy monumentality of the Maas Fjetterstrom school to create freely conceived sheer tapestries not unlike those woven by Tawney in the fifties.

Dora Jung (Finnish)
DOVES (detail) 1958
damask
linen; grays, brown, and black
Collection: Cooper-Hewitt Museum, New York

The technique of Jung's patterned damask series woven in the mid-1950s is double damask woven on a draw loom. The back of the cloth reverses, light on dark. Because certain areas are colored by discontinuous brocade, the short vertical re-peat is made to seem longer. The narrow scroll shape, the classicism, and the densely and me-ticulously woven fine yarns relate to the double cloths of Richard Landis (p. 204).

Eva Anttila (Finnish)
WHITE VEIL   1950
13½″ x 12½″ turned 90°
tapestry
linen and mixed fibers; multicolor
Collection: Cooper-Hewitt Museum, New York

This small head is typical of the post-war tapestries by Finnish artists Eva Anttila and Marta Taipale. The figures were often drawn with eccentric wefting, as in the cheek and the veil here. The scale of even the larger pieces is intimate, in brilliant colors played against natural gray linen. Unorthodox selection of materials from the whole fiber range and the blending of these yarns within a single shed make for a lively surface.

Ulla Tolluf (Swedish)
SHEER TAPESTRY (detail) 1957
tapestry
mixed fibers; neutral colors

This detail reveals how mixed fibers and fine
metallic threads are freely and eccentrically interlaced through an exposed linen warp. The concentric, saw-toothed lines are produced by hemstitching on the loom. The work is interesting in
comparison with contemporaneous works of Lenore Tawney (p. 46). At the time this piece was
done, its light-hearted freedom was a sharp break
with the disciplined refinement of Swedish design
and especially with the ponderous deep-toned
tapestries influenced by Marta Maas Fjetterstrom.

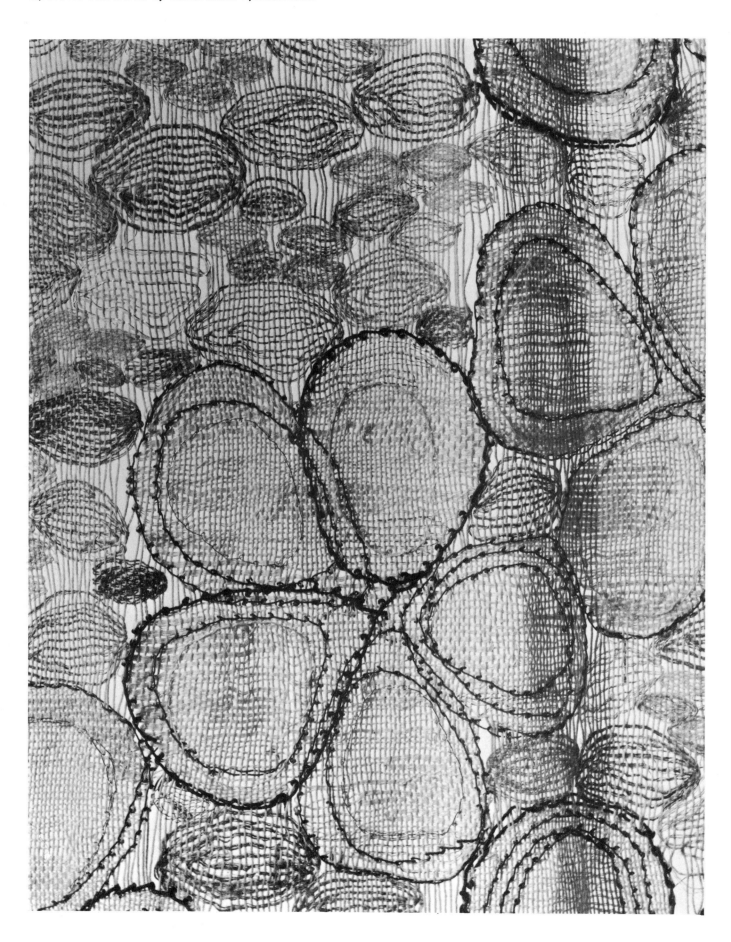

Immediately after World War II the Polish Ministry of Art and Culture organized programs to restore the native handcrafts, paying particular attention to the weaving country in the north of Poland, devastated by the war. This area has an ancient tradition of tapestry-woven rugs produced on the broad horizontal loom. Also supported as a national art was the important Cracow school of weavers working in kilim and Polish gobelin. Because the Polish weavers were taught early to respect materials and to believe that beauty of form was closely bound up with techniques, the progression in this century from traditional tapestry to free weaving seems to have been a logical one.

In the 1957 Milan Triennale Poland's sole presentation was Art Fabric and such as the western world had not yet seen. Although woven in gobelin technique, here was a weaver's art free of subordination to a painter's cartoon. Dominant were thick spongy surfaces of hand-spun wool, vegetable-dyed in glowing earth tones. With this material the scale became bold, the spirit free and vigorous, and, consistent with the avante-garde movement of that time, the importance of an image diminished.

At the 1958 Brussels World's Fair, Czechoslovakia offered another glimpse of East European Art Fabric, in a major exhibition of laces by a Prague school teacher, Luba Krecji. She had freed lace from its tradition of miniscule size and subservience to ornament and fashion. With rough-spun linen she expressed in a readable scale the excitement of its engineering aesthetic.

Luba Krejci (Czechoslovakian, born 1925)
LINEN LACE (detail)
knotted lace
linen; natural color

This detail indicates how deftly the artist combines structure and image. Although there are filet laces in which pattern is worked over a structure, this is not true here; the drawing and web are the same. Her filigree is enriched by balance of thready voids, the near solids, and the layered tracery of the bird.

For all the arts, the post-war years in the United States had begun a hale and vigorous new era. Dependence on the School of Paris for directions in painting and sculpture was over. The battle for modern architecture was almost won, and the International Style was the dominant vocabulary for building throughout the country. A new avant-garde in theater, musical composition, and poetry expressed and renewed confidence in progress and in innovative native talent. The high spirit of these times was contagious; there abounded a healthy cross-fertilization among the various art disciplines and media. Now that production could move from war materials to consumer goods, the industrial designer began his long and important rise to dominance. The economy of the country was booming and the demand for consumer goods—from pots and pans to works of art—was insatiable. A buoyant creativity particularly in the New York area carried its message to the nation and indeed to the world.

New York had never been very hospitable to craftsmen and it was often shunned by them. This American center for theater and dance, for fine arts and fashion seemed to dwarf the individualistic artist-craftsman. The city did support some ranking jewelers, and industrial designers such as Russel Wright and Eva Zeisel who sometimes worked in craft media. Although Anni Albers had been given her first one-man exhibition at The Museum of Modern Art in 1949, the work shown was not Art Fabric but prototypes for production: drapery and upholstery materials, room dividers.

In the 1950s came a breakthrough for the craftsman. The long pioneering efforts of Aileen O. Webb, first with America House and later with the American Craftsmen's Council (now the American Crafts Council), had stimulated craftsmen and created an audience receptive to their work. The Bertha Shaefer Gallery was successful in introducing *as art* the early Art Fabrics of Trude Guermonprez, Sue Fuller, Mariska Karasz, and Franklin Colvin.

Moving from the West Coast, Dorothy Liebes opened her New York studio in 1950 and Jack Lenor Larsen his the following year. Although their emphasis was on fabric design, decorative and utilitarian, the stimulation they each provided contributed importantly to the craft climate.

From 1950 to 1955 the Good Design Program, under the direction of Edgar Kaufmann, Jr., sponsored by the Merchandise Mart in Chicago and The Museum of Modern Art in New York, brought to the attention of a still wider audience the work of craftsmen and designers. Works by Sue Fuller, Lenore Tawney, Marta Taipale, Jack Lenor Larsen, and Lyn Alexander were included.

"Textiles U.S.A.," shown at The Museum of Modern Art in 1956, included industrial fabrics, home furnishings, fabrics for apparel, and a few Art Fabrics. As stated in the catalog of the exhibit, the work of the artist-weaver was included because: "Individual craftsmen still excel in the attention to detail that provides one kind of quality in textiles. But the craftsman's chief contribution now appears to be in the design of fabrics for mass production. Only a very few craftsmen have succeeded in producing new work genuinely original and readily distinguished from that produced in industry. Examples are Thelma Becherer's Velon and reed screen and Franklin Colvin's tapestry-like panel of nylon and mohair; both are exercises in pure design without utilitarian purpose."

Mariska Karasz (American, 1898–1960)
FIGURE EIGHTS (detail) 1957?
couched embroidery
linen; multicolor

Karasz illustrates the freedom with which the great needle artist approaches stitchery. She improvised on most known techniques and invented some others, working imaginatively with any material that could be threaded through a needle, on a ground, sometimes offbeat, always strong in character.

Sue Fuller (American, born 1914)
STRING COMPOSITION #119   1965
36″ x 36″
wrapping
nylon monofilament; translucent multicolor
Collection: Mr. and Mrs. Joseph L. Braun,
New York

For several decades Fuller has strung monofilaments to form layered curvilinear images within
a rectangular form. These works of symmetrical
precision possess the kinetic magic of a star
sapphire as they become more and more three-
dimensional. Often they are wrapped on an armature of clear acrylic and then the whole is cast
in a cube of clear acrylic so that only the monofilaments are visible.

In 1960 the traveling exhibition "Fabrics International" explored still further the potentials of technology, but Jack Lenor Larsen, director of the exhibition and advocate through his writing and lectures of some of the central themes, posed questions as to "which of the fabrics around us may serve to elevate our sense of quality? Which exploratory, specialized, or primitive constructions stretch the imagination and extend our vision?"

In addressing itself to the artist-craftsman, the exhibition suggested that the most flexible, least exploited fabric areas were not within loom-woven fabric but outside it. Having been developed for speedy consistency, the loom was an impediment to the freest range of individual expression. Larsen goaded weavers to consider the volumetric potentials of knitting, knotting, and basketry techniques and perhaps others that, in the long quest for production, evidently had been dropped or not even invented. Some such work was shown at the exhibition by pioneers such as Ed Rossbach, Ted Hallman, and Lilly Hoffman. Other work was directly or indirectly inspired by it, notably the knits of Mary Walker Phillips and the knits and crochets of Ted Hallman.

The results gave evidence in support of Larsen's other premise—that in the next industrial revolution, on which we are now embarking, the imagination and agility of the craftsman is invaluable not just in the peripheral areas of aesthetics and taste but in conceptualizing direct solutions to very basic needs. Because of his unclouded mind and the immediacy of being able to work directly from idea to realization, the artist-craftsman has advantages over even the super-organizations of post-industrial research. The poetic probings of adventuresome individuals was further demonstrated in the United States section of the 1964 Milan Triennale, as will be seen later.

Ted Hallman (American, born 1933)
INTERLACED FORM
Shown at Triennale, Milan, 1964

In the early 1960s, Hallman was creating with open knits a series of tall, organic hangings. All were essentially tubular or conical, all volumetric and monolithic. In the piece shown, both the element of gravity and the tension rings of heavy steel wire at the terminals are essential to achieve the taut form.

Mary Walker Phillips (American, born 1923)
NEAR EAST   1963
9'2' x 3'9½''
knit
wet-spun linen; natural color
Collection: The Museum of Modern Art, New York
Shown in "Wall Hangings,"
The Museum of Modern Art, New York, 1969

This piece was photographed at the entrance to the United States Pavilion, Triennale, Milan, 1964. The small weaving at left is by Anni Albers; another work can be seen on the right.

From the early 1960s, Phillips explored such non-conventional aspects of knitting as knit leather thongs, ropes, and beads. Then her interest turned to the lacy filigrees possible in shell stitches and other traditional fancy patterns. Her materials were wiry linens, blocked and starched when finished to form flat panels such as Near East.

A significant design event in 1962 was to provide the impetus for the phenomenal developments of the Art Fabric in the last decade. In Europe, in Lausanne, Switzerland, the first Biennale Internationale de la Tapisserie paid tribute to the revival of the ancient art of tapestry that began in the 1920s.

Working tirelessly for many decades in the modern tapestry movement, Jean Lurçat became the honorary president of the Association des Artistes Cartonniers Français in Paris. In 1962, when René Berger, director-conservator of the Musée Cantonal des Beaux Arts in Lausanne, invited him to "pursue this high mission of vigilance," Lurçat organized the first Biennale. As president of the Comité du Centre International de la Tapisserie Ancienne et Moderne (CITAM), he also became president of the first Biennale.

The high period of tapestry art is acknowledged (by Lurçat and the Committee as well) to be the medieval era. First limited to heraldry and simple ornament, Gothic tapestry evolved into hangings introducing figures and narrative detail. The great collections in The Cloisters, New York; the Victoria and Albert Museum, London; and the Louvre, Paris, offer superb evidence of this art form.

During the Renaissance, tapestry became a medium through which the painter's art, translated into cartoon and then woven, was reproduced. Even Albrecht Dürer engravings were the source for small tapestries woven as late as the seventeenth century.

By the eighteenth century the tapestry had become a woven picture within a woven frame, over-refined in both material and technique. The weaver's art had become completely subordinated to the iconography of the tableau and to what we consider today to be the decadence of perspective.

Beginning in the late 1920s, through the efforts of Jean Lurçat, Marie Cuttoli, and Pierre Baudoin, there was in France a revival of tapestry weaving, for which modern painting was considered eminently applicable. There were, however, many changes. In heavier yarns, the Gothic technique of hatching was used to structurally blend a range of color reduced to twenty-five to fifty tones in place of 30,000 shades used in the eighteenth century. Size, too, underwent a change. Instead of being a woven picture on a wall, tapestry became a wall. Lurçat called tapestry a mural; Le Corbusier, participating in the tapestry revival, considered it a "mural-nomad"—a portable mural.

The post-war success of the revival was due in a large part to the support of the French and Belgian governments, which subsidized the movement by purchases and commissions and by sponsoring exhibitions at home and abroad. When the French tapestry exhibition was shown in New York at the Metropolitan Museum of Art in 1947, the director of the Museums of France, Georges Salles, lauded the contributions of the modern painter to the art of tapestry.

Under the lively and dedicated direction of the late Pierre Pauli, Commissaire-General of the first Lausanne Biennale (and of all the subsequent exhibitions through 1971), the works were selected by an international jury. The participants came from Austria, Belgium, Canada, Czechoslovakia, France, Germany, Great Britain, Hungary, Italy, Japan, the Netherlands, Norway, Poland, Portugal, Sweden, Switzerland, and the United States. In spite of this nationalistic and geographical diversity, the reproduction in tapestry of the work of the modern artist still dominated. Only a handful of the weavers exhibited pieces that forecast the ferment of the present Art Fabric movement. The presentation of the Polish contingent—Abakanowicz (p. 76), Owidzka (p. 54), and Sadley (p. 234)—was electrifying indeed.

In that same year, a few dozen people, mostly friends and fellow-artists, crossed the New York harbor to the opening of Lenore Tawney's exhibition at the Staten Island Museum. Although off-off-Fifty-seventh Street, this was a triumph for the artist and a memorable celebration for those attending. The gallery scale was kind to the work; the audience, sympathetic and responsive. Here for the first time was a major exhibit of American Art Fabrics, with enough work shown to make the cumulative impact one expects in a one-man show. The series of quietly, intimately scaled personal pieces created a thunderous response.

For this exhibition, Tawney had selected from her long range of sheer impressionistic tapestries. She included newer works of attenuated shore birds and a bird form enfolded in a two-layered tapestry (pp. 268–69). But in the dozen weeks just before this show she had experienced the personal revolution described on p. 267. The new works, stark in form, austerely neutral in color, brutal by contrast and unrelated to her earlier work, without the overt sensuous appeal of the craftsman's hand, emerged out of the artist's total commitment and experience.

In the next year there were to be more of them, ever larger, more intricate, more refined. They were to become the core and the inspiration of "Woven Forms" in 1963 at the Museum of Contemporary Crafts in New York. But that event on Staten Island was the point at which Art Fabric was healthfully and joyously launched in America. Tawney's breakthrough, her style and innovation, stimulated a small, then larger and international following of weavers, critics, and an influential coterie of patrons. She opened eyes and imaginations and pocketbooks: from this time, the Art Fabric was considered so seriously as to be acquired by private collectors and public institutions.

New York's Museum of Contemporary Crafts, more familiarly known as the Craft Museum, had since its inception in 1957 included the works of artist-weavers, notably Guermonprez and Rossbach, and had acquired such key works as Tawney's *Bound Man* (p. 47). All this was taken in stride as part of the burgeoning crafts movement until, in 1963, director Paul Smith bravely mounted a revolutionary exhibition entitled "Woven Forms." Although Tawney dominated the lower floor, there were also fresh new works by Alice Adams, Sheila Hicks, Dorian Zachai, and Claire Zeisler.

The work of Sheila Hicks and Claire Zeisler is discussed later. Although Alice Adams's work is sporadic, sometimes unfinished, she is influential as a conceptualist, teacher and critic. In "Woven Forms" she expressed freedom from the rectangle in her shaped tapestries and the unorthodox approach to materials that forecast *Construction 1966*.

Lenore Tawney (American, born 1925)
THAW   1958
45″ x 36″
hand-spun wool, linen, goatshair;
brown and natural color
Collection: Cooper-Hewitt Museum, New York

Although the pastoral subject is less typical of
Tawney in this period than are the many shore
and woodland birds, several basic characteristic
elements are here: the sparse striped warp, the
textural importance of the weft yarns, the translucence, the direct but simplistic and unresolved
treatment of the warp ends.

The piece is unique in Tawney's use of the exaggerated variations within a single hand-spun wool
as an important element of the image. The economy of yarn types is also unusual. This piece uses
only a natural hand-spun wool, brown yarns in
several tonalities for detailing, and a supplementary linen weft for stability. The negative image,
which makes a memorable visual fugue, is as rare
in Tawney's work as in Art Fabrics as a whole.

Lenore Tawney
BOUND MAN   1956
about 9′6″ x 3′
discontinuous brocade
linen with other fibers; natural, black, and brown
Collection: Museum of Contemporary Crafts,
New York

The play of opaque and transparent passages in
this linen piece projects the drama of the crucifix
behind Bound Man. Heavy dark horizontals above
and below the figure give stability to the whole
composition and provide contrasts for the relatively sheer ground of the central panel. The
heavy roving that binds the figure is embroidered
through the whole cloth. In the weaving Tawney
has moved from order to chaos, calling attention
through structure particularly to the head, hand,
and foot.

47

Lenore Tawney
Installation of one-man exhibition, 1967,
Benson Gallery, Bridgehampton, Long Island

A broad range of large pieces from Tawney's
black-and-white period is shown here. From left
to right: painter David Porter in front of The
Queen; *Lenore Tawney behind* The King; The In-
nocent; The Bride; *sculptor Isamu Noguchi;* The
Cage; The Fountain *(side view);* potter Karen
Karnes; Inquisition; Motionless Dance.

Dominic di Mare (American, born 1932)
BOX   1963
six-layered weave
wool, linen, wire; gray, black, and white
Collection: Holt Collection, San Francisco
Shown at the Triennale, Milan, 1964

FORM   1966
70″ high
linen, jute, wool, feathers
Collection: S.C. Johnson & Son, Inc.

Since the early 1960s di Mare has probed the potentials of multiple-layered cloth. He discovered
that, unlike the double-weave traditions of Peru
and northern Europe in which layered cloths are
woven simultaneously one over the other, successive layers could be woven independently and
their warps cut off before starting to weave the
next layer. With this breakthrough he was able to
consider more layers and to treat them more independently. There is an interesting similarity
between this phase of di Mare layers and those
woven by Herman Scholten (p. 256).

In his six-layered Box, Californian di Mare has
emphasized depth by the bellow-like graduation
of rectangular apertures.

In a later period di Mare wove a long series of
layered space hangings that are sometimes so
lacy and sheer that the eye is carried through
them. More often he used shaped weaving and
feathers to achieve fetishistic totems. These are
voluptuous and sensual; sometimes, in their neo-
primitive exuberance, awesome or mysterious.

Rebellious, headstrong, and untamed, moved by elemental forces, Dorian Zachai was the only "wild beast" in the "Woven Forms" breakthrough. Although Tawney's forms were both large and strong, and Alice Adams's tapestries brutal in relation to that medium, none had the head-on impact of Zachai's. Here was primordial force just barely channeled into the discipline of woven form. Zachai in this period was tapping the same expressionist wellspring as key forces in American fine arts, and perhaps of all American weavers she was closest to them in gut expressiveness. She also possessed some of the vital strength of Magdalena Abakanowicz, but here the similarity ends, for somehow Zachai has not always been able to sustain the momentum to build a consistently valid body of work. That she is working outside the structural disciplines is certainly a factor. Of the five artists included in "Woven Forms," Zachai has been the most emulated, especially by student weavers. The spectacular immediacy of her style has appealed to them. So has a seeming disregard for technical competence. Her more recent work was included in "Deliberate Entanglements," UCLA Art Galleries, Los Angeles, 1971 (p. 61).

"Woven Forms" was heralded as the confrontation with a new kind of fabric and a new art form. As one critic remarked, "they [the artists] slash enough ties with traditional weaving to delight and offend and to set one thinking that weaving is older than the loom."

The thirteenth Milan Triennale in 1964 took as its all-encompassing theme the subject of Leisure—"free time." Edgar Kaufmann, Jr., president of the United States Exhibition Committee, stated in his introduction to the American catalog: "Technology, plus time to explore, yields unorthodox forms of abundance. The rich records of the past, plus time to explore, yields unexpected inspirations. These new freedoms are explored by United States designers in some examples presented here to show that leisure leads to play and play to creation, producing new resources for American design and American living. . . . stimuli to creativity come from all sides—from the technological ingenuity, from the economic challenge of marketing, from the needs of every day, from the ventures of insight." This last certainly applied to such artists in fiber as Anni Albers, Dominic di Mare, Ted Hallman, Sheila Hicks, Mary Walker Phillips, Ed Rossbach, and Lenore Tawney. Many of their works, interestingly enough, by that time were borrowed from museum collections.

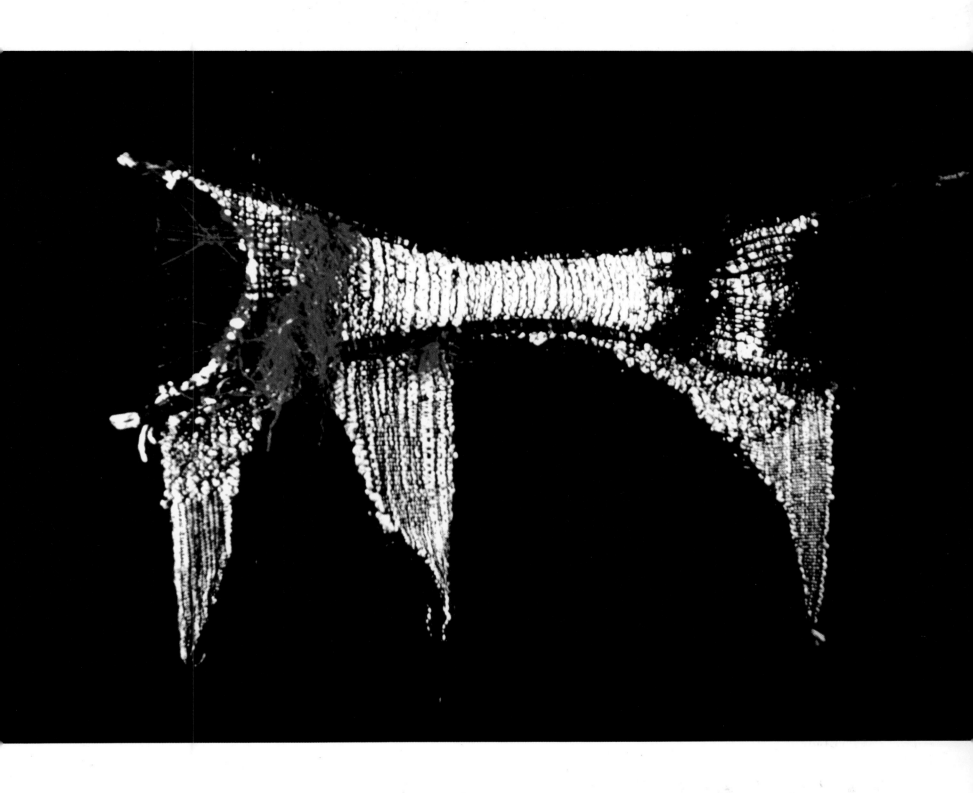

Alice Adams (American, born 1930)
CONSTRUCTION   1966
18" x 24" x 20"
coiling
steel cable and tarred rope; natural color
Collection: Ivan Biro

Adams, whose work was shown in "Woven Forms" at the Museum of Contemporary Crafts, New York, in 1963, was one of the first to make explorations in the full round. Her investigations have led to block-long outdoor environments of cords that not only caught trees and buildings in their giant web, but the audience as participant.

Construction is advanced in its basketry technique, in its full three-dimensionality, and in its brave attempt to manipulate material, which although durable and of strong character is extremely resistant.

Dorian Zachai (American, born 1932)
DOG   1962
49" x 70"
tapestry, shaped and stuffed with wool batting
wool, straw, cotton twine, and raffia,
with tree-limb reinforcements; red, black, natural
Shown in "Woven Forms," Museum of
Contemporary Crafts, New York, 1963

In this artist's work there is consistency in such diverse elements as the gnarled tree limbs, the expressive warp ends, the tubular body that terminates in a yawning mouth, and the humor in the knotted tail. The overall texture is the unifying element; so is the dominant rhythm of concave and convex curves. The triangular "legs" are not shaped weaving, in contrast to Tawney's long triangles of the same period. Rather they are tapered by warp ends dropped from the web and braided along the eccentric selvage.

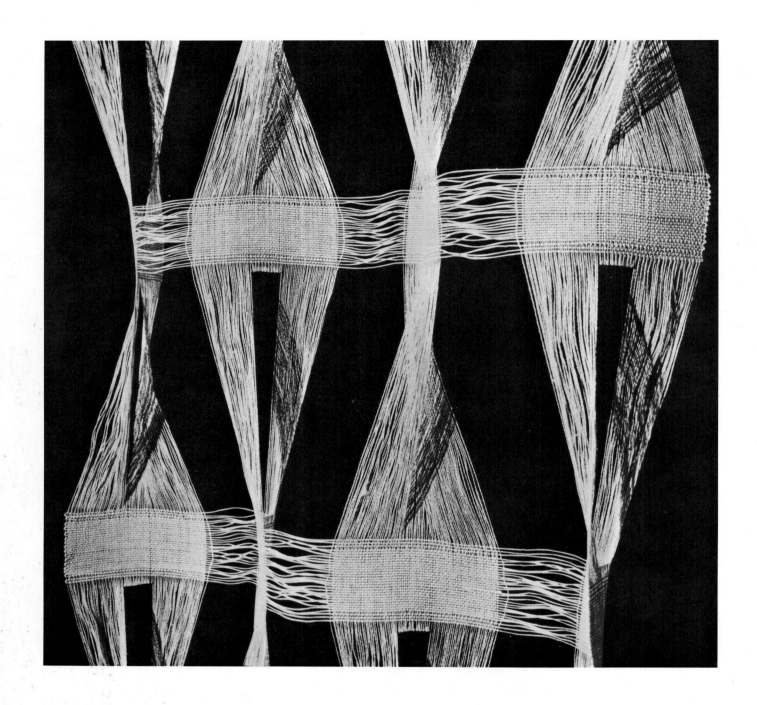

Peter Collingwood (British)
MACRO GAUZE 3D.1 (detail)   1968
wet-spun linen; natural

Collingwood is best known of the many weavers in the United Kingdom partly because of his prolific body of work and even more for his teaching and writing. Originally trained in science, his craft career has been dominated by the study of loom-controlled techniques that could so facilitate production of unique handwoven pieces as to bring them within average means. Some of these techniques are his own; others are the rationalization of very old ones.

Macro Gauze 3D.1 bears some relation to the controlled slits of Tawney and Schiele, and even more to the layered interlacings of Amaral (p. 98). Like them Collingwood is able to independently control the separate warp bands. The crossing and recrossing of the pairs of warp bands like Peruvian gauze weave is an innovation. Within the regular repeat and within a minimum of weaving the artist has achieved depth and a variety of silhouette. The handling of positive and negative space is masterful.

Helena Barynina Hernmarck (Swedish, born 1941)
SWEDEN HOUSE TAPESTRY (detail)   1968
9'4'' x 16'4''
brocaded tapestry
wool and linen; multicolor
Collection: Sweden House, Stockholm

Over a number of years Hernmarck has developed
the technique of combining tapestry joining with
"Rosepath," a traditional Swedish pattern weave
that like a brocade floats yarns over the surface
of the cloth.

When commissioned to weave a hanging for the
press room of Sven Markelius's Sweden House in
Stockholm, Hernmarck devised a means to use
her technique to express the halftone dot iconography of newsprint.

Jolanta Owidzka (Polish, born 1927)

In an open yard created by bombings during
World War II, Owidzka, Wojciech Sadley, and
Zofia Butrymowicz hung their works for a special
viewing when Jack Larsen visited Poland in
1967. Shown here are pieces by Owidzka, including (on the far left) Black and White, 1965,
shown in "Wall Hangings" at The Museum of
Modern Art, New York, 1969. Owidzka, a pioneer
in the new freedom of the Warsaw school, is especially known for the strong, pure manner in
which she has developed dark and light texture
patterns.

Bohdan Mrazek (Czechoslovakian, born 1931)
LEGEND AND LIFE   1966
86" x 175½"
shaped tapestry with weft loops;
sisal and cotton; black, blue, red, and beige
Collection: The artist
Shown at the Biennale, Lausanne, 1967;
"Perspectief in Textiel," Stedelijk Museum,
Amsterdam, 1969

By weaving on a vertical frame Mrazek is able
to achieve the skillful handling of a completely
shaped outline. Most of the warp ends have been
woven back into the web. But the unengaged
warp is expressed in the angles below the diamond at upper right. Movement is suggested by
the jet stream of concentrically ovoid shapes and
by triangles and feathered forms. The horizontal
flow and the shapes within it are echoed by the
periphery.

The growth of the Art Fabric movement in the ensuing years accelerated and moved beyond its original borders, stretching from East Europe to Australia to Bolivia and Colombia in South America, to western Europe and to the United States. The work of the artists has been nurtured through major international exhibitions and colloquia.   The Biennale Internationale de la Tapisserie in Lausanne has, since its beginning, been more than a measure of the growth of the movement in two-year intervals. It is a rallying point for the artists; it provides continuity in the evaluation of their development; it is an arena for the exchange of ideas. Not surprisingly, the proportion of Art Fabrics to the traditional tapestry has increased importantly.

That the 1957 Milan Triennale awarded a silver medal to Buic (Yugoslavia) and the São Paulo Bienal of 1966 awarded a gold medal to Abakanowicz (Poland) is a testimonial to the enlightened support from these artists' governments, as well as the courage of crusading jurors.

To collect work for The Museum of Modern Art's "Wall Hangings," co-directors Mildred Constantine and Jack Lenor Larsen visited Poland and western Europe. In 1968 the exhibition traveled to museums and colleges across the United States. When a larger version was given a major showing at the Museum in New York in 1969, it was stated in the catalog that "During the last ten years, developments in weaving have caused us to revise our concepts of this craft and to view the work within the context of twentieth-century art. The weavers from eight countries represented are not part of the fabric industry, but of the world of art. They have extended the formal possibilities of fabric, frequently using complex and unusual techniques." The directors of the exhibition were aware that the title "Wall Hangings" and the generic use of the word "weavers" were inadequate because many of the Art Fabrics shown were neither hung on the wall nor woven!

The Stedelijk Museum in Amsterdam opened its "Perspectief in Textiel" in the early part of 1969, and the prestigious endorsement of Art Fabric by both museums lent it authority and influence. From this time works by many artists found their way into public and private collections.

While European scholars and critics responded early to the art of fiber, relatively little critical notice came from the art critics of New York's major newspapers and magazines. But a year later, when Fred Tuten, critic for the New York *Times,* visited the 1970 Biennale in Venice, he wrote: "Jagoda Buic from Yugoslavia whose exquisitely crafted, gigantic knitted wool constructions resemble sagging cones and fragments of a medieval parapet, and the Japanese Nobuo Sekine with his monumental polished steel shaft topped by an oblong hunk of raw marble were perhaps the only balanced sculptors in the show" (July 12, 1970).

Recognition and further exposure came from the exhibition at the Museo de Arte Contemporáneo in Madrid which also sponsored an international colloquium in 1970. "Deliberate Entanglements," at the University of California in Los Angeles, 1972, was "assembled to assess as art the recent conceptual, formal, and structural developments in fabric forms." This brilliant exhibition was the nucleus of a program in which seven museums participated through additional exhibitions—for example, Abakanowicz's one-man show at the Pasadena Art Museum (p. 95)—and a week-long colloquium.

PERSPECTIEF IN TEXTIEL
Stedelijk Museum, Amsterdam, 1969

Installation photographs only partly reveal the enormous success of a sensitive mounting by curator Wil Bertheux. Of all major group shows during the last several years, "Perspectief in Textiel" was without peer. Part of its success derived from the generous space allowed—only two artists to each gallery—so that the works could be viewed independently. The respectful omission of all props and diversions and the soft, even flood of natural overhead light were also contributing factors.

In the gallery shared by Clare Zeisler and Marguerite Carau-Ischi (left), the shadow-producing separation between wall and hanging should be noted. The simple platform that lifts the Zeisler piece from the floor is scaled to be subordinate to the work. This photograph shows the affinity between the pendulous work of Sadley and the shaped weaving of Vohanka.

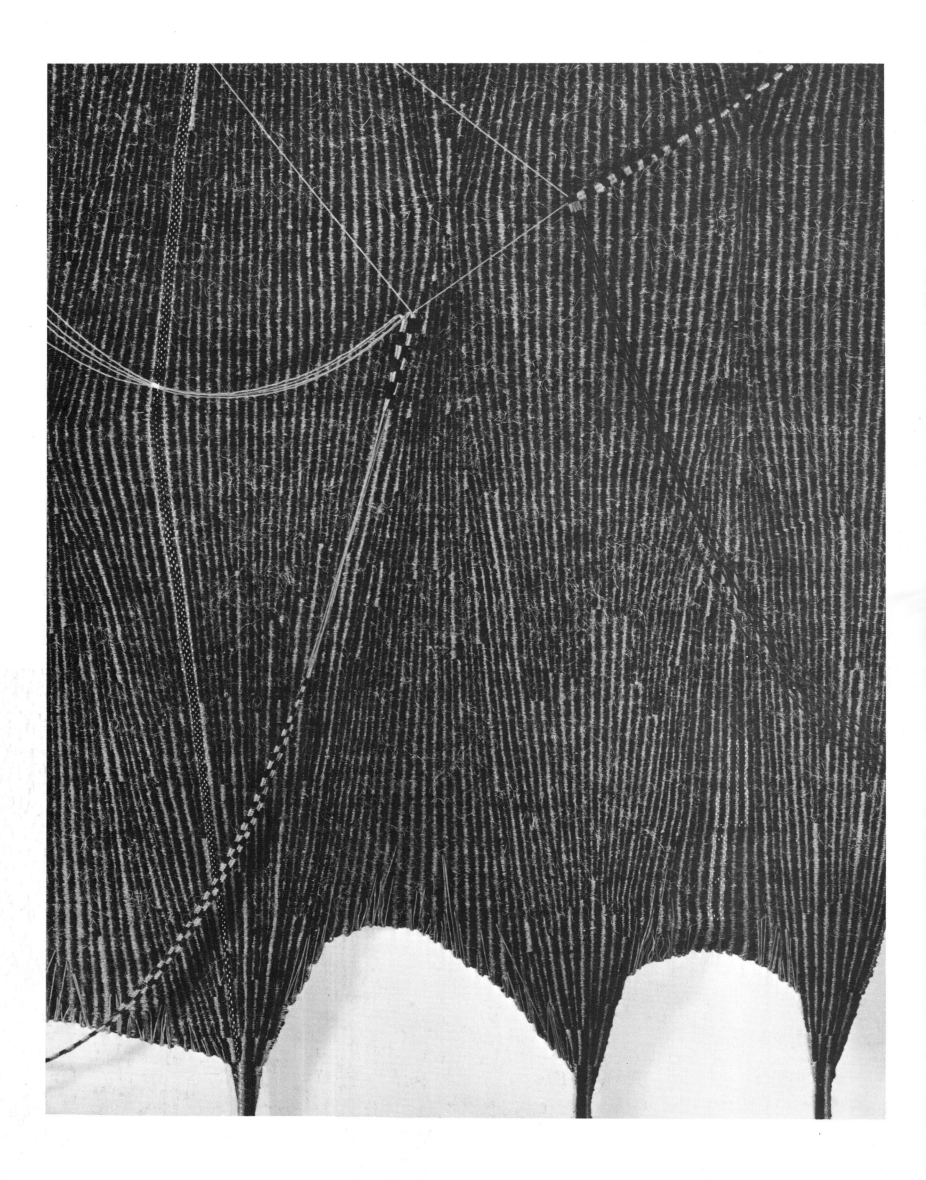

Jindrich Vohanka (Czechoslovakian, born 1922)
LA VISITE D'ALDEBARAN (science-fiction)
39″ x 58½″ (detail)
shaped tapestry with eccentric warp
wool, sisal, metal; gray and black
Shown in "Perspectief in Textiel,"
Stedelijk Museum, Amsterdam, 1969

The close-up photograph illustrates an approach to shaped weaving extraordinary enough to inspire a weaver of ancient Peru. Of the many elements working, none is so brilliant as the alternation of dark and light wefts which, in a weft-face construction, causes the dark/light ribs that underscore the sculptural complexity.

All selvages are, like a bat's wing, shaped and fluted. As the weaving progresses from the rope-like construction at the lower points, the warps are gradually spread to the width of one foot or more. They spread by branching out and separately engaging the weft so that forty-eight warp ends are first condensed into four groups, then branch into eight, then sixteen, thirty-two, and forty-eight. The inverse is true of the triangular sections between the points; here the warp ends condense like the veins of a leaf or the tributaries of a river. When the warp ends at the bottom were turned back into the web so as to form a firm edge, some were first floated over the surface. In this sense a process is expressed and a fine detail added.

The symbolic rigging of cords and guys is so aptly handled that it seems inextricably a part of the whole. Some of the cords are tape-woven in a small tapestry pattern.

It is interesting to note that the three great Czech weavers, Vohanka, Bohdan Mrazek, and Jiri Tichy, all work in shaped tapestry. To those in the West this first became apparent in the third Biennale in Lausanne in 1967. It was further emphasized in "Perspectief in Textiel" in Amsterdam in 1969, where Mrazek and Vohanka each showed three pieces of shaped weaving.

EXPERIENCAS ARTISTICAS TEXTILES
Museo de Arte Contemporáneo, Madrid, 1969

Major works, mostly European and mostly three-dimensional and sculptural, were suspended in a large gallery. To reduce to some extent the universal hanging problem—competition arising from seeing several works at one time—partial screens or baffles were used. The sculpture bases, perhaps used to protect the works, were white on a black floor and unfortunately distracting. Artists are (left to right): Aurelia Muñoz, Marie-Thérèse Codina, Wojciech Sadley, unknown, Sheila Hicks, Magdalena Abakanowicz.

Barbara Shawcroft
(American, born in England 1930)
GROUPING OF THREE INTERCHANGEABLE
PEOPLE   1967
height Black Man 9'; White Woman 8';
Green Child 5'
tubular double plain weave, stuffed
hand-spun wool; natural, brown, gray, and green
Collection: Mrs. Julius Epstein, Chicago
(Black Man and White Woman);
Mr. Spaulding Taylor, San Francisco (Green Child)

Shawcroft was one of the first Americans to produce large works in full three dimensions. Almost
invariably the task she sets for herself is complex,
involving both idea and tour de force of technique. Such is the case with Grouping of Three
Interchangeable People, in which she has carried
to new limits the size and complexity of tubular
weaving. In a monolithic woven fabric she is able
to achieve such complete anatomical details as
fingers and breasts, in figures articulated to stand,
kneel, and sit. She also has reserve for social
comment. Both accomplishments are extraordinary indeed.

Dorian Zachai (American, born 1932)
PROCESSION FOR A DEAD LOVE   1969
5' x 7'
double weave with a combination of plain weave,
twill, and tapestry, stuffed,
on wood armature and base

Today the artists continue their influence and interaction through contacts established over the years; they expose their discoveries and researches and share their struggles while their work is shown to an ever-growing global audience.

No aspect of the Art Fabric has moved faster than the development of single-element techniques. In a decade, the effects of a few major breakthroughs have been so widespread that in some quarters weaving on a loom is considered to be hopelessly old fashioned. By contrast, knitting and crochet have forever been released from the connotation of fustiness. Since the early work of Asawa, Phillips, and Hallman, it would seem that every scale and every material has been used to knit and crochet a broad range of forms. It is reasonable to speculate that these "new" media are still in a formative stage, as most of the many practioners are very young.

At the same time that macramé knotting has become an international pastime, it has been raised to an art by such talents as Zeisler (p. 287) and Grossen (p. 165). Warp twining, bobbin lace, netting, and weft looping are all being explored simultaneously in many places, but especially in the United States.

Obviously, some techniques have more potential than others, but most, either because they have never heretofore been considered as art media, or have not been used creatively since the late Bronze Age, present to these young people unlimited horizons.

Single-element techniques, in addition to the freedoms they offer the artist working in fiber, have always the inherent potential for volumetric form. While this aspect is still so new that most work is in relief rather than in the full round, it is unlikely to remain so.

On both sides of the Atlantic, most artists working in fiber have not only continued to use natural fibers but have sought out such organic materials as sisal, cordage, or hand-spun wool. Indeed the materials used have been the common denominator, far more than technique or style. Recently, however, there has been increasing openness, on the part of some artists, to new materials, and with them occasional incursions into brand-new technology.

Urszula Plewka-Schmidt (Polish, born 1939)
ORGANIZM (detail)   1970
14'11'' x 6'1''
knitting and wrapping
sisal, synthetic fiber, and hand-spun linen;
brown-bronze
Collection: Museum Bellerive, Zurich
Shown at the Biennale, Lausanne, 1971

For a large T-shaped monolith, two types of ar-
mature give a rigid stability to an otherwise pliable
single-element fabric. The peripheral frame is cov-
ered with a translucent knit of sisal. From the
frame spring the arcs of metal rod that create the
convex forms. The arcs in turn are wrapped in
woven ribbons of synthetic fiber.

Moik Schiele (Swiss, born 1938)
UNTITLED, 1972
26'3'' x 5'
slit tapestry on two warp beams
aluminum; copper color
Collection: Glaubtern Church Center, Neu-Affoltern; Architects: Ester and Rolf Guyer

Except for its copper color and larger size, this work is almost identical to Schiele's White Wave, shown on p. 246. The clean concept of the work, the richness of material, and the immaculate craftsmanship are appropriate to the precision of the architecture. In a space in which orchestrated light is the principal ornament, this piece offers the perfect, unifying element. Against unpolished stone, under the strongest dawn light, the modulated curves of light-reflecting aluminum are superbly appropriate.

Janet Taylor (American, born 1941)
TRIANGLES ON A CORNER   1969
40" x 80" turned 90°
tapestry
wool, rayon, cotton; red, blue, green, and yellow
Collection: The artist

Janet Taylor suggests environmental enclosure in a series of pieces designed to fit the right angles of inside and outside corners. The meticulous technique, the angular image, and the logic of her inverse progression of primary color are all consistent with the hard-edge purity of her graphic format.

Ron King (American, born 1943)
TRIANGLE REVOLUTION   1969
6' x 3½'
knitted
paper yarn; gray
Collection: Chandler Kudlip Associates, Inc., New York

When in the late sixties Ron King began to knit large forms in heavy yarns, he brought to the medium his own enormous scale and the formal discipline of a weaver used to working within set limits. This work is almost medieval in the mail-like texture and in the ordered strength of the triangular elements.

Walter G. Nottingham (American, born 1930)
BASKET SHRINE 1971
86" x 26" x 7"
coiling
mixed media, jute; natural and brown

Since his school days at the Cranbrook Academy
of Art, Nottingham has been working in the single
elements of crochet and macramé. Almost invariably his forms have a center from which spill symmetrical, pendulous cascades. In the years 1968–
72 his pieces tended to employ the form and
nomenclature of enclosed shrines. Such is the nature of this work. The detail here reveals a feathered and beaded haven for a spent bird. The enclosing wall of jute yarns is coiled, a basketry
technique. Although this technique is new to Nottingham, he handles it with the authority admired
in indigenous primitive craftsmanship.

Mariyo Yagi (Japanese, born 1948)
THE TWINE 1972
length 101½"
twining
wild hemp; bleached
Collection: The artist

Working in the isolation of Kobe, Japan, young
Yagi has been consistently involved with achieving tangible intimacy between object and man so
that he is no longer a viewer but a participant.
Yagi's first environmental pieces, fabricated of
woven pile, were hollowed-out walls to sit on and
shaped floors to nest in. More recently she has
used cords and rods to symbolize a shrine. Such
is The Twine. In a sense it is nothing more than
a tassle of many cord ends, cable-plied into a
mammoth rope. Through scale and sophistication
and an implied mystique, the work is raised to an
aesthetic level.

Developments can be roughly divided in two directions: artists such as Moik Schiele (p. 240) and Robert Kidd who have employed synthetic materials within existing, if non-conventional, techniques; and those who have been led by a new material into new construction or form. Typical of the latter is Kay Sekimachi (p. 258), who has used the inherent spring of monofilament to create rounded volume atypical of loom-woven fabrics. Ed Rossbach (p. 216) has very often employed plastic materials in very ancient constructions. He has also made patchworks by fusing the edges of plastic sheeting and in *Construction with Newspaper and Plastic* (p. 225) has created with pliofilm and newsprint a new vocabulary of materials which when woven are integrated into the fabric tradition.

With the growing multitude of materials, and with the reactivation of old and exploration of new techniques, the artists enjoy a multiple choice of expression: environmental, architectural, wearables, and the abstractions of pure research. Rarely are their works two-dimensional.

The movements that are active today in the arts have gone through their own periods of rebellion and liberation, sometimes reacting to the extremes of standardization and to the disarray of our society, and sometimes productive of major innovations. The Art Fabric artists can claim kinship with the spirit of these movements, but not influence, imitative or literal. Sculpture, strong in the decade past, may have contributed more to the vocabulary of the Art Fabric—for example, the work of Richard Lippold, Kenneth Snelson, Gego, and of course Buckminster Fuller.

Robert Kidd (American, born 1936)
KINETIC REFLECTIONS (detail)   1970
84" x 52"
Plexiglas, aluminum, Rovanna, wool, linen, nylon
Collection: Knoll International

The wall hangings of Robert Kidd retain the lush pile and organic composition characteristic of his hand-knotted rugs. But in the hangings, free of considerations of wear and tear, he is able to explore a new range of non-fibrous materials. These are primarily synthetic straws, slit films, and plastics for industrial application. In his massing of them, his juxtaposition of contrasting color and texture, he creates a fantasy richly organic both in concept and effect.

Glen Kaufman (American, born 1932)
SCUTUM   1972
10' x 3'4"
weft twining
vinyl film and polypropylene; black
Collection: The artist

Kaufman uses a new material in a new way for a new form. By shirring, he exploits the soft draping quality of vinyl and maximizes the brilliant highlights of the myriad folds. The lighter center is formed by contrasting the smooth, highly reflective face of the material against the satin-finished back.

Marlise Staehelin (Swiss, born 1928)
PLASTIC WALL ELEMENT (detail)   1972
64″ x 60¾″
wrapping
polyurethane film; translucent white

In an extremely heavy hanging Staehelin has exploited the potentials of wrapping and of a new material. At the top one sees vertical cords which grasp the supporting rod. These are so densely wrapped as to become opaque. In contrast the weft wrappings, combining six vertical cords in each rib, are more loosely wrapped with a wider film strip. Here the diagonals between the ribs become translucent, light-reflecting membranes.

Debra Rapoport (American, born 1945)
KNITTED ENVIRONMENT 1970
cable-plied wool
Collection: The artist

Designed to take any shape depending on the
body in it, this heavy knitted garment of seemingly tangled string also has openings of more
rigid construction for head and hands.

Sam Gilliam (American, born 1933)
CARROUSEL MERGE   1971
over 15' long
synthetic polymer paint and aluminum powder
on canvas, draped from ceiling to floor
Collection: The artist

Gego (Venezuelan, born in Germany)
RETICULAREA 1969
Collection: Museo de Bellas Artes, Caracas

Although Gego's environments of linked steel wire
are not technically fabric, they do succeed in a
fabric-like manner in pointing the way to other
applications. When this piece was exhibited at the
Center for Inter-American Relations, New York, it
was hung within the ballooning whiteness of a
cloth tent to erase the corners of the room and
heighten the sense of being within a starry con-
stellation. Gego's purity is polar to the intimate
environment-as-raiment of Debra Rapoport.

The influence is perhaps felt more through the various movements within the arts rather than the work of a particular artist. Expressionism, Dada, and Surrealism; Duchamp, Man Ray, and the Found Object; Assemblage; the New Surrealism; Environmental Art—all the adventures of modern art and the confluence of all the media are shared today by painters, sculptors, graphic artists, and artists of the fiber medium.

There are of course artists working in unclassifiable disciplines: Is Claes Oldenburg a craftsman or a sculptor? Is Sam Gilliam a painter or an artist working in fabric? Robert Morris and the late Eva Hesse worked with synthetic materials—fiber glass, rubber, twine—are they sculptors or . . . artists? Like the artists working in fiber, they all are able with their mingled components to generate a power that has changed our concepts of art. We as viewers share all their imaginative visual experience and in doing so we liberate our own.

While the legendary School of Paris and the New York School of painting of the fifties were nurtured within the boundaries of a particular quarter in one city, the School of the Art Fabric flourishes throughout the world, even in countries with few or no precedents relative to this art form. The artists have much in common. Many of them are aware of the challenges of the future, posing questions they ask of themselves. One of the artists, Ed Rossbach, states some of these questions succinctly and eloquently: "The whole fabric field needs to burst wide open. We are all inhibited somehow by certain nice standards. I don't know how such a breakthrough can be accomplished. We are weighed down with such a baggage of preconceived ideas about fabrics—and what is acceptable. . . . we are in such a new time when hand fabrics are suddenly relieved of all science—of all utility—of all functioning other than aesthetic. We still don't know what to do with the new freedom. It is an exciting time in fabrics. We have moved through the functional fabric, then the 'art object,' and now such restrictions seem inadequate except as something to be returned to only as desired, and on occasion. I think of today's large-scale knots—many are pure decoration, but some indicate a new important direction—not functioning as fabrics, not decorative fabrics, and not objects. I am intrigued by process art in fabrics."

Where this future will take our artists cannot be forecast. They belong in the mainstream of modern art. Their work presented here—its wholeness, the inseparability of all its fundamentals, its materials, its techniques—demands to be experienced aesthetically as art beyond craft.

Ed Rossbach (American, born 1914)
BASKETS 1970
plaited
polyethylene tubing, Mylar, opaque white plastic,
anodized aluminum
Collection: The artist

"A tribe of baskets" is what Ed Rossbach's de-
signer-wife calls them. She says, "they differ from
baskets from Asia, India, and America in that they
are luminous, shiny plastic, gold, silver, copper,
and white." Rossbach's basketry uses plastic as
a structural material much as the Pacific Islanders
use palm or pandanus. The material, tubular or
folded, is plaited into a variety of shapes, some
with fringes, some with serrated rims. These are
quite different from an earlier work in which Rossbach wove plastic raffia over a palm and ixtle
basket (p. 221).

abakanowicz

Magdalena Abakanowicz with La composition des formes blanches *shown at the first Biennale Internationale de la Tapisserie, Lausanne, 1962. The piece measures 19½' x 6½'.*

A conventional gobelin, with several tapestry joinings, is contained in a rectangular format. This painterly composition, developed with a variety of materials over an exposed warp, demonstrates her early bravura approach to technique.

MAGDALENA ABAKANOWICZ
Polish, born 1930

Studied at Fine Arts Academy, Warsaw. Teaches at the Fine Arts Academy, Poznan, since 1965. One-man exhibitions in Warsaw, 1960, 1963, 1965, 1967; Cracow, 1971; Paris, 1962; Galerie Alice Pauli, Lausanne, 1967, 1971; Kunstindustrimuseet, Oslo, 1967; Stedelijk van Abbe-Museum, Eindhoven, 1968; Stedelijk Museums, Arnhem, Schiedam, 1969; Södertälje Konsthail, Södertälje; Nationalmuseum, Stockholm, 1970; Pasadena Art Museum, Pasadena, 1971; Kunstverein für die Rheinlande und Westfalen Düsseldorf, 1972. Group shows at Biennale, Lausanne, 1962, 1965, 1967, 1968, 1969, 1971; The Museum of Modern Art, New York, 1969; Stedelijk Museum, Amsterdam, 1969; Museo Español de Arte Contemporáneo, Madrid, 1969; Camden Art Center, London, 1971. Represented in collections of National Museum, Warsaw; Stedelijk Museum, Amsterdam; The Museum of Modern Art, New York; Museu de Arte Moderna, São Paulo; Kunstgewerbemuseum, Zurich, as well as other public and private collections. Awarded the Gold Medal of the Bienal, São Paulo, 1965; as well as many Polish government prizes.

Abakanowicz's studio in Warsaw, 1967. A high warp loom and components for Assemblage II *(p. 84).*

Magdalena Abakanowicz has a rebellious spirit. She protests against preconditioned responses to the meaning of her art, and its traditional classification and limitation as "applied" or "decorative" art. What she feels so strongly in the creation of her work, she would also have us feel strongly and personally as participants.

Her latest works are environments—textile "situations" into which the spectator is introduced and involved. He and the space are metamorphosed by his participation in the "object" created (p. 90).

Looking back upon the development of the artist's highly original art, it is not surprising to note that in Warsaw in the early fifties she belonged to an artistic and intellectual community that expressed a new, united, dynamic energy. In 1955, the World Youth Festival held in that city marked the first break in the social-realist official line imposed on the East European countries since the end of World War II. Sponsored by the students, an exhibition of the work of young painters was related to aspects of German expressionism, with the addition of social and political overtones.

In that same year the artist was graduated from the Fine Arts Academy. She had naturally responded to the teachers on the faculty and to the general ferment that prevailed. The artistic-intellectual community was a strongly united group, and the efflorescence of all the arts was accompanied by expressions of intellectualism and emotionalism. In painting there was an outpouring of color—brilliant, turbulent, thickly textured—resulting in works of enormous tactile values. Undoubtedly this was an influence on the emerging young weaver.

Abakanowicz was trained in the disciplines and traditions of weaving. However, even in her early work, such as the woven abstract picture (p. 76), her direction tends to be metamorphic rather than mimetic.

BLANCHE 1966
58½" x 78"
tapestry weave
sisal, horsehair, nylon cord; white and black

Still within the conventional gobelin joinings and rectangular format, this early work presents major innovations. A black sisal form emerges from the long slit. Great contrast in weft size relieves the flatness. The surface is further enlivened by suspended wisps of horsehair and coiled braid that intermittently pierce the plane. Here is the first glimpse of the central apple shape to emerge in such shaped pieces as Abakan Rouge *and* Abakan Jaune *(pp. 86–87).*

In this work the artist breaks with the tapestry tradition of juxtaposing color areas. The detail on the following page illustrates her orchestration of a range of white wefts to produce a sculptured surface. Fine cords are interlaced singly, in pairs, and in groups. Coarse cords are eccentrically woven with sufficient density to anchor the coils of braid. Some of these are wound with shiny nylon cord so as to vibrate with reflected light.

The artist demonstrates, using her hands as the only tools, her direct and primitive involvement with the materials of her art. She uses a vertical warp, without an open shed. Instead of a shuttle or a butterfly, she interlaces a grouped weft of linen and sisal yarns. After interlacing, her fingers function as a sword to push the weft into the web of the cloth.

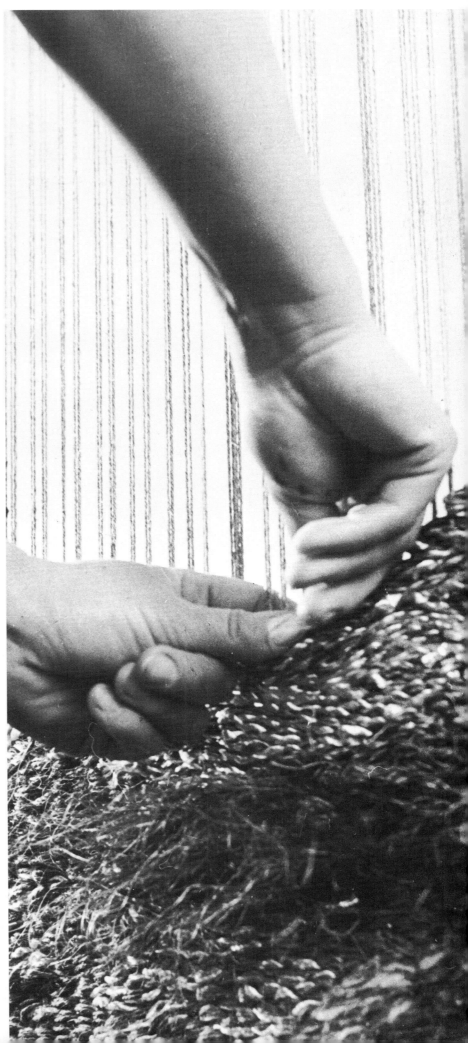

ASSEMBLAGE II   1966
10' x 9' turned 90°
tapestry weave
sisal and fur; black
Collection: The artist

The work shown is hung on its side, so that the
selvages are top and bottom as seen here. The
curved profile is actually the last weft woven,
secured by darning the warp ends back into
the cloth, thereby realizing another selvage. This
is the technique that permits the development
of Abakanowicz's later freehanging works. The
shaggy filigree of horizontal yarns is made up
of warp ends unengaged with weft. These together with the random superimposed fringes and
patches of fur appliqué evoke a sense of mystery
heightened by the murky blacks. This is the artist's first use of the expressionist color characteristic of all her later work.

ABAKAN 27   1967
57⅜" x 71¾"
tapestry weave
sisal; black and brown
Collection: Jack Lenor Larsen, New York
Shown in "Wall Hangings,"
The Museum of Modern Art, New York, 1969

Although it is a small tapestry rectangle, in this
piece two themes are further developed: the split
circle defined by a weft fringe raised above the
ground of gobelin relief; and the vertical slit embellished by two lips woven separately and applied. A number of the weft fringes are twisted
into a single strand. These strands are grouped
and wrapped to form spikes. It is evident that
these elements are a natural outgrowth of spontaneous creativity. In this piece the first color to
relieve the neutrals is introduced.

ABAKAN JAUNE   1967–68
12'9'' x 9'9'' x 4'10''
shaped tapestry with crochet
sisal; yellow-orange
Collection: The Museum of Modern Art, New York
Shown in "Wall Hangings,"
The Museum of Modern Art, New York, 1969

In this shaped three-dimensional piece, the artist
breaks with tradition by abandoning the flat rectangular plane. The elephantine elements, woven
in parts, are sewn together and supported on an
armature. Varied surface treatments include tapestry joinings, changes in the scale of yarn and
interlacing, gradations of tone within a single brilliant color, and protruding weft fringes, clipped
and unclipped. Crochet rondels are applied as a
further embellishment.

ABAKAN ROUGE   1969
13' x 13' x 11½'
shaped tapestry
sisal; red
Collection: Nationalmuseum, Stockholm

Apertures left and right are a new element, as are
the supplementary entrails, which foretell the later
developments shown in Sweden (pp. 90–91). The
freedom from the rectangle, the introduction of
gargantuan forms, and the use of full-blooded
primary color—these outbursts in a single work
mark it as a milestone in the artist's development.

While she was influenced by the palette of the painters, and by their organic, abstract compositions and rich elaborations of surface, her weaving is neither painterly nor linear. She speaks to us more as a sculptor. She is intensely concerned with the identity and nature of the materials she uses—cords, horsehair, sisal (p. 85)—and the frank physicality of her forms, shapes, and spaces. The composite effect of all these elements produces an acutely personal expression, rather like a volcanic eruption of organic energy. Its power is enhanced by the insistently monochromatic color she almost always employs. These colors are given surprising variety when she moves from light-absorbing to light-reflecting fibers or creates high relief by contrasting fine yarns tightly woven against large elements that are barely interlaced. The phenomena of great scale and weight are given further emotional impact by the monochromatic color. Visual response is heightened also by the use of unweaverlike materials, such as fur, and by large, flapping jungle-like elements (p. 87) that prompt the viewer towards involvement if not contemplation.

In her latest "textile situations" the controlled movements she uses are almost choreographic. Time is of the essence in these compositions—there is a still, static state with no transformation in process; then there is a sudden movement when rope is allowed to run free until it is enmeshed again. An unforeseen awareness of space and materials offers sequences effective close up and at a distance (p. 93).

The mammoth wall in Holland illustrates Abakanowicz's response to a rare commission. She was invited to create a wall for the reception room of a new State Building in Holland (p. 97). Her solution is not limited by the program set for this commission but, in the spirit of rebellion, espouses the cause of her own creativity. In violating the existence of the wall itself, she defies the nature of modern architecture and re-asserts her disdain for the fastidious.

The panels are potent exaggerations of the organic forms and coarse materials of her vocabulary. They are arresting in their giant scale and tensions, outrageous in their relationship to the architectural elements of the building. The "composition grows black from the black stone floor to the dark wood ceiling," she says. Her emotions and outpourings speak loudly; they are full of sounds. The total composition is an adventure, a confrontation that inundates the viewer with projected elements that are on the borderline of dream and reality.

Invited to present a one-man exhibition at the Pasadena Art Museum, she utilized a narrow, block-long space for a single work. This, an environment in three parts, is again made up of her characteristic organic forms and massive ropes composed on site. Both the elements and the galleries themselves are a sequential non-narrative drama powerfully staged. As in the earlier environment in Sweden (pp. 90–91), the first cavernous, congested space serves to awaken emotional responses. This then propels the viewer into a great empty space in which the single focus is a bed heaped high with a mass of tangled ropes (p. 95). The artist's unprecedented use of an everyday artifact underscores her overt symbolism.

Today there is an extremely wide gap between the work of Magda Abakanowicz and that of her contemporaries, even those in Poland. In her resolve and drive to explore, she is like other great artists of our day. Her involvement with techniques serves only to allow a creativity that comes from gut compulsion and from imagery without precedence.

ENVIRONMENT   Kunsthalle, Södertälje, Sweden, 1970

From the open-air exhibition on the dunes, it was a logical step for Abakanowicz to go beyond the environment for objects to an environment composed by creating "woven situations" in a system joining ceiling and floor. She wished to draw attention to the diverse means of weaving beyond its classification and limitation as applied or decorative art. To do this, she eliminated single objects. In the first situation sixteen spatially woven works are environmentally composed. While each might have an individual plastic importance, the system created gives the spectator a collective impression of the total composition.

SITUATION 2 (detail)

Exhibition, Nationalmuseum, Stockholm, 1970
The raw material at a moment when its possibility
for transformation is greatest.

*ENVIRONMENT Kunsthalle, Södertälje, Sweden,
1970*

SITUATION 3 (detail)

CONSTRUCTION WITH ROPE (detail)

*The artist explains: "In a hall, the empty room is
divided by ropes running on the floor and under
the ceiling in several predetermined directions.
Each rope, after a certain period of free run, is
transformed into a knot. The spectator observes
this phenomenon in its static state—no transformation is in process. However, the movement can
be started again and be stopped only after the
free run of the rope is completely enmeshed. The
division of the room is thus eliminated and in its
place there is a single new object—the environment—formed by all the ropes interlaced."*

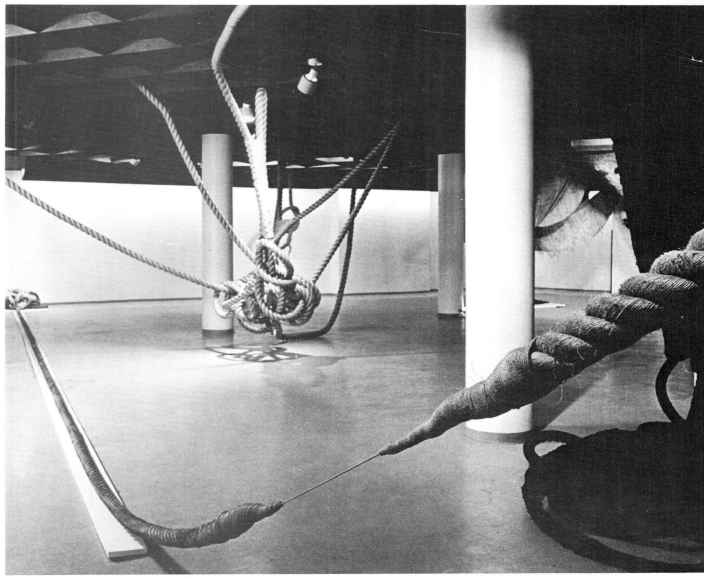

ENVIRONMENT, SITUATION 4

ABAKAN ROUGE II (detail)

An object, orange in color, is placed horizontally over the head of the viewer. This is a temporary phase of the object, since it is not certain if the dangling rope has been extracted out of the object, or if it is meant to be taken into the object.

Installation at Pasadena Art Museum, California, 1971, part of "Fiber as Medium" program.

A heavy single rope cuts a swath to the brass bed that is the climax of the environmental drama. Beyond is a dim, near-empty space with a dreamlike quality of infinity.

ENVIRONMENTAL WALL   1970–71
71' x 24'
sisal and wool; black and brown
Commissioned for the reception room of a new
State Building in North Brabant, s'Hertogenbosch,
the Netherlands

The artist stands below her gargantuan work
The work is not only unprecedented in scale
and impact but in being entirely woven in situ,
with help from three Polish assistants and four
from Holland. On warps suspended directly from
the ceiling, the weft has been freely worked
without heddles or shuttles. The photograph on
the left indicates how, with a special scaffold,
this was accomplished.

amaral

OLGA DE AMARAL
Colombian, born 1932

Studied architectural design at Colegio Mayor de Cundinamarca, Bogotá, and fabric design at Cranbrook Academy of Art, Bloomfield Hills, Michigan. Director of Textiles, Universidad de los Andes, Bogotá. Exhibited at Sociedad Colombiana de Arquitectos, Bogotá, 1957, 1961; Galería El Callejon, Bogotá, 1961; Galería TAB, Bogotá, 1966; Museo de Bellas Artes, Caracas, 1966; Biennale, Lausanne, 1967, 1971; Jack Lenor Larsen Showroom, New York, 1967; Museum West, San Francisco, 1968; The Museum of Modern Art, New York, 1969; Biblioteca "Luis-Angel Arango," Bogotá, 1969; Museum of Contemporary Crafts, New York, 1970. Group shows at Gallery Buchholz (with Sheila Hicks and Else Bechtelev), Munich, 1970; "Deliberate Entanglements," UCLA, 1971; Museo de Bellas Artes, Bogotá, 1972; Galerie Demeure, Paris, 1973. Represented in collections of the Dreyfus Fund, New York; Hyatt House, Chicago; Stanley Marcus, Dallas; Ruth Kaufmann Gallery, New York; Jack Lenor Larsen, New York; J. H. Hurschler, Pasadena; Instituto Colombiano de la Cultura, Museo de Arte Moderno, Banco de la República, Bogotá; Bienal de Arte de Coltejer, Medellín.

View of one-man show at Biblioteca "Luis-Angel Arango," Bogotá, 1970. Central piece is Woven Wall #69, Ashes, *plaited with woven tapes of hand-spun horsehair and wool.*

Olga de Amaral is a phenomenon. Of the artists working in the burgeoning fiber medium she has been, for a number of years, the only South American to be internationally recognized. With her 1970 New York show and in her participation at the 1971 Lausanne Biennale and at the "Fiber as Medium" program in Los Angeles, she emerged as the most dynamic force in the Americas, and a prodigious artist.

Amaral is second generation in that her Art Fabrics began after Tawney and Hicks and before the third and fourth generations of recent years. A Colombian living at the crossroads of Andean ferment, her technique is a result of stimulation rather than influence of pre-Columbian weaving. She is the well-organized director of a large handweaving emporium in Bogotá, a center of many handweavers. She is married to a North American, Jim Amaral, who is a painter. Emotionally she moves in the world of art, but daily she gains from the rationale and the functional bias of her upholstery and carpet production. Perhaps because she has skillful assistance at her command, she is able to be prolific, developing many ideas, trying them in variation, probing in her experiments to modify pattern and color to satisfy her intellectual curiosity. This intense productivity has enabled her to move quickly, to grow and expand far faster than the solitary artist.

Like the first works of Tawney and Hicks, the early Amaral studies were playful, small ideas, little more than narrow yard goods. They employed the same color, texture, and pattern manifestations that characterized her fabric design. From these she developed the special techniques, personal explorations, and architectonic constructions that characterize her mature work. Using the textured wools and somber colors of her atelier, she developed first wrapping and slit tapestry, then the crossed warps and layered pattern development that are her style.

Painfully, she learned to see her work as sculpture, considered and complete in all details. It was no longer "weaving on a stick." There developed stability and finish, depth, and finally scale. Her newest works are both monumental and monolithic, with great depth and presence. They are woven walls, stout bulwarks, sometimes free-standing (or rather, free-hanging). They exist fully in the round, because of their dimension and thickness, and because they are in fact horizontal tubes extravagantly rounded at top and bottom. And, unexpectedly, many of them are *Janus*-type: each side is a face, different in technique and style.

The two- and four-layered, slit and cross-warped weaving typical of Amaral (p. 101) has, almost imperceptibly, given over to other revolutionary techniques. Primary among these are the lavish, all wrapped coils that interrupt the woven strips or snake through them horizontally—or, as in *Linear Woven Wall* (p. 104), are used alone, *in toto,* like a great crashing waterfall.

Newer, and still more forceful, are those walls plaited of prewoven strips. Patterns deriving from the plaited constructions are complex or simple, dazzling in contrast, or, with the fused low-key colors of eucalyptus bark, gain a heightened sense of highlight and shadow, and of depth.

By employing as yarns the thick, full-bodied elements already wrapped or woven as tapes, she is able to realize the final constructions in magnified dimension. She feels that the strength of these elements and their structural textures support the scale and bulk of the woven walls. At the same time the hard cords and slick-surfaced horsehair have increased the range of tactile and visual texture. Most recently she is exploring the translucent and light-refracting possibilities of plastic films and horsehair employed as a monofilament.

INTERLACED IN BLACK AND WHITE   1965
103″ x 97½″
hand-spun wool;
black and natural grays and white
Collection: Ruth L. Mayer, New York
Shown at the Biennale, Lausanne, 1967

In its combination of structure and optical illusion, this basically simple plan, repeated over and
over, is never completely revealed. The construction is as intriguing as that of a pre-Columbian
work. Both layers are woven with such long tapestry slits that the web takes on the appearance

of interwoven tapes alternately joined by two
inches of common weft. The layers were woven
simultaneously but are not interwoven; rather they
are occasionally attached with tapestry joining.
Along the top and bottom rods, the piece has
been stretched beyond its woven width; therefore the vertical slits are pulled to form a diamond
grid.

The emphasis of the strong value contrast, the
knowing use of weft striping, the simple black
"frame," all contribute to the compact rhythm of
the whole. Compare this use of split tapestry with
that of Tawney (p. 272) and Schiele (p. 244–45).

Of her work she has said, "The need to create textures that clearly show the materials has led me to form my woven walls for architectural spaces with my own materials. These materials allow me to realize the structures in larger dimensions. Their function is very clear and of great importance for the proportions of my work. The strength of the elements of constructions previously made and the construction of the texture itself facilitate their integration in architecture with self-sustaining bold strength."

The countercurrents in Olga de Amaral—passions versus logic; sensitivity versus organization; spontaneity versus discipline—are in effect the exhilarating experience of interaction of intent and result. Underneath all the shagginess visible in her work is a clean, sharp eye and mind exploring the endless puzzle of process.

DETAIL #44 FOUR LAYERS INTERLACING   1966
51" x 12"
layered tapestry with wrapped warp
hand-spun wool;
red, blue, and natural black and white

The woven bands cross and recross as the piece is developed. Construction is similar to Orange Weaving, *except that one layer is not woven, but all spirally wrapped.*

ORANGE WEAVING   1966
39¾" x 25⅞"
double-woven slit tapestry
wool; orange and acid green
Collection: Jack Lenor Larsen, New York
Shown in "Wall Hangings,"
The Museum of Modern Art, New York, 1969

The two warp layers are woven simultaneously with long tapestry slits, much in the manner of the larger and simpler Interlaced in Black and White *(p. 101).* The significant difference is that here the two layers are *interwoven, often and with a variety of crossings.* The narrow widths rise and fall from the surface, combine and split at will, change color permanently or alternately in stripes. This modulation of repeated elements, splitting and regrouping, bears resemblance to The Principal Wife *(p. 186),* by Sheila Hicks. The piece is also notable for its richness of finish, but most important is the invention of the devices that permit the interweaving of the two layers.

LINEAR WOVEN WALL #65   1969
80'' x 98''
spiral wrapping and soumak
hand-spun horsehair and wool;
grays, purples, and gold
Collection: Hyatt House, Chicago

Amaral's long involvement with spiral wrapping culminates with this piece in which the wrapped elements are looped over the supporting rod and fall in a giant cascade. The band of soumak visible from the back serves only to anchor the looped elements and to maintain their sequence.

LATTICE WOVEN WALL #66   1970
8' x 8'
woven and plaited
horsehair and hand-spun wool;
natural black, gray, white, and blue

The shaped form of this wall is determined by the two constructions employed. The narrow pre-woven tapes that are plaited in the upper section become the warp for the wider, thicker woven section below. The spirally warped wefts extend the form horizontally, then eloquently terminate. The fragmented dark and light pattern derives from striping the woven tapes.

WOVEN WALL #42   1968
70″ x 29¼″
layered tapestry
hand-spun wool; white, beige, lavender, and black

The artist's series of small, narrow hangings (1966–68) culminates in this handsome three-dimensional work employing layers of tapestry with long slits and spiral wrapping. The front layer is ingeniously joined at right angles to the base layer so that a deep reveal is formed. Like the corrugated and pierced metal reliefs of sculptors Antoine Pevsner and Yaacob Agam, #42 produces different images when viewed frontally or in profile. Particularly in the base layer, the tapestry pattern is emphasized and formalized. The disciplined treatments of the warp ends distinguish this work.

WOVEN WALL #79: PARAMUNA   1972
12′ x 7′
plaiting
hand-spun horsehair and wool; purple and yellows

Like #69, p. 99, Paramuna is all plaited, but here the two layers are of different elements—one of solid-color prewoven tapes, the other of spirally wrapped multicolored rope. The two are, in some areas, plaited together and, in other areas, against themselves, creating lively thrusts and counterthrusts. The strong contrasts of flat and round elements as well as of colors create a sense of movement within a weighty piece. The two faces of this wall offer a sharper contrast than any of the earlier woven walls (p. 105). While the piece is similarly looped over a bar, the two faces are entirely different in construction, in density, and in termination.

anselevicius

EVELYN ANSELEVICIUS
American, born 1925; resides in Mexico

Studied at Black Mountain College, North Carolina; Institute of Design, Chicago. Designed fabric, under the name of Evelyn Hill, for Cohama & Knoll, 1950s. Worked in Mexico, India, Bolivia, 1960s. Presently works in San Miguel de Allende, Mexico. Exhibited at The Museum of Modern Art, New York, 1969; one-man show at Jack Lenor Larsen Showroom, New York, 1970; Biennale, Lausanne, 1971.

Evelyn Anselevicius with one of the many contour studies for The Face of the Earth *(opposite).*

THE FACE OF THE EARTH 1970
99'' x 104''
braided and coiled sisal; golden bronze
Collection: The artist

The technique used here is without precedent, except perhaps in sisal rug squares. The sisal braids are folded back on each other and coiled to achieve the curvilinear contours of the original graphic concept. Finally, the stitched-through, modular sections are pieced together in the manner of a jig-saw puzzle.

Except for the black line, all the colors derive from the tints and shades of the admixtures of two near-complementary dyestuffs, gold and violet. The color placement and the shadow lines of the coiled braids reinforce the composition. The Face of the Earth is remarkable not only for its new technique but for the development in a single piece of a work of this scale and perfection (see cartoon, opposite).

Before embarking on her career as an artist, Evelyn Anselevicius designed for Knoll Associates a remarkable collection of worsted and Velon upholstery.

Since she has been weaving "for herself" she has become one of the most unswervingly forthright of the American weavers. Her works combine concept, impact, and scale with a convincing execution. A decisive innovator, she disciplines each work to a single idea and subordinates all else to it. Although a superb colorist, she most often works in black and white so that the charm of color will not dissuade her from the prime objectives of technique and form. Her use of graduated pile to delineate image is an invention that serves her well for the forceful yet simple compositions she chooses.

In all her pieces the graphic concept is developed first, then a technique selected or invented for it. "For several years, I have been greatly involved in structural problems that are related to thoughts. The approach I end up using is determined by the problems that are created by the idea. The decisive moment in the creation of a piece is the first thought that inspired me to begin. The crisis is over when all of the parts begin to fall into place." But the process is more complicated: "One idea grows out of the process of another and new insights and experience make it possible to use ideas that have been dormant."

THIRD EYE   1960
38" x 42"
knotted pile
wool and linen; black and natural color
Collection: Mabel Curtis, St. Louis

In contrast to Linear Face, *the pile here is knotted and cut. The shaggy ends hang freely downward. The detail shows the relation of pile to the twill-woven linen ground and to the horizontal continuation of the black weft.*

LINEAR FACE   1960–69
(the third in a series)
84" x 77" turned 90°
looped pile
wool; black and white
Collection: Mr. and Mrs. Harold Cohen,
Chevy Chase, Maryland

Rows of black knotted pile were woven between bands of white wool in blanket weave. The pile is in varying lengths so that the resulting irregular black profile produces the illusory image. The cut weft pile projects crisply horizontal. The composition is given force by the contrast of large areas of dark and light, and unity by the continuity of narrow, flat verticals.

becherer

THELMA BECHERER
American, born 1916

Studied at Manchester College, Indiana; Temple University, Philadelphia; University of Maine, Orono; school of the Philadelphia Museum of Art; Penland School of Crafts, North Carolina. Taught at Putney School, Vermont; High Mowing School, Wilton, New Hampshire. Exhibited at Victoria and Albert Museum, London, 1962; The Museum of Modern Art, New York, 1965, 1969; Suffolk Museum, Stony Brook, New York, 1964. Represented in collection of The Museum of Modern Art, New York, as well as private collections.

In her studio, feeding a porcupine quill into the shed, 1970.

Studio showing warp, grasses, and loom.

A nature lover, Thelma Becherer starts with found materials, forms and colors in nature—grasses, seed pods, shells, bones, feathers—snow on trees, clouds, insect markings, animal footprints—to find "a way of capturing my particular feeling for beauty and passing it on to others."

She possesses a wonderfully selective eye, with which she isolates and reveals the beauty of some fragile element. Her compositions have a rare quality: combining the free organic configuration of her selected materials with a sophisticated placement within a rectangular format. By focusing our attention on the surprising beauty of the details, she sharpens their poetic forms.

Weaving is a full-time avocation although she is also involved with a profession far removed from her art. Because for many years she has steadfastly pursued a single theme and technique, this continuity has served to enrich her vocabulary and polish her expression. For over two decades she has been using clear monofilaments, exploiting their transparency and light-refracting potential. By using elements not normally connected with textiles, linking things some see as disparate, her work appears calmly thoughtful, "pictures and ideas stored in my mind." Most of her pieces fall into the category of fragile poetic exercises in pure design, each "to be admired in itself, like an ornamental vase."

UNTITLED 1969
36" x 14½"
plain weave
Velon monofilament, black cotton thread,
wood shavings
Collection: Evan T. Williams, Brooklyn, New York

The surprising dynamic profiles of the wood shavings and their textures make a rich contrast with the Velon monofilaments used for warp and weft and with the fine black weft. Deft use is made of the dark and light transparent materials, which have been packed together to make a dot-dash pattern.

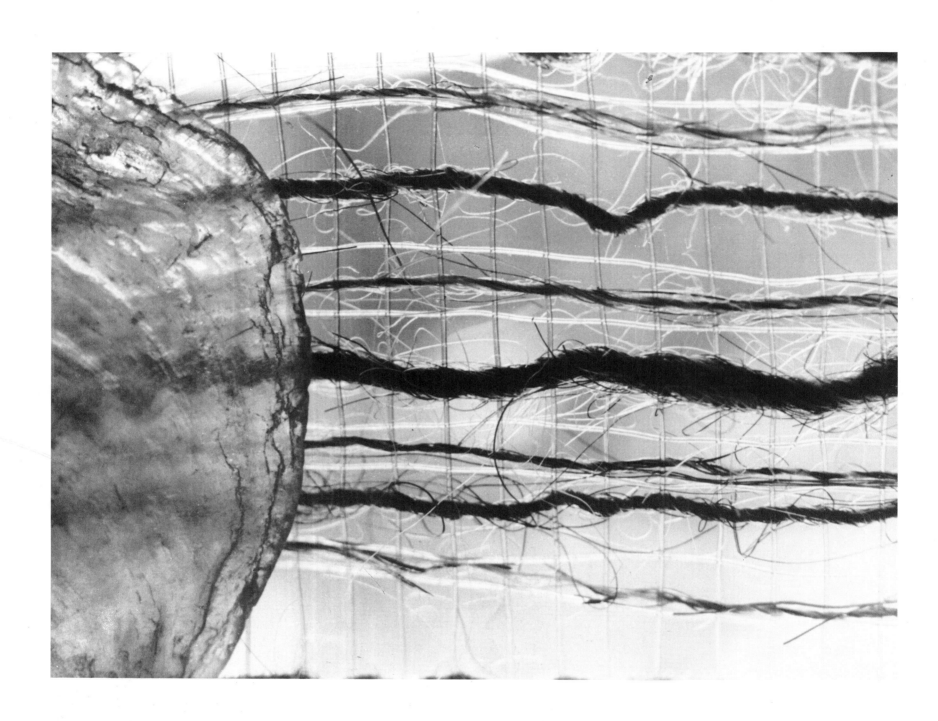

JINGLE SHELLS 1970
34" x 24"
plain weave
transparent Velon monofilament, hand-spun silk,
wool, mohair, and jingle shells
Collection: Thomas B. Williams,
Brookhaven, New York

Modulation of transparency, translucence, and color is further developed with smooth and shaggy yarns, exploiting their profiles and silhouettes. The jingle shells were tied onto Velon, which was then woven into cloth. The integration of the large, round superimposed forms, their color, and the variations within them creates a shimmering, gossamer work.

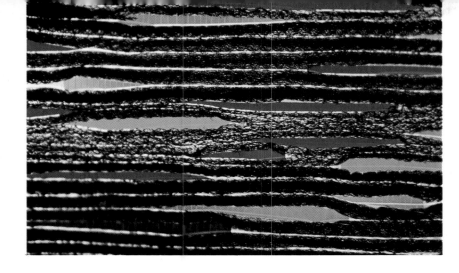

UNTITLED 1970
32" x 25"
plain weave
transparent Velon, black nylon net,
acrylic transparent paper
Collection: The artist

The artist handles these man-made materials as she does the natural ones, selecting them for form and color. The shaggy, opaque black nylon net unifies and frames the jewel-like transparencies.

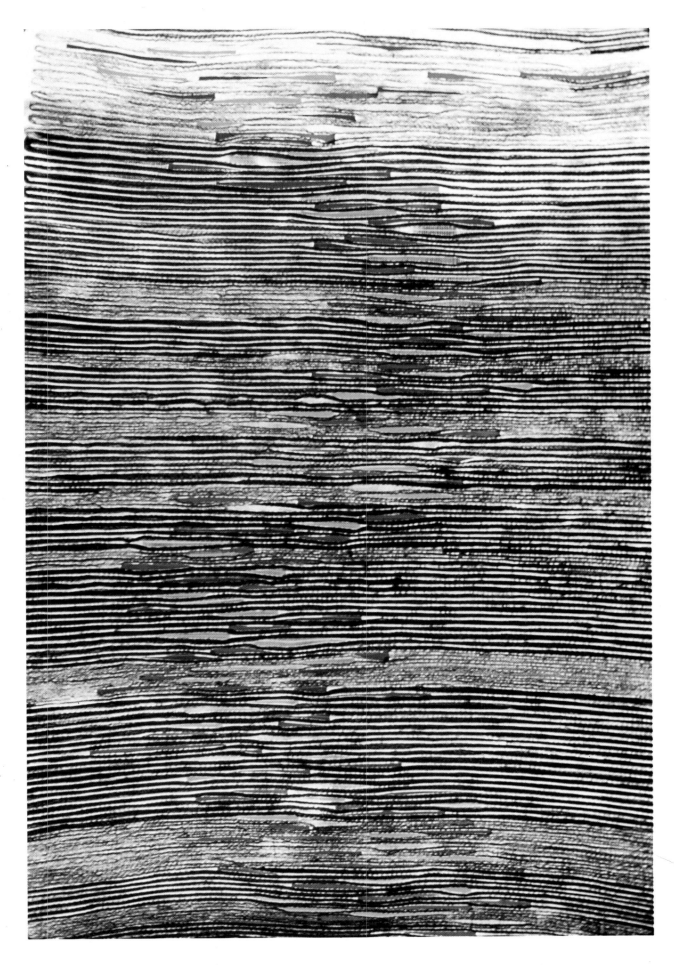

beutlich

TADEK BEUTLICH
born in Poland, 1922; resides in England

Studied art in Poland, Germany, Italy, and England. Started weaving in 1950. A weaver, printer, and sculptor in wood, and lecturer at Camberwell School of Art, London. Author of *The Technique of Woven Tapestry*. Exhibited at Grabowski Gallery, London, 1963, 1967, 1969; Craft Centre, Manchester, 1969; "Weaving for Walls," Victoria and Albert Museum, London, 1965; Biennale, Lausanne, 1967, 1969; British Designer-Craftsmen, Smithsonian Institution, Washington, D.C., 1969; "Modern British Hangings," Scottish Arts Council Gallery, Edinburgh, 1970; "Deliberate Entanglements," UCLA, 1971.

Britain's great artist in fiber is Polish-born Tadek Beutlich. Although long established in England (since 1947), and seemingly without continental dialogue, his work still seems to harken back to his heritage. It is strong, sensuous, personal, and original. At best, as in *Archangel I* (opposite), it is also elegant and monumental.

His mature work has developed in a line so direct that it is easy to follow. It has moved from inverted arches superimposed on a flat woven rectangle to voluptuous cascades of unspun material that push far beyond the still rectilinear woven base. That the work has grown in scale, depth, freedom, and power is characteristic of the international movement. His means, however, are personal; so are the finesse and polish of his surfaces.

Beutlich often makes rough sketches or models of paper, cardboard, and fabric to study the possibilities of his designs. Although he does not make drawings or studies of plants, insects, or landscapes, he is much drawn toward them rather than toward abstract ideas. "I like to give freedom to my individuality within the limitations of the medium. Because of the materials, like unspun jute, sisal, and the way I handle them by twisting, looping, letting the loose ends hang, the simplicity and directness of the design emerge." There is a definite continuity in his pieces because as he resolves one piece, different approaches and solutions suggest themselves to him, which lead to still other handling of the same materials and techniques.

The artist stands before Archangel I
(detail), 1971.
8'7" x 8'3"
plain weave
sisal and mixed fibers; bleached white
Collection: The artist

The piece was woven on a horizontal loom in three parts. The two outer sections are rectangles seamed to the center isosceles triangle. The cascade of unspun sisal at the seams is created by the weft ends of the join. This construction is similar to that of Eruption *(p. 121), but a further development of both technique and aesthetic.*

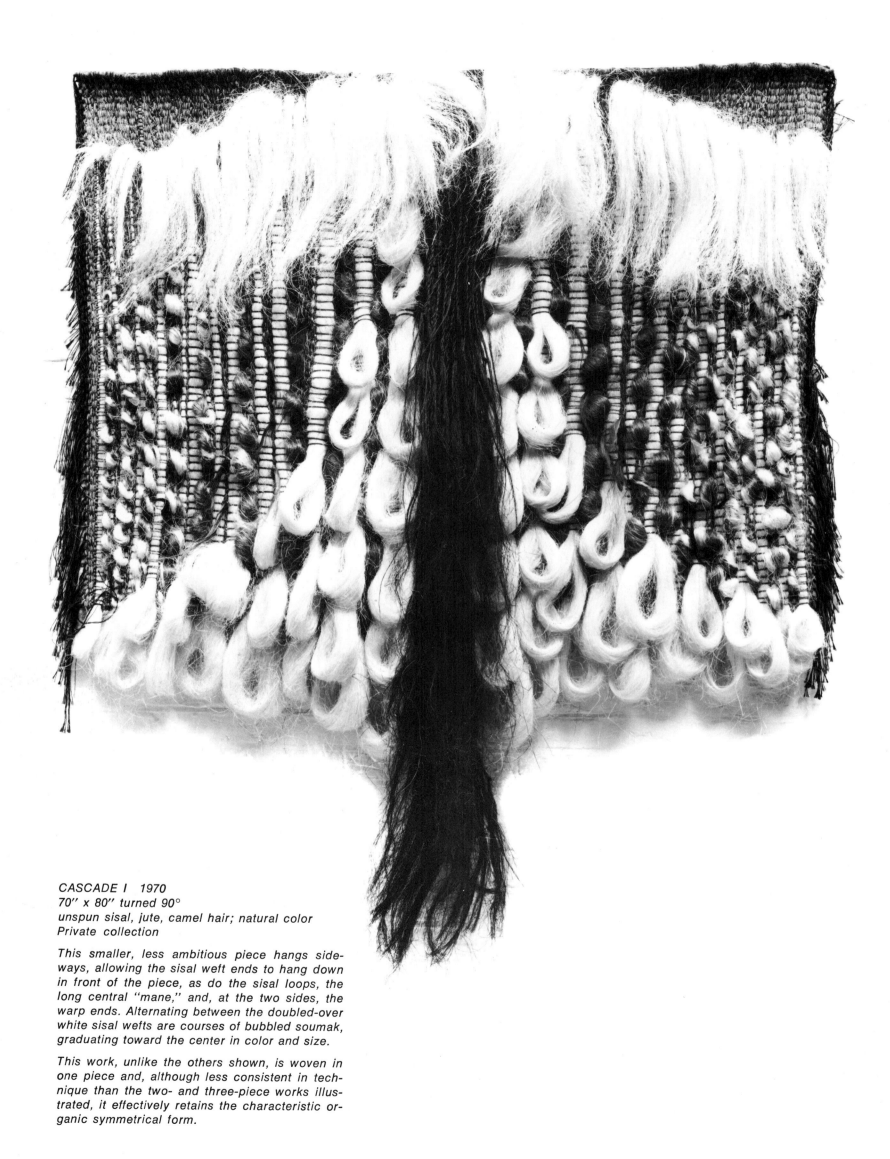

CASCADE I 1970
70'' x 80'' turned 90°
unspun sisal, jute, camel hair; natural color
Private collection

This smaller, less ambitious piece hangs sideways, allowing the sisal weft ends to hang down in front of the piece, as do the sisal loops, the long central "mane," and, at the two sides, the warp ends. Alternating between the doubled-over white sisal wefts are courses of bubbled soumak, graduating toward the center in color and size.

This work, unlike the others shown, is woven in one piece and, although less consistent in technique than the two- and three-piece works illustrated, it effectively retains the characteristic organic symmetrical form.

ERUPTION 1970
9'4" x 10'10"
unspun sisal and jute; red and black
Collection: The artist
Shown in "Deliberate Entanglements," UCLA, 1971

The hanging is woven in three pieces—the two wide wings and the narrow ribbed center channel. Then it is seamed so that the fringed weft ends of all four selvages push forward, into the bilaterally symmetrical composition. This fabrication also causes the center to be concave, and so to emphasize the three-dimensional effect.

Reading left to right from the center, the four surfaces are: the ribbed center section, produced by alternating bundles of red fiber with woven black bands; the double mane of weft end "fringe"; a wide band of bulbous relief produced by a variation of soumak technique; longer loops of the same material and method. The effective use of pendulous, extra-long loops at the bottom transforms the woven rectangle to a weighty shield. The almost zoomorphic blending of color within the fiber bundles is graduated in a manner consistent with the elongation of the loops.

VENUS II   1970
80″ x 60″
woven, with weft pile
unspun jute and other bast fibers; natural color
Private collection

A whimsical treatment of a familiar subject, this work relies on the voluptuous fiber-forms for its anthropomorphic details. The bubbly surface is an uncut weft pile for which a handful of unspun bast fiber was inserted in an open shed. In this way both the length and height of the loop could be controlled. The lively color shading was produced by combining natural and dyed fibers. The overlay of heavy yarn near the top of the piece was formed with fibers pulled out of the weft loop, twisted firmly to produce a hard-spun yarn, and then laid over the surface. The fringes are of warp and weft ends.

DREAM REVEALED   1968
8′4″ x 10′
unspun jute, horsehair, camel hair, cotton;
white, black, and natural
Private collection
Shown at the Biennale, Lausanne, 1969

The work is woven in two pieces, joined from the center of the hanging downwards, leaving the top inside selvages open. The resulting curves reiterate those of the inverted arch that dominates the composition. The raised arch of bulbous forms (note detail, left) is created by the artist's improvisation on the twisted wefts of soumak technique. Their satiny, golden surface and the tangle of furry weft ends derive from the rare use of unspun jute fiber. Its soft luster is emphasized by the spiny glisten of black horsehair in the A-form at the bottom of the piece. This leads the eye to the ombré weft, which shades lighter from bottom to top.

buic

JAGODA BUIC
Yugoslavian, born 1930

Studied at the Academy of Applied Arts, Zagreb; later in Rome and Vienna. Exhibited at Triennale, Milan, 1954; Helsinki, 1963; Oslo and Copenhagen, 1965; Biennale, Lausanne, 1965, 1967, 1969, 1971; Museum of Applied Arts, Zagreb, 1966; Musée Grimaldi, Antibes, 1967; Expo 67, Montreal; Bienal, São Paulo, 1967; Biennale, Venice, 1968, 1970; Stedelijk Museum, Amsterdam, 1969; The Museum of Modern Art, New York, 1969; "Rosc" ("Poetry of Vision"), Dublin, 1971. Awarded Silver Medal, Triennale, Milan, 1955; prize of the city of Zagreb, 1957, 1962; First Prize for textile design at the International Exhibition for Design, Belgrade, 1961; First Prize for Yugoslavian wall hangings, Sombor, 1965. Represented in public collections in Zagreb, Belgrade, Split, Sarajevo, Yugoslavia; hotels in Dubrovnik; Kennedy Center for the Performing Arts, Washington; Dreyfus Fund Collection, New York; Continental Bank Inc., New York; Stedelijk Museum, Amsterdam; and other private and public collections.

It is no accident that Jagoda Buic was among the international artists invited to participate in the 1971 "Rosc" ("Poetry of Vision") exhibition in Ireland. As James Johnson Sweeney wrote in the catalog of the exhibition, her work fulfills the "breadth of exploration of both materials and concepts, a persistent search in fresh directions, a hospitality to fresh directives, an appetite for fresh horizons" that the jury sought in its selections.

Buic is deeply rooted in the heritage of the old Mediterranean, of the Dalmatian stones, flora and fauna, and the rugged soil of the Balkans. The art-craft tradition of the east-west culture from which she comes carries with it a ritual formality. Her personal expression of all this speaks of an intimate relation between her materials and the poetic and cerebral process that combine to make up her vision. In her volumetric forms her poetry is expressed with an awe-inspiring solemnity. Working in monumental scale, mostly with wool and sisal, preferably in blacks, browns, and grays with an occasional touch of gold, or an occasional use of silk to counterpoint the ponderous materials, Buic seldom departs from traditional weaver's techniques.

In speaking of the avant-garde tapestry she has said: "It is nothing more than a return to the primary qualities of weaving and its laws, a love for the material and the act of directing it to tactile sensibility. However, I foresee new possibilities of interlacing. When I say interlacing, I think of the weft and of the infinite mathematical possibilities of the ligature of the thread. These possibilities represent the instrument of the tapestry worker, the possibility of finding a veritable textile existence. On the road of this technical evolution from tapestry to weaving, tapestry loses even its name, but it gains its place in the plastic movement of today."

Jagoda Buic standing before Composition in Space. *(three elements)*

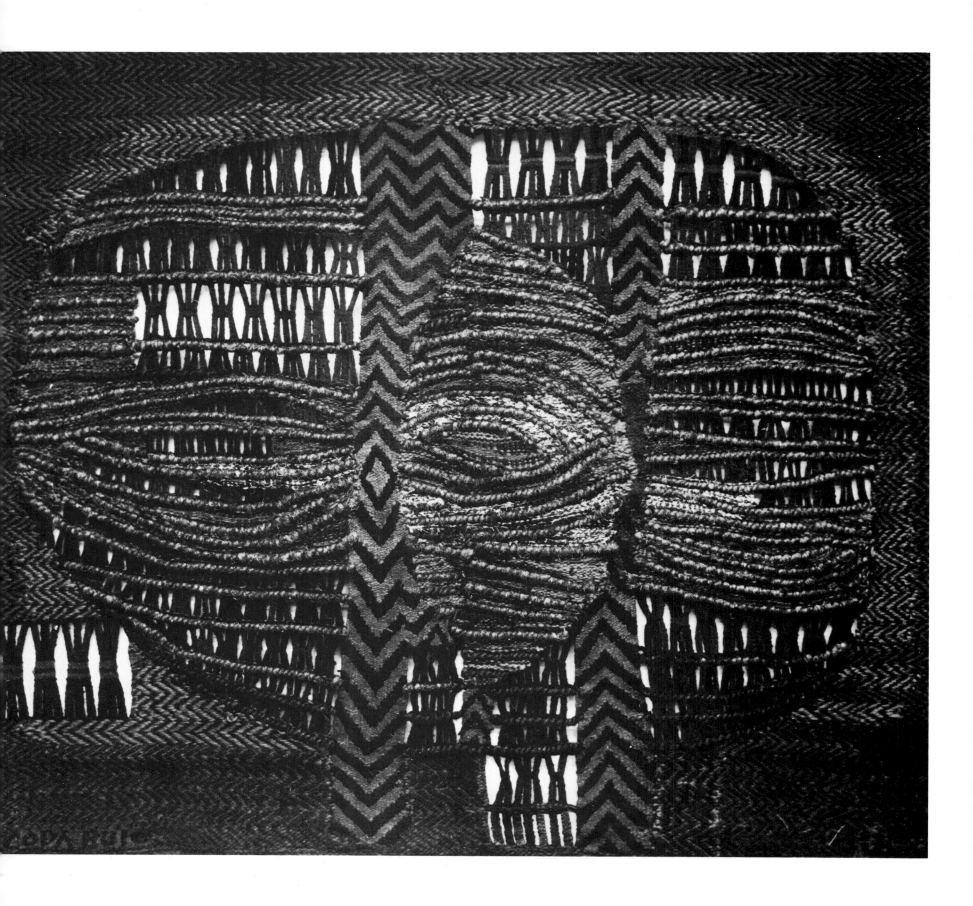

TRIPTIQUE STRUCTURAL   1966
about 97½" x 117"
tapestry
wool, goatshair, cordage, sisal;
brown, black, gray, and gold
Collection: J.H. Hurschler, Pasadena
Shown at the Biennale, Lausanne, 1967

*This is the first of Buic's works with voids to en-
gage the wall behind it as a part of the composition. The artist has used a traditional Yugoslavian
weaving technique called Vutlak.*

Woven in reverse twill, the dense weft-faced
frame is "in front of" the finely woven tapes. Because of their actual relief and implied or optical
dimensionality, the spiral-wrapped horizontals appear to advance. Tapestry joining is used for the
chevron of the vertical bands and for the solids
between them, as well as for the chevrons of the
vertical bands. In a complex composition of repeated rectangular, ovoid, and diagonal elements,
Buic has stretched the dimensional play of woven
fabric.

As a catalyst for her art form she seeks modernization not through mechanization but, as her drawings show, through a thought process. An integration and organization of thought is combined with vestiges and memories of bygone periods of rustic mythology that enables her to render the invisible visible. However, her work is above all modern in purpose. "Today, I see the meaning of all the new movements in the synthesis of architecture with the other branches of plastic creation. In this sense, the tapestry, as well as all the other spatial elements, cannot be only decorative; it is conditioned by space and creates for itself an ambiance. The tapestry exists in counterpoint to the "warm" and "cold" surfaces of modern architecture, in counterpoint to the emphatic materials like stone and steel. The fibers also stifle sound. I do not wish to cover the walls with tapestry; I would like them to exist together, so that the wall is present in the composition. Therefore the numerous perforations in my weavings. But I would like to go further, working at weaving which exists freely in space. I embrace works in three dimensions which live in the space which conditions them."

There is no narrative pictorial element in Buic's work, neither a depiction of an actual event or object or person. Such imagery as appears is in the nature of heraldic symmetry, of emblems made emphatic and emotional by expanded scale and persistent use of a dark color. Diagonal lines, diamond shapes graduated in size, horizontal lines made bolder by being raised from the flat surface, the circle —all of these are arranged in what might seem symbolic phenomena if indeed one could "read" a significance from these ancient, almost universal signs. The color is generally monotone without strong contrasts to relieve the insistent whole. But variations in surface, a rhythmic use of apertures or slits, the shaped compositions, all offer a vital ceremonial character of timelessness.

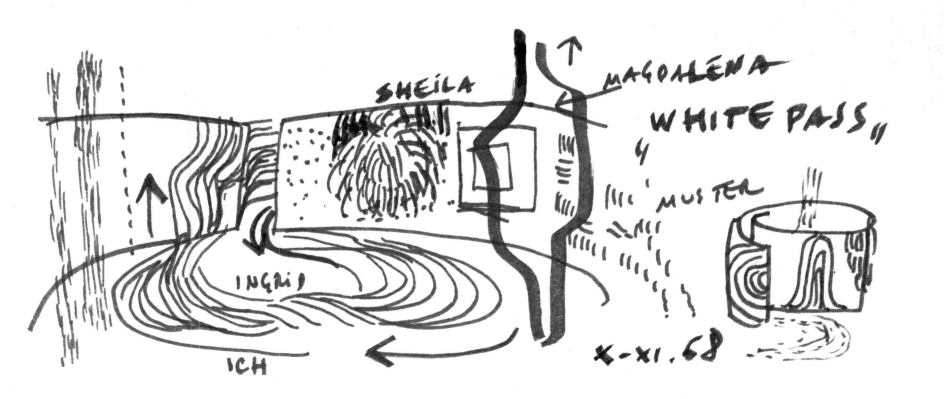

Undeniably, Buic's work in costume design and scenography has been an indispensable source of inspiration. For years she has been associated with the Dubrovnik Theater Festival which presents many of its programs in medieval buildings and in the open courtyards surrounded by medieval architecture, cliffs, ledges, where the air is clear and suffused with the pungent scent of pine and flowers. In this indigenous atmosphere, theater is embellished by her materials, which help to create new dimensions in scenery and costumes. This creative liberty surely liberates Buic in her thoughts about new perspectives, and new relationships in space with regard to her weaving.

As a person, she is warm, voluptuous, and gregarious; as an artist she is intensely involved with all the different aspects of her work. As an artist, she does not always go her lonely way; rather she dreams of situations in which shared beliefs can work in harmony. Thus, in 1968 she envisioned a dialogue with some of her fellow artists—an environment in the form of a snail in which the work of Magda Abakanowicz, Sheila Hicks, Ingrid, and "Ich" could come together (p. 127).

There is also a kinship with the sculptors working in her own country during the past decade, whose use of inorganic materials—iron, steel, and other metals—illustrates a strong consanguinity of form and scale. All of Buic's work is directed toward the sensibilities of the contemplator, making great demands on his involvement, yet, as a work of art, retaining a separate existence.

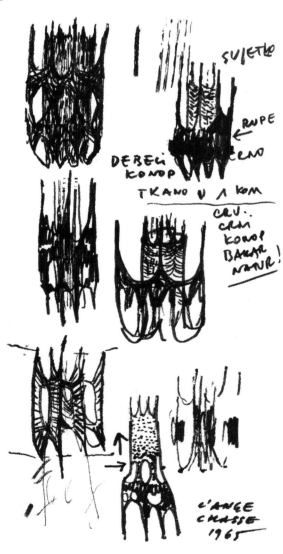

Sketches in pen and ink, L'ange chasse, *1965*

FALLING ANGEL   1967
120½" x 57"
slit tapestry, weft twining
sisal; black and brown
Collection: Stedelijk Museum, Amsterdam
Shown in "Rosc" ("The Poetry of Vision"),
Dublin, 1971

Two concentric layers of slit tapestry are hung
from an armature. Both the inner and outer structures are ornamented by weft bands which together with the introduction of color produce the
structural variations, while the change in the size
and rhythm of the slit tapestry provides interesting
"fenestrations."

Characteristic of Buic's architectonic predilections, the scale, weight, and sense of permanence
in this piece are like a castle keep.

129

UNTITLED 1972
approximately 54" x 80" turned 90°
tapestry; handspun wool; reds, brown, and black
Collection: The artist

With this strong brilliant piece Buic returns to two-dimensional tapestry and to color, here admixed with the browns and sooty blacks she knows so well. Recurring too are the crenellations and chevron motifs that dominated her work in the sixties. They are employed here, however, as an over-all pattern without the relief of intermittent flat areas or tapestry slits. In this work it would appear that the Slavic roots of Buic have reasserted themselves.

POLYPTIQUE   1967
7½' x 18'
shaped tapestry
black sisal; goatshair, wool; gold silk
Shown at the Bienal, São Paulo, 1967;
Biennale, Venice, 1970;
"Deliberate Entanglements," UCLA, 1971

Buic is concerned with architecture; she also
weaves it, complete with crenellated turrets, and
the essential and permanent strength of its basic
materials. Here the structural patterns are handled
like those of a master mason; as the eye moves
across the large surfaces, it is carried along by
rhythmical repetitions; their logic and progression
providing moments for quiet contemplation.

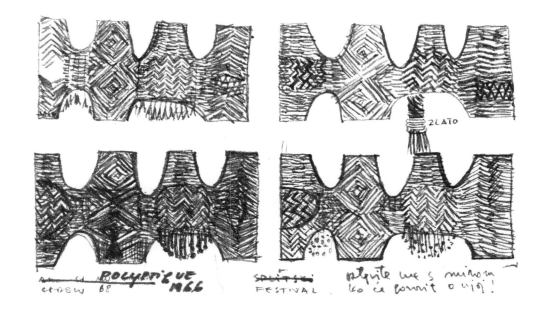

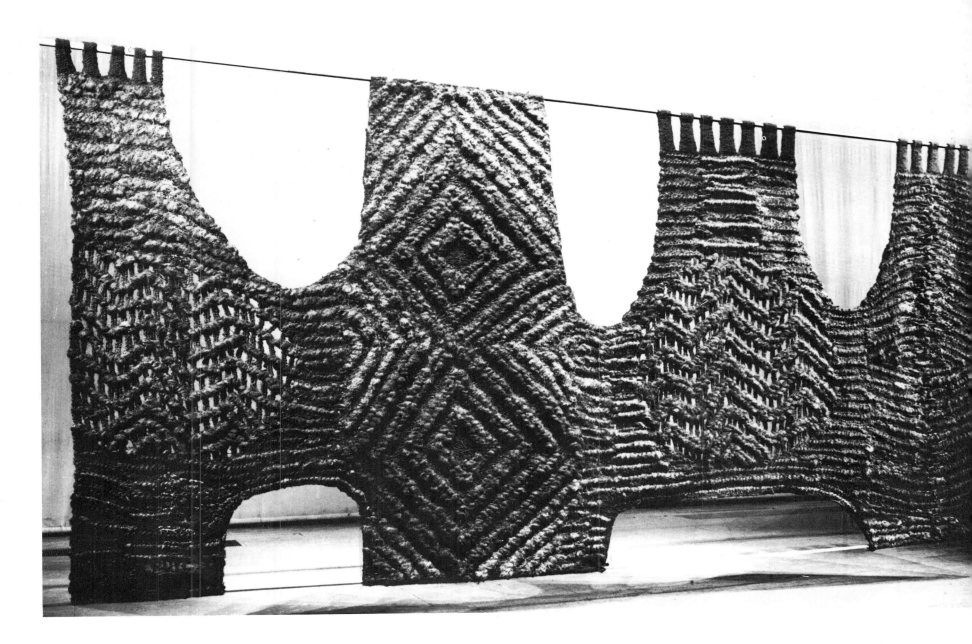

pen drawing, Eglise

FLEXIONS "HOMMAGE TO PIERRE PAULI"
seven elements
11'8" x 14'7"
shaped tapestry, with weft wrapping
wool, sisal, cordage; black and brown
Collection: The artist
Shown at the Biennale, Lausanne, 1971;
"Rosc," Dublin, 1971

The seven elements of Hommage, individually woven, are composed with ritualized formality and infinite variety. Although Buic's familiar patterns —horizontal, vertical, diagonal lines—appear in these pieces, there is no sense of the rectilinear, since the elements seem to flow with the authority of some ancient pillars. In the elements on the extreme left and right, the essentially two-dimensional character is relieved by an actual rounding of form. The piece is woven in an A shape, turning one up and one down. Gravity pulls it out of the flat horizontal. Weft wrapping is used as high relief for pattern and texture. In the early sketch for this work and in the second stage shown in the watercolor, Buic begins to feel the growing rhythm of the rounded form.

The interstices between the individual elements and the openings within some of them offer glimpses of an unseen landscape. From the outside this Hommage is a bulwark; inside it is a haven, a sanctuary.

watercolor sketch

133

PRIMARY FLEXION   1969
27" x 66" turned 90°
soumak and looping
sisal and wool; brilliant red
Collection: The artist

This floor piece, turned 90°, brings the selvage up to the top in the collar. Here also horizontal rows of soumak are reversed, right to left and left to right, to create the bold rib. The loops are cut to form the pile. This recumbent object full of a lively frenzy is a departure from Buic's customary freestanding or wall-hung works.

COMPOSITION 64   1964
70" x 97½"
shaped tapestry
wool and "cordage"; black
Shown at the Biennale, Venice, 1968

Nostalgic of Near Eastern saddle bags, Composition 64 is notable not only for its implied symbolism but for its early development of woven dimensionality and for its rich texture. The surface throughout is created by two supplementary weft elements of sisal cordage. One is laid across the web—the second is spiral-wrapped around the first so as to bind it to the warp ends. The rectangular bag fronts were woven with long, unenlarged weft ends, which were later woven into the sheds of the piece proper.

*Jagoda Buic with a partially finished work
woven and wrapped
hand-spun wool, cotton; natural colors*

It is rare for Buic to work without heavy density,
without heavy dark colors and without stiff sisal.
Here with frail delicacy she is manipulating a very
open filigree. The sparse, bumpy warp serves only
as the armature on which she builds. The weft, a
heavy handspun roving wrapped around a core,
determines the surface texture and delineates the
patterned silhouette.

The continuous wefts are often eccentric, forming,
when finished, a large ellipse similar to that of
her Triptique Structural (p. 126). These wefts are
buttressed by the staggered verticals, which are
not woven but are of weft wrapped around eight
warp ends down one leg and up the other.

The photograph clearly demonstrates the unusual
freedom with which she is weaving—not in the
traditional sequence of bottom to top but beginning and finishing where she pleases. In part this
freedom derives from her method of breaking and
tying the warp.

butrymowicz

ZOFIA BUTRYMOWICZ
Polish, born 1904

Studied at Fine Arts Academy, Warsaw. Awarded grand prize of the Polish government, 1967. Exhibited at Zacheta Gallery, Warsaw, 1953, 1968; Stewart Hall, Montreal-Pointe Claire, 1969; group shows at Kunsthalle, Mannheim, 1964/65; Kunstmuseum, St. Gall, 1964/65; Gemeemtemuseum, Arnhem, 1964/65; Stedelijk van Abbe-Museum, Eindhoven, 1964/65; Kunstindustrimuseet, Oslo, 1965; Grabowski Gallery, London, 1966; Palazzo delle Esposizioni, Rome, 1967; Biennale, Lausanne, 1967; Palais des Beaux Arts, Brussels, 1967; University Museum, Mexico City, 1968; Hermitage, Leningrad, 1968; The Museum of Modern Art, New York, 1969; Palazzo Corsini, Florence, 1969; Museum Folkwang, Essen, 1970; "Exempla 70," Munich, 1970. Represented in collections of Lodz Museum; National Museums, Warsaw, Poznan; Museums of Modern Art, Skopje, Rome, Mannheim.

The artist at work in her studio. To insert a weft of unspun sisal, she opens the shed of her high warp loom.

Zofia Butrymowicz is the eldest of the Warsaw School. Her verve and the spontaneity of her work belie this fact. So do her colors: although they are often so somber as to be charred plays of black on black, the reds she so often, so skillfully handles, burn with a lively inner fire.

The wisdom of years is more evident in the ease with which she—like Josef Albers and Henri Matisse in his late work—knowingly manipulates a narrow range of forms into full, robust expression.

Like her Warsaw colleagues Barbara Falkowska and Jolanta Owidzka, and like the traditional tapestry weavers of Cracow, Butrymowicz retains the single weighty thickness of wool gobelin. This technique she dominates. The small gouache sketches she works from are themselves free. And freely she interprets them on the loom. Her materials are hand-spun wools—often very heavy and irregular and sometimes barely spun at all. "I try to use only noble and durable materials which provide a deep tone of color. I try to discover laws which rule over the material." Although the solidity and earthy color of her work is very different from the pale webs of Susan Weitzman, there are similarities in the importance of irregular spinning and the adherence to a single sphere so large as to fill the rectangle.

Butrymowicz is ever searching, ever receptive. "New experiments in art have always been of interest to me . . . whether I agree with them or not, and therefore I never pass by or I am never indignant at any expression in art. I strongly believe that in the wide range of experiments there will also be some elements of the development of culture."

Butrymowicz Warsaw Show, 1968

Because most of the pieces are turned 90° to the direction they were woven, the weft striations are vertical. The tapestry joinings are minimal. The artist has spliced wefts of different colors and characters to modulate the areas within and without the suns. Additional relief is given by occasionally raising some wefts to the surface.

The masterly installation employs only hand-hewn weathered beams to visually and physically support the weighty pieces and to emphasize the rhythms of repeated circles within rectangles. The exhibit is forceful because all the work hangs freely in space; it is unified because all the pieces are parallel and facing in one direction, and because the work itself is consistent. Most important, the impact of the work is cumulative.

carau-ischi

MARGUERITE CARAU-ISCHI
Swiss, born 1928

Self-taught. Exhibited at the Biennale, Lausanne, 1957, 1969, 1971; Stedelijk Museum, Amsterdam, 1969, and The Museum of Modern Art, New York, 1969. Awarded scholarships and prizes by the Swiss government.

Born in Zurich, Marguerite Carau-Ischi lives in the small village of Castagniers, in the south of France. This isolation has perhaps encouraged the consistent development of a pure style, with an insistently rectangular format. A woven frame begins the geometry and controls the composition, defining the content and the space around it. Marguerite Carau-Ischi frankly professes to "paint with textiles using the richness of their materials and their textures." She works from sketch or collage, keeping in mind the relation of color, scale, material. When these are fully determined, she is ready to execute the actual work. Using her materials to reach a synthesis of expression through simple technique, she reduces details to an understatement of essentials. Although she is interested in animal, vegetable, and synthetic fibers, she concentrates on sisal. What emerges is unbelabored, fresh and pure, with a calculated simplicity.

HORIZONTAL-VERTICAL 1969
70'' x 112'' turned 90°
tapestry
bleached sisal
Shown at the Biennale, Lausanne, 1969

The large relief, immaculate and pristine, is consistently pure in its use of one material—sisal, bleached to a single luminous ivory. The glistening surface emphasizes the shadowed relief of the fine ground and the heavy ribbed frame. The narrow horizontal-vertical slits counterbalance the dense composition.

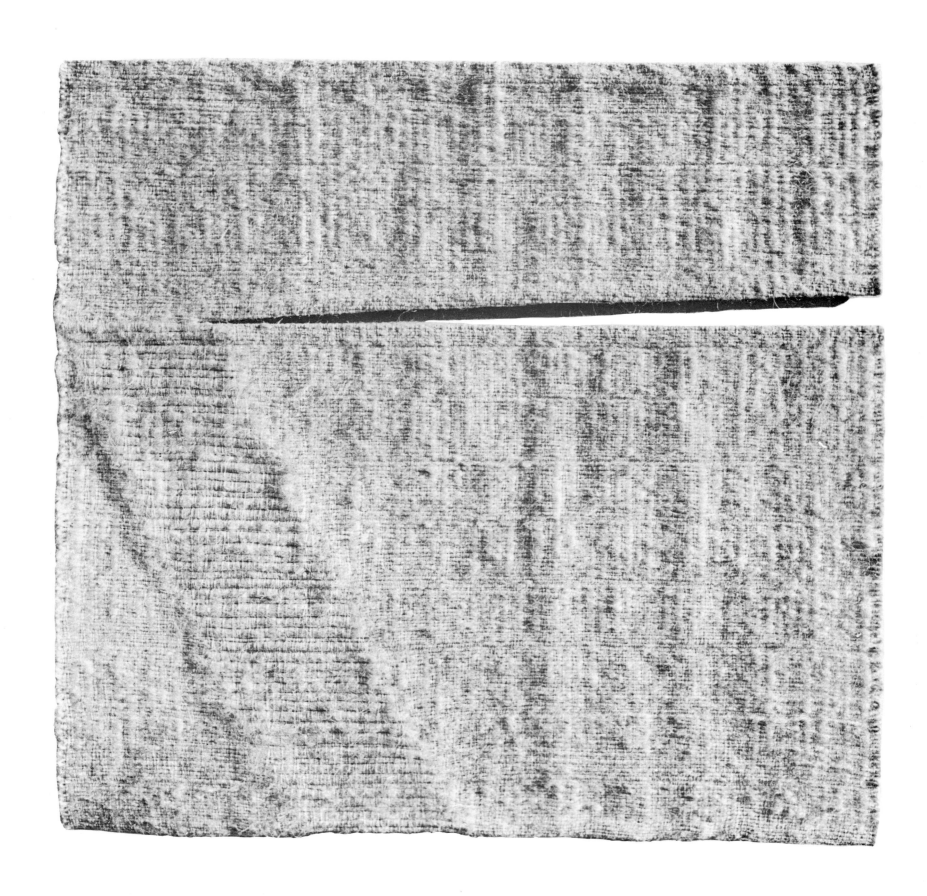

INCISED COMPOSITION   1969
68¼″ x 71″
tapestry
bleached sisal
Collection: Ruth Kaufmann Gallery, New York

*Two diagonals—one a broad raised band, one a
deep slash—interrupt the elegant surface. The
composition is carried to the edges, without the
woven frame of earlier work.*

YELLOW AND IVORY COMPOSITION *1969*
66″ x 70½″
tapestry
sisal; bleached and yellow-orange

Here the sisal relief is further developed, with more depth and variation. The asymmetric placement of the large textured area in the rectangle is balanced by two small squares of ivory.

COMPOSITION IN IVORY AND YELLOW *1971*
5′6″ x 10′3″ turned 90°
tapestry
sisal; bleached and yellow-orange
Shown at the Biennale, Lausanne, 1971

With the dynamism of a diagonal thrust, the strident yellow form moves across an ivory ground. In the spirit of hard-edge painting, Carau-Ischi's usual woven frame is eliminated, and the movement pushes beyond the edge. The composition of large open surfaces is relieved by horizontal and vertical texture patterns.

falkowska

BARBARA FALKOWSKA
Polish, born 1931

Studied at Fine Arts Academy, Warsaw. Exhibited in one-man and group shows throughout Poland; in China, Mexico, Denmark, Belgium, and Italy; in Leningrad, Cologne, Prague, Stuttgart; and at the Biennale, Lausanne, 1965; The Museum of Modern Art, New York, 1969. Represented in collections of National Museum, Warsaw; History of Weaving Crafts Museum, Lodz, and private collections in Europe and the United States.

Barbara Falkowska in a grain field.

The artist's studio—a clutter of "living things."

A medieval ferment and a quiet ruminative passion for the feel, the look, the smell of nature blend in Barbara Falkowska's work. She creates elegies to fields of corn, meadows of lupine, sunflowers, beans, ammonites, to the past penetrating into the present.

Her work is an amalgam of her meditations: "When I am about to weave a branch of lupine, I feel myself walking along a field of lupine made hot yellow gold by the sun."

There are timeless aspects to the dialogue she conducts with all kinds of things. Surrounded in her studio by barks, birch leaves, photographs of lizards long dead, and ammonites 150 million years old, she thinks "of the mysterious life, fascinating and bewitched, in the stone (ammonites), this strange melange made of things dead and alive of which our enviroiment is composed. When it comes to ammonites, it seems unjust to speak of them as 'things dead.' They live, but in another form. And life emanates from them without stopping. . . . One can share these emotions and impressions through the intermediary of words, by silence, writing, singing, weaving. It is precisely in weaving that I participate in all that."

She uses earthy, traditional, durable materials—flax, wool hand-carded and hand-spun, sisal, and strongly twisted agave fiber. She dyes her materials with the ancient natural dyes: madder, indigo, barberry, oak bark, birch leaves, greenweed, and cochineal. "I feel the smell of the bath in which the wool is dyed, observing the way in which it changes color, how it drinks the color of the plants, all this excites my imagination. When the wool leaves the dyeing vats, the skeins drying in the air, suspended one alongside the other, form a composition which I regret having to destroy when I select one for weaving."

Like the earthy romantic colors that fuse to carpet a primeval forest, her colors are blurry and somber. Here and there one can see an occasional flickering of luminous gold thread, or a fleck of bright color moving to the surface. She is unerring in her choice of palette.

"It is in the course of weaving that the creative work takes place. I never prepare a detailed cartoon of my projects; I only make a general scheme of the composition. I make some studies which help me to affirm my impressions, the ambiance, the color, and to know in detail the construction which interests me. After, in the course of weaving, I am sure of myself."

Important to her creative vocabulary are several techniques she has made her own. Unlike the covered warps of classic gobelin, her warps ride over the weft as an important compositional element. Moreover, because she does not use the evenly spaced reed (using instead a comb or sword) to beat in the weft, her warps are not vertical lines but eccentric or pulled to form a lively organic texture that reinforces the surface. When Falkowska weaves stiff, raw sisal through spongy wools as can be seen in the full-scale detail from *Sunflowers* (p. 147), she has set up an unusual surface tension with staccato rhythms derived from the forward and back weft movement.

Of the Polish artists discussed in this book, Falkowska is most closely allied to gobelin technique and to the strong folk-art tradition of her country. But unlike the tapestry weavers of Cracow, she is not working *within* the tradition. Instead she projects a very personal, eccentric, and contemporary style on an ancient technique, more medieval in spirit than in essence. Within the gobelin framework, Falkowska improvises on construction and in unorthodox combinations of materials. "I am and I feel united with tradition, that is to say that if I adhere to the medieval development of this branch of art . . . I intercept what has been elaborated by numerous generations. I respect and esteem the realizations of my predecessors— great, or anonymous. I do not need to make a revolution in the domain of the means of expression. I believe that some changes are produced as a function of the development of man. . . . I do not believe in a so-called progress of art which begins by revolutionizing the formal means."

Her work cannot be taken casually: it expects and demands attention on the part of the viewer. It reflects her thoughts, her pursuit of meaning and of the interactions which take place among the natural elements around us.

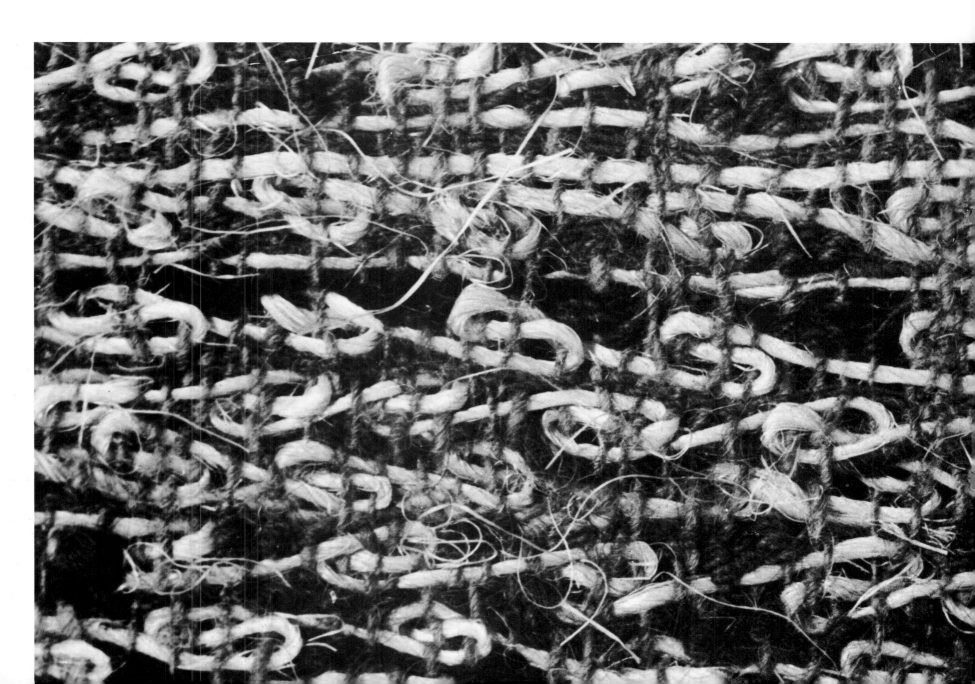

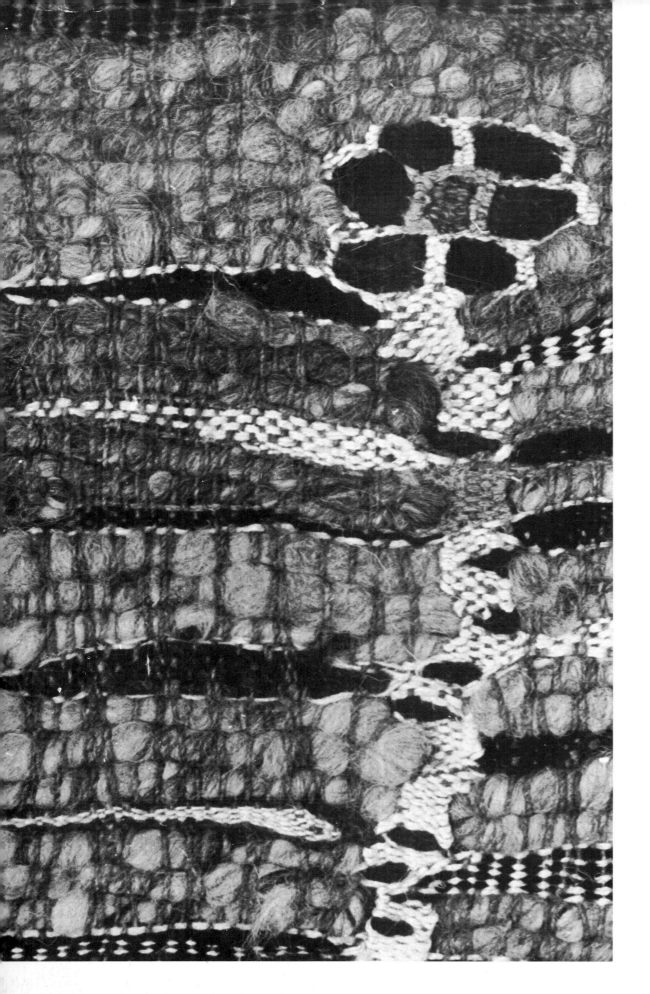

GRAY FLOWER   1966
12" x 10½"
tapestry
wool, linen

This small study reveals the quality of Falkowska's surfaces. Because the motif is woven of fine smooth yarns that tend to cover a warp otherwise exposed, it seems embedded in the thick spongy surface. Especially effective are the reversals of dark and light yarns, including the outlining of the leaves. The palpable character of these simple materials gives essence to the whole.

BEANS   1966
76" x 47"
tapestry
wool; beige and gold background, dark blue, brown, black with touches of red
Collection: Robert Peterson

The vigorous forms of this homely subject are masterfully structured within the simple woven frame finished with long, varicolored tab fringes. This work owes its success to the vigor, the consistency, and the variety of its execution. The organic permutations within her hand-spun, hand-dyed yarns contribute to the almost calligraphic forms; so does the eccentric wefting technique. Most unusual is the eccentric or "pulled" warp, which creates a textured pattern sufficiently strong to integrate the entire surface.

AMMONITES (detail) 1967
50'' x 108¼'' shown as woven
tapestry
hand-spun wool, sisal; earth colors

Within a complex major work, the artist has seemingly dwarfed giant prehistoric trees with the volu-
tion of fossilized ammonites. Actually, the trees
are seaweeds sheltering fishes. The technical improvisation is not only as free as the graphic fantasy, it is essential to it. Image and material and
craftsmanship are inseparably integrated. Also
contributing are contrasts of scale and the play
of color values she introduces with her materials.

AMMONITES IV (detail)
55½'' x 15½''
tapestry
wool and sisal; earth colors

Bubbling up between the spaced-out warp yarns,
the large soft weft provides contrasts of scale
and a play of negative and positive forms. The
repeated spirals and the mossy earth-tone palette
that are typical of Falkowska derive from the shadowed arboretum of her mind's eye and from the
narrow color range of her dye-pots.

fruytier

WILHELMINA FRUYTIER
Dutch, born 1915

Self-taught. Formerly Director of Design of the de Ploeg weaving factory, Bergeyk. Exhibited at World's Fair, Brussels, 1958; Stedelijk Museum, Schiedam, 1964; Biennale, Lausanne, 1965, 1967, 1969; Biennale, Venice, 1968; Museo de Arte Contemporáneo, Madrid, 1969; The Museum of Modern Art, New York, 1969. Represented in collections of KLM, Amstelveen; Crematorium, Ockenburgh; Provinciehuis Noord Brabant, the Netherlands; Dreyfus Fund Collection, New York.

As an artist in service to architecture, Wilhelmina Fruytier, a tall, handsome woman, is well cast. That she is persuasive, responsible, and to the point has convinced many building committees to accept her desire to contribute. As important as her physical strength are her personal qualities of being open and direct. "The basis of my work is the commission, that is the given space in the existing architectural environment; the people that visit and work in the building; the functional and social circumstances on the spot."

First a painter, then a weaver of conventional gobelin tapestry, in 1957 she undertook a series of experiments in material and construction. Seeking expression sufficiently strong to serve Holland's rising new buildings, she wove her first rope tapestry in 1961. This heavy material, exaggerated by the scale of her technique, made it possible for her to intensify the character of the weave when it was viewed from a great distance.

Feeling that her abstract images and bold structures called for sharp contrasts and clean demarcation, she combined only neutral tonalities in order to avoid shaded confluence of color. As her style matured and the pieces grew in size, Fruytier developed relief by floating wefts over the surface (p. 154). As these became so pronounced and produced heavy shadows, her range of materials grew simpler and her color contrasts more subtle. Finally there emerged the series in immaculate white that serves to accentuate the highlight and shadow of the relief. Within the simplicity of a single weft, she developed first a series of small slits (p. 157), then large elliptical ones (p. 158).

Fruytier's large, weighty tapestries are essentially architectural. They are specific to the vast public spaces for which they are designed. Architectural, too, are her clearly visible structures with their direct expression of materials. So is her simplicity, clarity, strength, and monumentality. She says, "for me the essential point of departure is each given architectural and environmental situation. In that given situation a wall hanging must intensify and complete the existing space through simplicity, structural power and clarity of design. In that way I hope to contribute to the restoration of tapestry as a monumental art form. I strongly feel that that can only be done when the limitations of material and weaving techniques are faithfully observed and used in such a way that the resulting work has its own life, yet is in healthy and strong harmony with its surroundings."

Wil Fruytier in front of the long horizontal of a rope tapestry commissioned by the University of Nijaegen, the Netherlands, for their meeting room, 1969. The vertical warp is tied to a weaving frame; the weft is laced in and out, without use of heddles.

UNTITLED 1966
*commissioned for a crematorium,
Ockenburgh, the Netherlands
4'11" x 26'3"
tapestry
ropes of manila hemp and cotton;
natural and dark neutrals*

*Fruytier's "ropes" vary in size and twist, in fiber
and surface. Some were patinated by the sea or
darkened with oil and creosote. Always they are
sufficiently hard to maintain their character when
packed into the web. The heavy relief is produced
by the soumak technique of diagonally wrapping
wefts or pairs of wefts around successive warp
ends. The depth is exaggerated by the relative
flatness of the white ground and by the black
areas that suggest deep shadows. Particularly successful are the handling of composition and the
relation of the alternating woven pattern to the
brickwork.*

This detail from a tapestry contemporaneous with the piece for the crematorium illustrates the variety of both Fruytier's materials and the manner of their interlacing. Finer wefts weave over and under single warp ends while heavier material is carried over two, three, or more warps, sometimes in the diagonal progression of a twill. The black jute in the center and the natural jute at center left densely cover the warp with soumak wrapping. The weft is eccentric in that it deviates from the horizontal. Some areas, such as the "eye" at the center, employ an outlining technique.

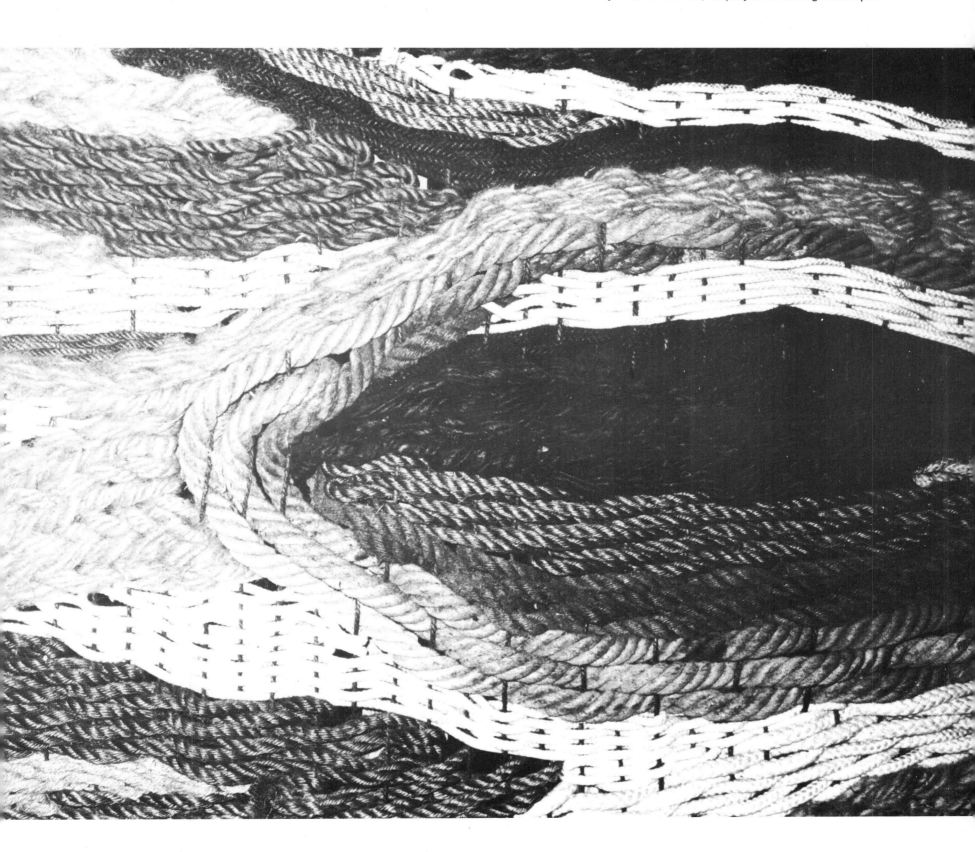

Small preliminary sketches such as this one in conté crayon are used for study and presentation. The sketch is not enlarged into a cartoon but squared off into sections of one-third of a meter. The graphic tonalities of the drawing are freely interpreted in the weaving.

EXPERIMENT #12   1969
13' x 14'7"
tapestry
polypropylene film and cotton; black and white
Shown at the Biennale, Lausanne, 1969
Photographed in the artist's studio

For this experimental work, Fruytier developed a weft of polypropylene sheeting compressed into a much-pleated rope. This gave her a new, satiny surface, more durable and soil-resisting than white cotton. In the white areas, note the varied pattern caused by uneven wefting. A single bold image is enlivened by the structural pattern of a weft joining, which reads as a dark and light dovetailing. This derives from weft loops that do not engage each other but circle back on two adjoining warps. The resulting dark and light fret is relieved by the knife-edge severity of the long vertical slits. These are sufficiently open to pierce the flat plane and carry the eye in and around the composition.

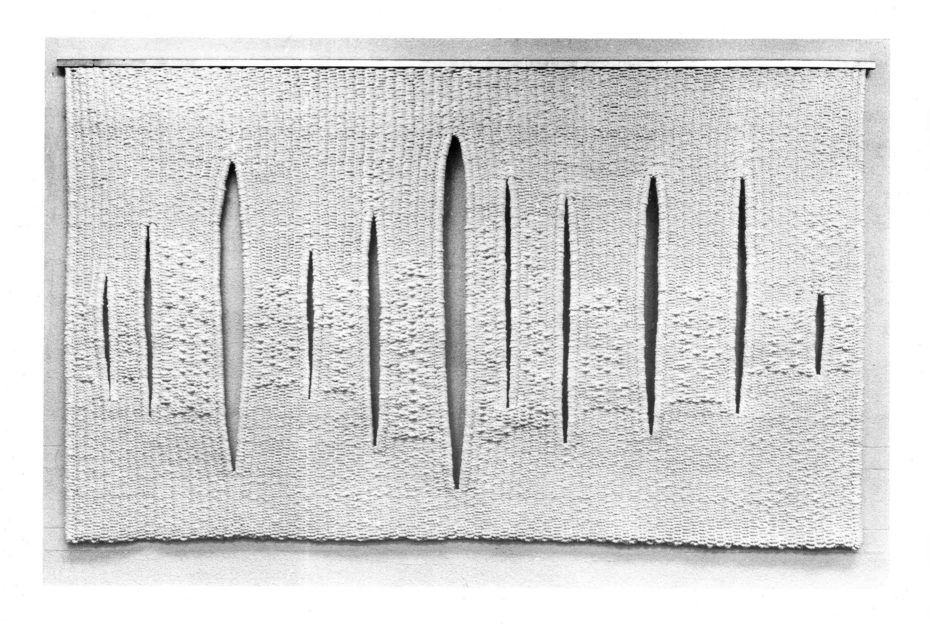

UNTITLED 1970
70'' x 117''
slit tapestry
cotton; white
Collection: KLM (installed in the KLM Building
in Amstelveen, the Netherlands)

The white frieze, hung from an aluminum bar, is
pierced by eleven large slits. The widely spread
warp permits the cotton weft to be packed very
tightly, producing a fabric of great body and
substance. Its thickness is exaggerated by the
wrapped reinforcing of the slits and selvages.

giaque

ELSI GIAQUE
Swiss, born 1900

Studied at the Kunstgewerbeschule, Zurich, with Sophie Tauber-Arp. Taught at the Kunstgewerbeschule, 1944–70. Exhibited extensively in Switzerland; at the Exposition Internationale des Arts Décoratifs et Industriels Modernes, Paris, 1925; Triennale, Milan, 1951, 1954, 1957; World's Fair, Brussels, 1958; Biennale, Venice, 1958; Biennale, Lausanne, 1965, 1967, 1969, 1971; Stedelijk Museum, Amsterdam, 1969; The Museum of Modern Art, New York, 1969; retrospective exhibition, Museum Bellerive, Zurich, 1971. Represented in collections of theaters, schools, churches, and the Museum Bellerive, Zurich. Awarded gold and silver medals at several Milan Triennales.

At work in her studio, Elsi Giaque interlaces weft through taut vertical warps. These elements were later combined in Pure Spatial Element *(p. 13).*

A contemporary of Gunta Stadler-Stölzl and Anni Albers, Elsi Giaque is in spirit a contemporary of the young weavers, some of whom she taught in her prolific and meaningful tenure as professor at the famous Kunstgewerbeschule in Zurich (among her pupils is Moik Schiele, p. 240). The work that she has produced in the last five years reveals the contemporaneity of her philosophy and her performance. She has recently retired from her long career in education to devote herself to her work as a creative artist.

Her experience, she explains, began with the theater. "As a young student I worked with the marionette theatre in Zurich. Action, color, light, the three-dimensional, the word and the music . . . all formed me. In the theater everything is possible, especially in an 'unreal' theater that lives from fantasy. My teachers, Sophie Tauber-Arp and Otto Morach, had created the most modern plays in the marionette theater. At the same time we worked with thread on textile creation, because in that material there are also infinite possibilities."

Even today she feels that "at the basis of everything there isn't only a simple technique, but fantasy, creativity. It is from this gift, this light, that any new work springs."

It is surely the movement and light so necessary to the theater that became a dominant factor in the development of work Elsi Giaque has produced in recent years, such as the environmental work of 1969 (p. 13) and most recently *Hourglass* (p. 164). Characteristic elements appear in each of these works in varying degrees: the use of iridescent color, linear wrapping, metal frames, contrasts in degrees of transparency, vibrations produced by overlapping planes. Sometimes the work functions by the physical act of setting the layers in motion, and sometimes by the eye as the viewer moves through the spaces created by the kinaesthetic compositions.

SPATIAL ELEMENT   1970
11'4" x 10'5" x 15'7"
wrapping, tapestry
mixed fibers; multicolor
Shown at the Maison de la Culture, Grenoble

This three-dimensional composition creates a non-confining environment similar to the Spatial Element *discussed on page 13. This is still another variation on a very personal concept.*

THE COLUMN IN COLORS THAT SING
13'6" x 14" x 14"
silk wrapping on metal frames; polychrome
Collection: Museum Bellerive, Zurich
Shown at the Biennale, Lausanne, 1967

The tall, free-hanging tower of tautly wrapped yarns was an early experiment in the kinetic vibration of transparent iridescence. Red and fuchsia, gold and green play back and forth through the blue vertical of the middle section. At the top and bottom, the yarns are gathered and weighted to maintain tension.

HOMAGE TO MAX BILL   1966
47" x 47"
gobelin tapestry
wool and silk, framed
Collection: Florin and Pia Andri, architects
Photographed in the home of the architects

Giaque's tribute is a complex one, and profound.
She has built one surface precisely in tight, flat
geometry and rendered the other wildly in the
shaggiest of weft-pile surfaces. The fiery reds
contrasting with forest greens reinforce her ex-
plicit reference to a fellow artist who is painter,
sculptor, architect, and critic.

HOURGLASS 1971
60½″ x 78″ x 12″
shaped weaving with supporting tapes and frames
Terylene; neutral color
Private collection

The false perspective of a woven image dominates this three-layered piece. The concave selvages of the hourglass derive from the rare shaped-weaving technique used here in combination with grouped warp ends. Discontinuous weft- *ing is used in the curves at top and bottom. To continue the vertical curves, the warp is spread on frames at top and bottom. The three-barred bottom frame is sufficiently wide to hold the supporting cloth tapes in a triangular sling.*

This is a most sophisticated piece. No physical movement is required of the three layers; only the movement of the eye and the illusory movement and dimension of the layers provide the dynamic effect.

grossen

FRANÇOISE GROSSEN
Swiss, born 1945; resides in United States

Studied textile design at Gewerbeschule, Kunstgewerbliche Abteilung, Basel; received M.A. in Art Fabrics at University of California, Los Angeles, 1968. Awarded Swiss government fellowship, National Competition for Applied Arts, 1967. Exhibited at Jack Lenor Larsen Showroom, New York, 1968; The Museum of Modern Art, New York, 1969; Biennale, Lausanne, 1969, 1971. Represented in the collections of Hyatt House, Chicago and San Francisco; Dreyfus Fund Collection, New York, and private collections.

When Francoise Grossen graduated from the Gewerbeschule in Basel, she had a well-rounded education in the aesthetics and technology of textile design, a developed sense of color, and that combination of inventiveness and organization to serve her well as a designer. She had also completed a first small macramé hanging, knotted of hand-spun wools in a manner revealing her personal and poetic aspirations.

There followed a summer in Africa, and then the opportunity to work at the University of California in Los Angeles—a period more conducive to personal probings than to design. With this uninterrupted concentration, her style developed quickly. Bold pieces grew easily out of the great manila ropes she salvaged from shipyards and deserted beaches. Other times, as in *Swan* (p. 168), she manipulated the unyielding wiry materials into the exacting disciplines of a preset plan. Although this tested both her skills and her perseverence, from it resulted the best early work. She says, "the beauty of the material pre-exists and I try to make the material assert itself to the fullest degree, in an almost intellectual manner."

More recently she has vacillated between the early formal plan and a more organic approach in which she seeks to uncover the potential within materials and process. She has not abandoned either direction. In speaking of her working process, she says, "the working process is a kind of musical improvisation on a given theme. The starting point happens when improvisation—inspiration—and materials coincide. Very often one piece derives from the other." She acknowledges the influence of Eva Hesse, the sculptor, and quotes her: "I am interested in finding out through working on a piece some of the potential and not the preconceived . . . as you work, the piece itself can define or redefine the next step; or the next step combined with some vague idea" (*Art Forum,* May 1970, an interview with Eva Hesse by Cindy Nemser).

Some of the pieces produced for her work at UCLA were almost of the order of found objects. Other pieces, such as the monumental *US#2* (p. 169) and a giant commission for Hyatt House, Chicago, are complex in organization of techniques, materials, and colors. They are improvised within a selected thematic limitation; as the work develops, there are repeated options.

In spite of her youth, Françoise Grossen has accepted her early success and recognition with modesty. She still has a deep commitment to probing her art and her life, simultaneously.

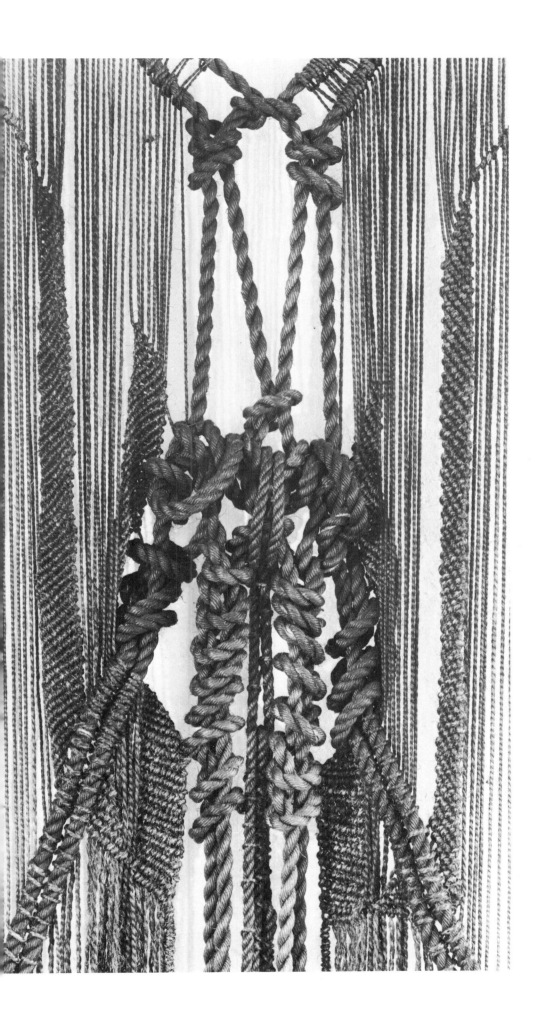

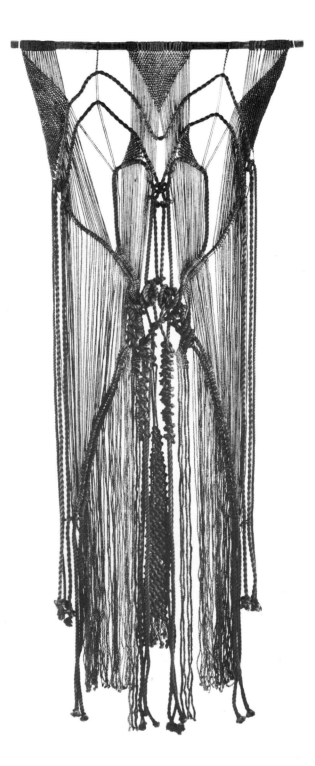

LOCUST   1969
11'4" x 5'8"
macrame
sisal; black-brown
Shown at the Biennale, Lausanne, 1969

In structure, Locust relates to the earlier Swan
(overleaf) in that fine verticals support the heavy
diagonals. These lead the eye to the dense massing of macramé knots in the center. The zoomorphic form with wings defined by the diagonals
relies on the pull of gravity; the lower ends are
not "finished" but relate to the floor. The large
knots are balanced with areas of small ones. The
artist says, "color, material, shape, and scale are
one. The small knot was lost in itself, but the
larger knots began to count as expressions of
their shape. The heavier knot has a distinct identity and also provides structural strength."

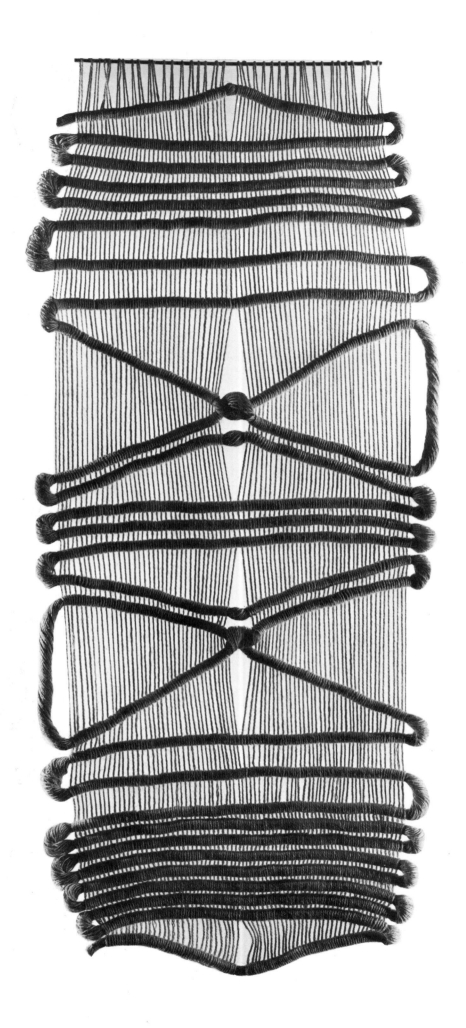

SWAN   1967
6'10'' x 3'10''
macramé knot
sisal; undyed
Collection: Jack Lenor Larsen, New York
Shown in "Wall Hangings,"
The Museum of Modern Art, New York, 1969

The strength of the formalized symmetry derives
from the simple directness of the plan and the
contrast of single verticals with heavy grouped
horizontals. These continue their meandering ways
to become diagonals crossing at the center to an-
imate the symmetry. Although knotted, this piece
is developed with the logic of weaving.

US#2   1970
about 8' x 10'
macramé knotting
sisal; reds
Collection: Mr. and Mrs. Jacob M. Kaplan,
New York

A completely asymmetrical composition that can
be adjusted according to the heights at which the
loops are hung, this unrestrained, almost barbaric
piece is made with a variety of knotting techniques, varied weights and twists, in tonalities of
orange, pink, and red. The piece, which recalls
some of the overstated encrustations of Antonio
Gaudi's Sagrada Familia in Barcelona, produces
immediate response in the viewer.

INCHWORM   1972
20′ x 13′
macramé
cord braided over core of multiple elements
of cable-ply cotton; white
Collection: The artist

A commercially available, manufactured material is employed to produce the startling anthropomorphic form. The enormous scale of the material itself contributes to the size of the piece. The knots changing direction and contrasting with areas of unengaged cable help to give the bilateral symmetry of this form a convincing sense of motion. The fringes are created simply by peeling back the braided casing.

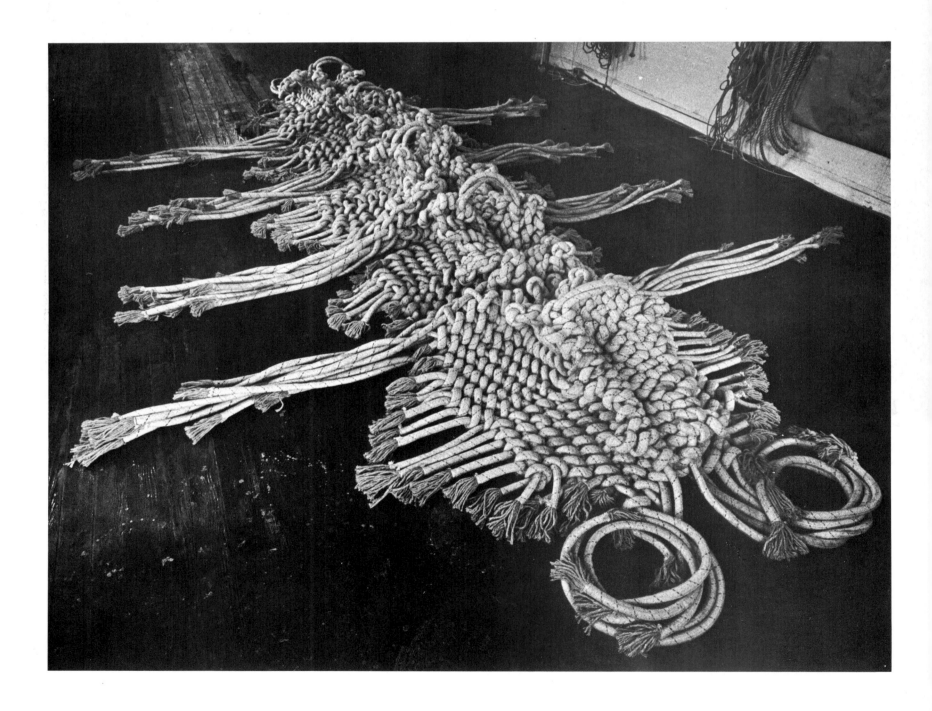

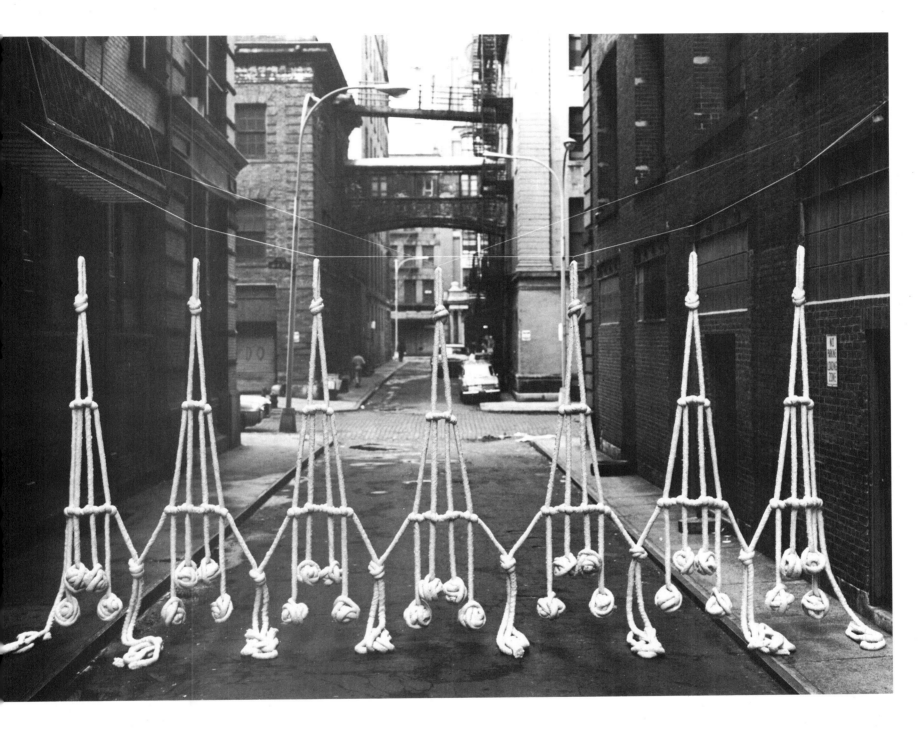

CONTACT 1971
9' x 22"
macramé
cotton wadding encased in plaited filament;
offwhite
Shown at the Biennale, Lausanne, 1971

This composition, like Swan, is formal in structure; but material and technique are much simplified. Each of the seven elements is made up of two looped ends, plus a horizontal element that connects one element to the other with an overhand knot. Gravity is an important component. The number of elements is arbitrary; the very large yarn is an expedient and successful means for creating such a large piece.

hicks

SHEILA HICKS
American, born 1934; resides in France

Studied at Yale University, New Haven, Connecticut. Awarded Fulbright grant for research on pre-Incaic cultures, 1957; Fribourg Scholarship to study painting and weaving in France, 1961. Taught at University of Mexico; worked with Luis Barragan, Mexico. Established Atelier des Grands Augustins, Paris, 1968. Exhibited at The Museum of Modern Art, New York, 1962, 1967, 1969; Oldenburg Museum, Germany, 1964–65; Stedelijk Museum, Amsterdam, 1969; in Mexico, South America, Europe, and Morocco; Triennale, Milan, 1964; Biennale, Lausanne, 1967, 1969, 1971; "Douze ans d'art contemporain en France," Grand Palais, Paris, 1972. Represented in collections of CBS, New York; Cooper-Hewitt Museum, New York; Kunstgewerbemuseum; Zurich; Art Institute of Chicago; National Museum, Prague; Banque de Rothschild, Paris; Ford Foundation, New York; Rochester Institute of Technology, New York; TWA, Kennedy Airport, New York; The Museum of Modern Art, New York; American Airlines, St. Louis; Air France 747 Jets; Hotel Camino Real, Mexico; Societé Francis Bougues, Paris; Préfecture Val de Marne, France; Wilmington Trust Bank, Delaware; IBM, La Defense, Paris.

In each of her works, Sheila Hicks articulates her theoretical knowledge, technical proficiency, intellectual and creative incentives. She arranges her own reality with thread, feeling at times like a carver who has an idea of the whole but who in detail lets himself be guided by the grain of the wood. "By looking always for means of expression in significant form by means of fibers, visually and in the most important sociological sense, the fiber being basically elemental, ordinary, trivial, one can manipulate it and structure messages, surprising and at times phenomenal." Her imaginative cast of mind leads her to make sketches and detailed drawings of forgotten images suddenly illuminated, of botanical subjects, wooden fences, colors swimming in and out of grass, the wigs of mummies, brushes, stone walls.

American by birth, coming from the vast Midwest and then briefly Chicago, Sheila Hicks remained essentially American until she went off with a Fulbright grant in 1957 to do research on pre-Incaic cultures. She studied painting with Rico LeBrun and Josef Albers (a strange apposition) at Yale University. There her interest in the arts of weaving were whetted by the presence of Anni Albers and Dr. George Kubler, the noted historian of pre-Columbian Arts.

As early as 1955 she made a backstrap loom, which she tied to the bed post in order to weave her first work, now in the collection of the Art Institute of Chicago.

When she chose to do her graduate work in the field of pre-Columbian weaving, Dr. Kubler recommended that her thesis adviser be Dr. Junius B. Bird of the Museum of Natural History in New York. The early influences of the two painters, the weavers, the historian, the archeologist, would remain with Sheila Hicks in her life and work. It was during this period that she resolved to live within the context of all civilizations and "to aim at taming the thread, to becoming a part of its nature."

A most illuminating commentator on her own work, Hicks has said in her notations of a would-be weaver (J. J. Belgon, *Waarjekijkt Erotiek,* Amsterdam, 1967):
> Where one thread becomes attached to another
> or where one linear element transverses a second
> When fibers overlap and twist actively binding
> together
> or passing over and under each other
> And when a simple knot or loop manages to hold a
> network of threads interlaced, meshed,
> fused
> I observe and marvel
> how a textile is made
> A continuous thread traveling up and down
> in between,
> around a tautly stretched harp of threads
> becomes a pliable plane
> a fabric, a cloth
> a weaving, a tapestry
> a message
> of hierographs written with wool
> netting, knitting, twining, wrapping may result
> in a wig
> a bundle, a band
> a ball, a braid, a hammock
> using these as implements
> there remains but to speak

Sheila Hicks in Mexico in 1960 working on the backstrap loom.

In Mexico, where she remained for five years (1959–63), she began to weave in her own home on an apiculturist's ranch in Taxco el viejo. She worked on a small weaving frame (she carries one with her wherever she goes—a recent work was made flying across the ocean). She also continued to work with the backstrap loom, as well as to do works that show the influence of the macramé of Mitla as well as the wrappings and the tassels applied to Peruvian tapestry. Although these small works are in the nature of "studies," they are in themselves complete objects of art. For her daughter she made clothes—knitting, knotting wonderful threads in combinations. She also made fabric objects—shirts, sleeves, bouquets (in the Kunstgewerk Museum, Stuttgart), and skirts (in the collection of the Art Institute of Chicago, where she had a one-man exhibition in 1963). In that same year she showed at Knoll Associates in Chicago and Knoll International in Stuttgart. Her work began to grow in scale, from miniatures to a series starting with *The White Letter*, 38″ × 47 1/2″ (p. 176) where, using warp and weft in the same fiber and color, she "wrote" her "messages" with subtle variation of weave. The wrapped warps and braided warp endings, first seen in her Mexican period, were later to reappear in a tremendous exploratory essay (pp. 186–89).

By 1964, Hicks had left Mexico and moved to Paris, where a totally different kind of exposure brought her to another, more expansive phase of her life and work. She had been in 1961 in France accumulating the experience of the great European tradition found in the museums and cathedrals. These iconographical references of painting and sculpture as well as the archaic and primitive wealth entered into her bank of ideas. She immersed herself in fabrics in all of their metamorphoses and diverse uses.

In Europe, during an exhibition at the Kunstgewerbemuseum in Zurich, she was engaged by a rug manufacturer, Arterior Textile GmbH, who invited her to produce a series for this company. Here she developed the technique of combining the braided and wrapped pile with tufting by electric pistol. It is not surprising to note here that Hicks was the artist to welcome and respond to this tool. Unafraid of machine techniques, stretching her inventiveness to supplement the flat formal format of her earlier work, her ingenuity produced an idiom to serve her purpose. The *Red Prayer Rug* (p. 180) is one of a series in this technique. Others are in the collections of The Museum of Modern Art, New York, and CBS. This series was all made of abundantly hirsute cascades of tassled wool. They were never meant to hug the wall but to gush forth, to spring freely from the wall.

Claude Lévi-Strauss, the eminent French scholar, anthropologist, and philosopher, writes of Hick's work, "Her wall hangings have the living warmth and the thickness of fleece; their complex structure and their shadows seem to chisel out perspectives attributable only to dream palaces; they offer the mellow depth, radiance, and mystery of the starry sky.

"Nothing better than this art could provide altogether the adornment and the antidote for the functional, utilitarian architecture in which we are sentenced to dwell.

MHAMID 1970
9¼″ x 7″
tapestry
silk, vicuña, razor-clam shell;
natural and magenta
Collection: Mr. and Mrs. R.W. Bettelheim,
New York

In spite of its size, this miniature projects monumentality, impact, completeness, with a range of materials and techniques. At the top, continuous wefts of natural silks are striped with a magenta floss. At the bottom, slit tapestry combines the several tonalities and textures of silk and vicuña. The shaped selvages reinforce the solidity of the strong shell that separates the two areas.

WHITE LETTER   1962
38" x 47½"
plain weave
hand-spun wool; natural color
Collection: The Museum of Modern Art, New York
Shown in "Wall hangings,"
The Museum of Modern Art, New York, 1969

WALL (detail)   1967
Lounge of the Alumni Union, Rochester
Institute of Technology, Rochester, New York
11' x 25'
tufted and embroidered
wool; ivory white

In her Paris studio, the artist works on a panel for the Air France 747 lounge, 1970.

In the early 1960s Sheila Hicks was working on a weaving frame without heddles. Through this slow process she was able to compose patterns freely without the restraints imposed by a loom. The order of the interlacing could be improvised: whether over one, under one or over six, under four or some other variant could be determined as the weaving progressed. Out of the groupings of warps and wefts she developed in relief a free imagery responsive to the play of light.

Woven on a modest scale, in a single yarn and color, the composition of White Letter depends upon contrasts of size and variations in the direction and placement of large and small groups.

The Rochester wall employs essentially the same imagery, but here the technique is embroidery with long stitches over a looped pile ground.

In a recent development, for the lounges of Air France's 747s, the image is again embroidered, but solidly, in natural Chinese wild silk over an open scrim.

It enlivens it with the dense, patient work of human hands, and the inventive charms of a creative mind constantly stimulated by experiencing the gamut of those new materials which modern industry supplies, while remaining faithful to the immemorial rules of the most ancient perhaps of all the arts of civilization."

No place in the world would be alien to Sheila Hicks. Her particular sensitivity absorbs and selects, from each voyage of discovery, experiences, and visions that she stores in her mind's eye for some future use.

The flow of Hicks's work is intermingled with the fullness of her experience of working in many places in the world. In each of the places in which she has worked she has absorbed the tone, respected its tradition, and responded to its potentials. The canvas of the tent, the canopies of mats and vines, the structures of screens, the harmonies of the sinuous movements of dance are the inspirational seed for her images. There are no contradictions in her mind, whether she is concerned with Greek coiffeurs, French passementerie, or the manufacture of nylon stockings.

In inspiration as in execution, Sheila Hicks works collectively as well as individually. With her deep respect for traditional handcraft and with the modern perspectives which guide her, she accepted an invitation in 1966 to go to Calicut, Kerala, in the south of India, where she worked with a hand-loom factory designing for commercial textiles. She worked closely with the Malabar craftsmen, selecting silks, flax, and jute but mostly commercial counts of fine cotton. She designed directly on existing warps with inventoried materials and plain weave employing a technique so simple that it could be carried on by the artisans (see *Badagara,* p. 185). She has been back to Calicut several times to continue her work there.

Back in Paris, she established her studio, the Atelier des Grand Augustins. Her long association with Warren Platner began with a commission to design and produce two major walls for the Ford Foundation Building in New York (p. 183). Later, using the same theme as her earlier *White Letter* and *Hieroglyphs,* and again in collaboration with Warren Platner, a great wall was realized for the Rochester Institute of Technology (p. 176).

The walls by Sheila Hicks are, in a sense, a complete contrast to her individual works, yet there are solid links between these expressions and her single hangings. Her walls are made to cover existing walls, or are walls in themselves. They are composed of single elements multiplied, components that are repeated and assembled. They are commissioned for specific places and are essential to the architectural spaces they occupy.

At one time Hicks wanted to work only within architectural spaces, but her devotion to further exploration of thread potential left her impatient and eager to delve further into her medium.

During a walk in the Luxembourg Gardens in Paris, she was struck by the magic of a single brick transformed through structural multiplication into a wall. Her fertile mind saw the equivalence of the simple brick to a single pliable thread. Structure began to take form, to be manipulated, and to be composed. For Hicks, an idea that has its own logic may start with just such a single element. Realization began with two different kinds of forms: *Banisteriopsis* (p. 184), composed of over 3,000 similar elements which she describes as pony tails; and *Principal Wife* (p. 186), which began as single, unrelated elements made by wrapping massed warps. In *Trapèze de Cristobal* (p. 188), these single elements became more controlled and disciplined. The same wrapped components are evident in the great wall for the Banque de Rothschild, Paris (p. 189).

In contrast with this experience, in 1968 the artist participated in setting up a workshop in Chile devoted to stimulating the production of handcraft. The Taller Artesanal was formed as a cooperative. It is a remote village in Huaquen on the coast in central Chile. In this mountainous region where wool and hides are a natural resource, Sheila Hicks's family joined with twenty-four others in a cooperative program sponsored by the Fundación Artur Matte. Some of them worked at home, some in the school and workshops. Hicks directed the production of rugs and hangings utilizing alpaca and wet-spun linen and pointed the direction toward a continuing project that provides for economic and aesthetic growth.

In 1970 she was invited to Morocco to help revitalize a strongly traditional rug industry. After traveling throughout the country, she chose workshops in Rabat and Tangiers to start her series of Moroccan prayer rugs (pp. 190–91). This Moroccan series has a density that relates to the heaviness of the architectural details that inspired them—doorways, tunnels, portals, the rounded household arch, the pointed Moslem arch. Sometimes the differences in pile depth of a single piece recall the stalactite detail in architecture made up of successive layers of plaster. Like the "Moroccan forms which flatter the eye with proportions and symmetry which appease the spirit," the prayer rugs transcend convention and iconography: in spite of their ordered quiescence they have magic, mystery, and metaphor.

When the artist started to work on the Moroccan series of prayer rugs she conceived of them as rugs for the wall, floor, or ceiling. The material was to be all wool; the techniques all knots, scissor-carved to various levels; the motifs or themes all architectural elements. These self-imposed conditions she entered in notebooks, sometimes with words, sometimes with sketches and swatches. The rectangular format and the large solid areas of color bring to mind the magnificence of Mark Rothko's paintings of the fifties, but with notable differences. Hicks's unshaded color areas are boldly, if softly, defined. Sometimes deep within a carved valley a thin outline of contrasting color separates major areas. The extreme density of the knotted pile is exploited by the several depths and thicknesses in a single composition. This play of color and depth is intensified when a single work is composed as a diptych or triptych (see pp. 190–91).

Sheila Hicks works out of her Atelier des Grands Augustins in Paris, and moves from continent to continent, giving demonstrations (Edinburgh, 1970; Los Angeles, 1971), spontaneously making a happening in what she calls "Fêtes du Fils" (Rennes, 1970), returning to Mexico to see a reconstructed colonial building for which architect Ricardo Legorreta comissioned a prayer rug, 1972; traveling to Tangier and to India.

Her searches bring her empirical and theoretical knowledge of the historic past. She is also open to search and research her own past efforts. She always has "one or two dozen odd—very odd—things hanging around which I keep through the years for one reason or another—ideas I want to go on with, or half-successful fragments of good possibilities." These themes and the techniques she ardently disciplines so that they appear and reappear in her work, emerging as outgrowths of her own creativity. In the work of an artist like Hicks, the "mistakes," the half-finished, the preliminary sketches are not without interest to those of us who would fully understand her development. Sheila Hicks is a consummate artist who has a special kinship with human and aesthetic ties—an artist who has the specific power to liberate her ideas and give them bodily form.

RED PRAYER RUG   1964
89¾″ x 39″
tufting
wool pile on cotton base cloth; reds
Produced at Arterior GmbH, Wuppertal, Germany
Collection: Dr. Mittlestein Sheid

The long tassels looped through the back cloth are spirally wrapped with wool. They cascade out from the flat arch of uncut wool pile. The voluptuous composition is consistently rich in form, surface, and color, with the many tones from pink to red relieved by cool accents in the wrapping. The exuberance of expression flourishes within the formality of a traditionally symmetrical form.

MEDIEVAL CLOAK   1965
74″ x 47″
tufting and knitting
wool pile on cotton base cloth;
greens, red, and violet
Collection: Arterior GmbH, Wuppertal, Germany

With an unusual degree of conscious abandon, the artist has created an illusion of age and mystery. The lush palette of mossy greens, relieved by red and violet, further enhances this illusion.

Constructed with an electric pistol, the long unruly loops are, for the most part, uncut. The heavy roving was knitted with oversize needles. The artist says that she was inspired by contemporary coiffeur, so that this piece becomes a social artifact as well as a work of art.

WALL   1968
originally designed for
George Jensen Center For Advanced Design,
New York
about 9' x 20'
wet-spun linen; natural gray

Sheila Hicks collaborated with Warren Platner in composing a cohesive environment in which all the elements—Hans Wegner furniture, walls, floors —in natural colors and organic materials, unite to create a lively exuberance.

The linen room has two long facing walls of wiry wet-spun linen tassels looped at one end and cut at the other. They are stitched onto the linen base cloth.

Hicks's preoccupation with the spirally wrapped tassel, first seen as an integral outgrowth of pile construction in the earlier prayer rug series, is here developed into independently constructed elements applied in a rich, random composition.

WALL 1967
Ford Foundation Auditorium, New York
(view of installation of single panel in auditorium)
designed by Sheila Hicks and Warren Platner,
made by the Atelier des Grands Augustins, Paris,
Henri Tronquoy, technical consultant
10' x 35'
linen and silk; natural gray and gold

Over a ground of natural linen canvas, gold-colored plied silk yarns are embroidered so as to create a relief. The wall becomes luminous when washed with light. The precision of the stitching is pertinent both to the regular rows of medallions and to the formal severity of the architecture. To ensure a perfect circle, the silk was stitched over an aluminum disk.

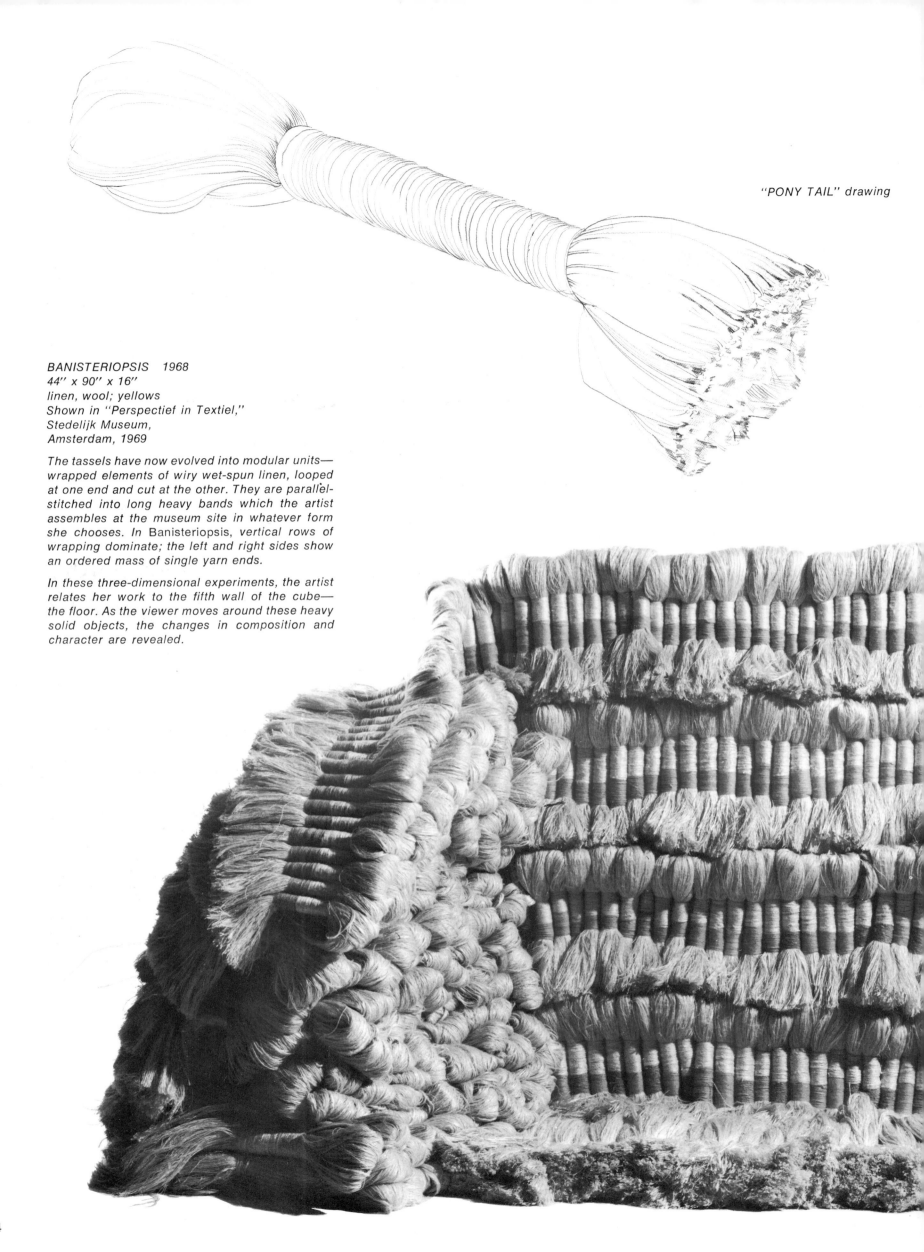

"PONY TAIL" drawing

BANISTERIOPSIS   1968
44″ x 90″ x 16″
linen, wool; yellows
Shown in "Perspectief in Textiel,"
Stedelijk Museum,
Amsterdam, 1969

The tassels have now evolved into modular units—
wrapped elements of wiry wet-spun linen, looped
at one end and cut at the other. They are parallel-
stitched into long heavy bands which the artist
assembles at the museum site in whatever form
she chooses. In Banisteriopsis, vertical rows of
wrapping dominate; the left and right sides show
an ordered mass of single yarn ends.

In these three-dimensional experiments, the artist
relates her work to the fifth wall of the cube—
the floor. As the viewer moves around these heavy
solid objects, the changes in composition and
character are revealed.

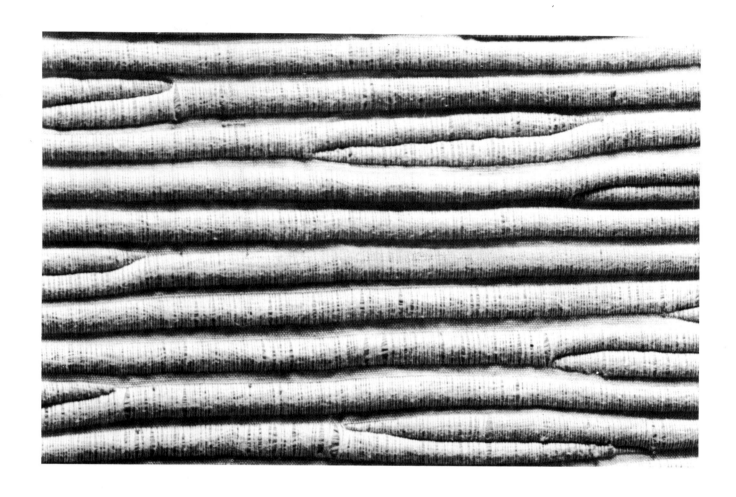

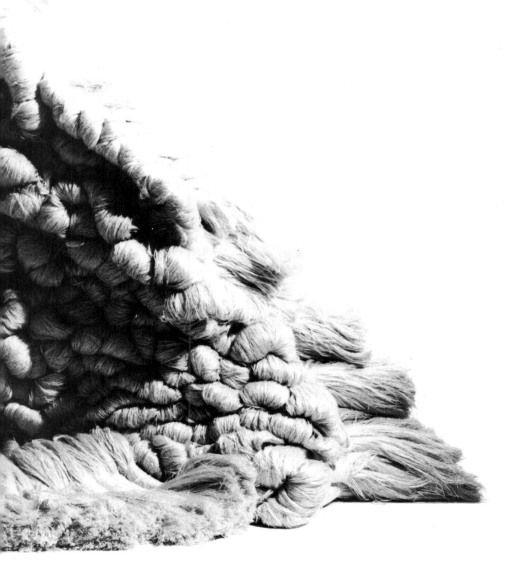

BADAGARA (detail) 1968
woven at Commonwealth Trust Company,
Calicut, India
for the Parry Murry Company
plain weave with discontinuous wefts
cotton; bleached white

On an assignment to design cotton fabrics for a handweaving factory in southern India, the artist has taken a daring and successful approach. The yarns, the weave, and indeed the warp are standard with the mill. The innovation is the unprecedented scale, bulk, and weight of the weft, in which hundreds of fine yarns are carried as a single element. These enormous wefts, large as fingers, randomly terminate within the cloth to provide a sculptured relief. The smooth warp-faced cylinders are reminiscent of the wrapped "warps" beginning with The Principal Wife (p. 186).

THE PRINCIPAL WIFE (detail)
as shown in "Wall Hangings,"
The Museum of Modern Art, 1969
single elements 15'9" long

THE PRINCIPAL WIFE drawing

TRAPEZE DE CRISTOBAL (detail) 1971
10' x 4'
wrapping
wool, cotton, linen, synthetic fibers; multicolor
Collection: Stedelijk Museum, Amsterdam
Shown at the Biennale, Lausanne, 1971

WALL 1970
Executive suite, Banque de Rothschild, Paris
10' x 16'
natural linens wrapped with silk,
wood and synthetic fiber

Another innovation in the artist's development of wrapped yarn elements is the long, separate, chainlike constructions. These were first shown at the Stedelijk Museum in 1969; a similar composition of ten elements (see p. 186) was shown at The Museum of Modern Art later that same year.

At first the warp chains of rough natural linen were wrapped with gleaming silks. The neutral areas in these first works surfaced with much less baroque zest than is evident in the wall for the Banque de Rothschild. Clearly the artist has realized the potential of these random chains. In the bank wall the luxurious surface and color of the cylindrical verticals are relieved by the bulbous twisted linen forms. Like large stones rippling in a stream of fast water, they play in counterpoint to the smooth luster of the verticals. The blues and greens emphasize the cool fluidity.

The unwrapped linen at the top and bottom serves to isolate the composition from the ceiling, floor, and furnishings in the room. The wrapped elements are stitched to the panels, hung so that no joint is visible.

The progression from the single sinuous component meant to be composed in situ, to the ordered group shown in Lausanne in 1969, to the controlled cadence of the disciplined wall in the Banque de Rothschild demonstrates how the artist is carefully testing for qualities—for congruence between the spirit and physical form of her work.

In a sense the earlier chains with their cylinders randomly separated into twos and threes do not have the sophisticated surface interest of the chains in the bank wall, where the precision in the handling of the material has a great deal to do with the resulting form. The dimension of the wall is both visually and physically experienced. And the total is replete with the rhythmic cadence of music.

RABAT 1971

The artist standing at the entrance of the Galerie
Bab Rouah, in Rabat, Morocco, on the occasion
of her exhibition in 1971. Behind her, the Tapis
Maghreb *triptych can be seen in the first hall.*

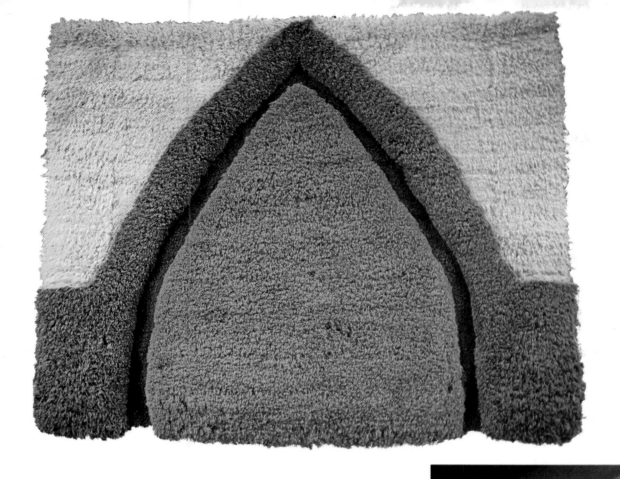

CAID MANSOUR   1971
58½'' x 78''
wool; natural, green, gold, and rose

TAPIS PORTE   1971
93½'' x 70''
wool; natural, black, and red

L'EPOUSE PREFEREE OCCUPE SES NUITS 1972
diameter 160''
wrapping
nylon, silk, gold and linen threads;
red, scarlet, gold, and natural
Shown in ''Douze ans d'art contemporain de France,'' Grand Palais, Paris, 1972

The cotton core is wrapped with nylon, silk, gold and linen threads, stitched on a linen canvas base composed of two half-circles joined together.

This great circle is the most recent of Hicks's work in wrapped gimp. The technique is actually not in the fabric vocabulary but enlarges the broad art of assemblage. The twisting and winding together of actual thread elements and the contrapuntal balance within the sphere set up emotional rhythms. For Hicks this is an unusual, ecstatic outburst; the total is accomplished by a free composition that also succeeds by virtue of its colors.

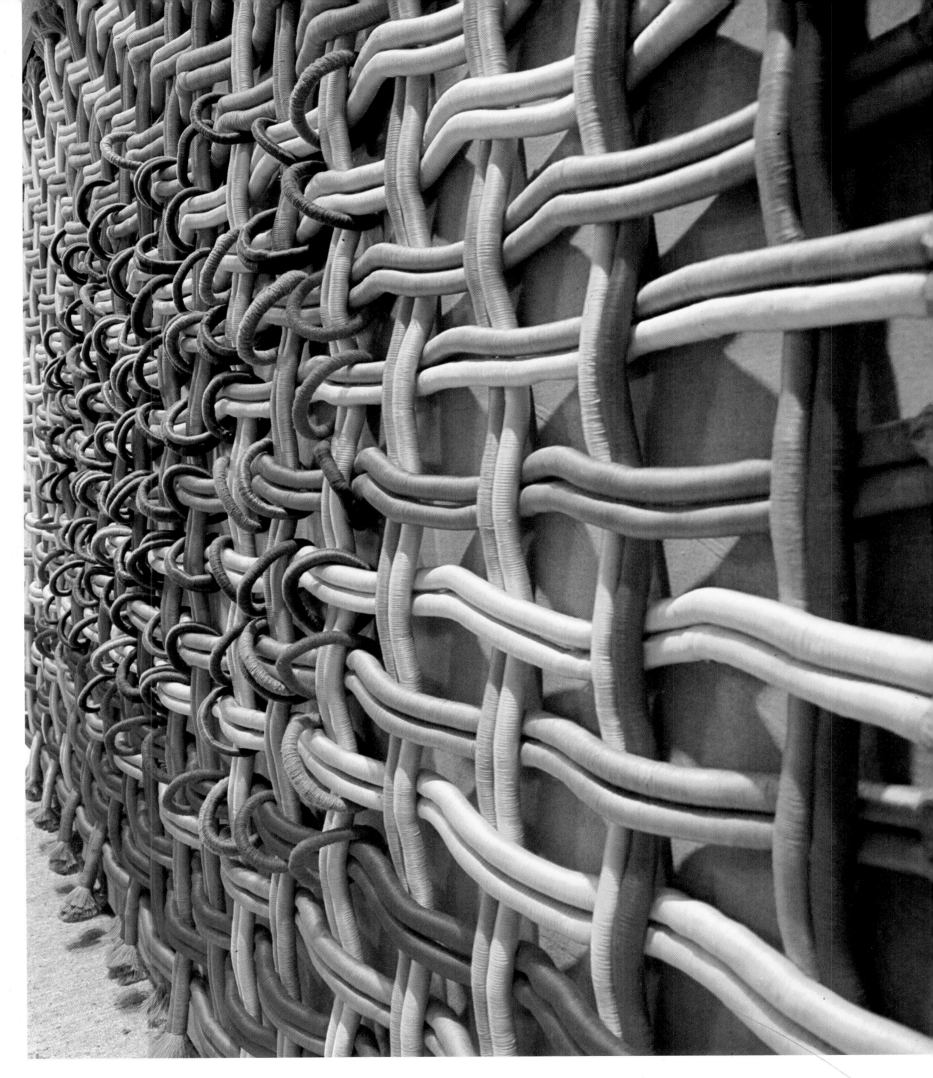

LA MEMOIRE 1972
10' x 14' 10''
wrapping and interlacing
linen base, nylon and wool
Collection: IBM, La Defense, Paris

jacobi

RITZI JACOBI
Romanian, born 1941

PETER JACOBI
Romanian, born 1935

Ritzi Jacobi received the Diploma of the Fine Arts Institute, Bucharest, 1966, in tapestry techniques. Peter Jacobi received the Diploma of the Fine Arts Institute, Bucharest, 1961, in sculpture; one-man shows, 1962, 1965, 1967, 1968. Married in 1966. German citizens since 1971. The Jacobis worked individually from 1964 to 1967, each in his own discipline; they began working collectively in 1967 and exhibited at the Biennale of Middelheim-Anves, Belgium, 1968; International Sculpture Exhibition Legnan-Castellzana (Galeria Enzo Pagani), 1968; "Interfauna," Düsseldorf, 1968; Triennale, Milan, 1969; Biennale, Lausanne, 1969, 1971; Maison de la Culture, Grenoble, 1970; as well as in Chicago, Washington, Prague, Copenhagen, Alexandria, Berlin, Budapest, Belgrade, Moscow, Warsaw, and in Mexico. Represented in collections of National Gallery, Bucharest; Museum of the XX Century, Vienna; Museum für Kunst und Gewerbe, Hamburg; Museo di Arte Moderno, Rome; as well as private collections.

The Jacobis are a swinging couple, yet surprisingly they follow three traditions: a Romanian tradition of the tragic leading to the absurd as in works by Eugene Ionesco and Saul Steinberg; work produced within the traditional weaving disciplines so that the essential elements of most pieces are woven on the loom with natural fibers of somber colors; and the traditions and conventions of modern art from Pop Art to the New Surrealism.

It seems natural that the weaver and the sculptor together should be influenced by Claes Oldenburg's happenings, environments, and objects. It is also logical and natural that his "soft" or stuffed sculptures, which were first shown in the summer of 1962, should be precursors of the woven forms and environments of the Jacobis. Just as Oldenburg's art objects always "present something," so the Jacobis' work also has a narrative quality, if hidden.

They both studied the folkloric traditions of their country, particularly from the period 1500 to 1700. But this knowledge does not produce esoteric themes, nor are the artists victimized by a devotional attitude to the past. Their work is not novelty, but a formal statement of extreme individuality.

The Jacobis consider their work art, craft, and decoration. A work may start from discussion between them in which they explain their ideas to each other by miniatures and cartoons. This allows opportunity for improvisation "as the flute of our ideas in realizing the work." From the time they began working collectively they introduced environmental elements. They also produced textile objects, textile multiples, and textile mobiles. For these they use natural goatshair, combined with rubber cables, sometimes covered with wool, sometimes exposed. The Jacobis are helped by assistant weavers, joiners, and ironmongers.

In speaking of the weaver, R. C. Kennedy says (in *Art International,* May, 1969), "Ritzi has a tendency to create visions of a landscape which reminds one of the frightening woods of the fairy tales by the Grimm Brothers. The viewer of the Ritzi vision is made to awaken his own fantasies and to travel back into the dream world of his own childhood, composed to frighten as well as enchant in unknown flower landscapes."

Both of the Jacobis possess boundless imagination; they are free of inhibition. To be able to combine these qualities with discipline and diligence is rare indeed. The Jacobis present their own art magic.

RELIEF TEXTIL   1968
25" x 48" turned 90°
tapestry with wrapped elements
wool; natural and browns
Collection: The artists

The rectangle of the traditional tapestry format
has been broken by the shaped selvages. The
freely moving ropes follow and so reinforce the
tapestry-woven image to provide a calligraphy,
dimensional and voluptuous.

ENVIRONMENT, VARIABLE II (details)   1970
panel size 53" x 66"
tubes, height and diameter: 69½", 11"; 56", 17½";
59", 10"
heatherspun wool; gray
Collection: The artists
Shown at the Biennale, Venice, 1970

The vertical monoliths and wall are formed by
loom-woven fabric of somber gray covering metal
and wood armatures. The spirally wrapped ropes
are sometimes fat and sometimes tapered. At
times they divide to become two and three separate elements with color changing from light to
dark. The apertures in the wall are lined with
narrow woven tapes in darker tones. The innovations in this sophisticated fabric landscape combine the best elements of art and craftsmanship.

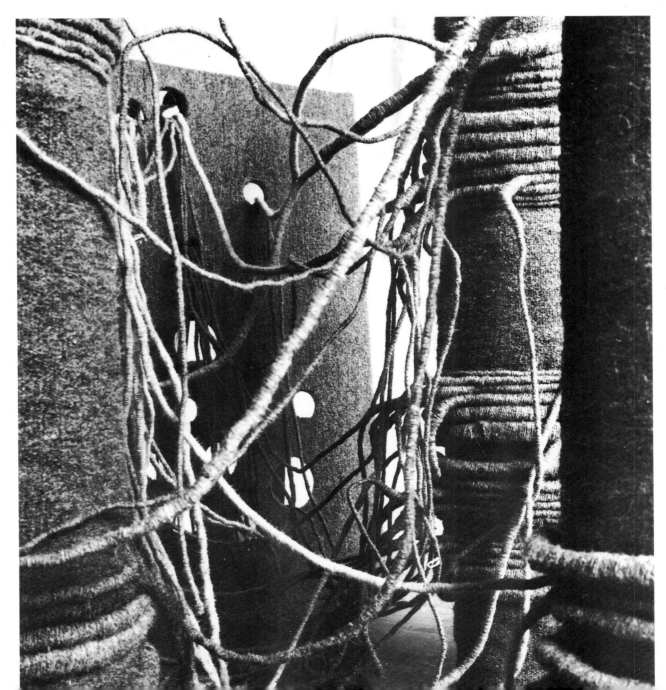

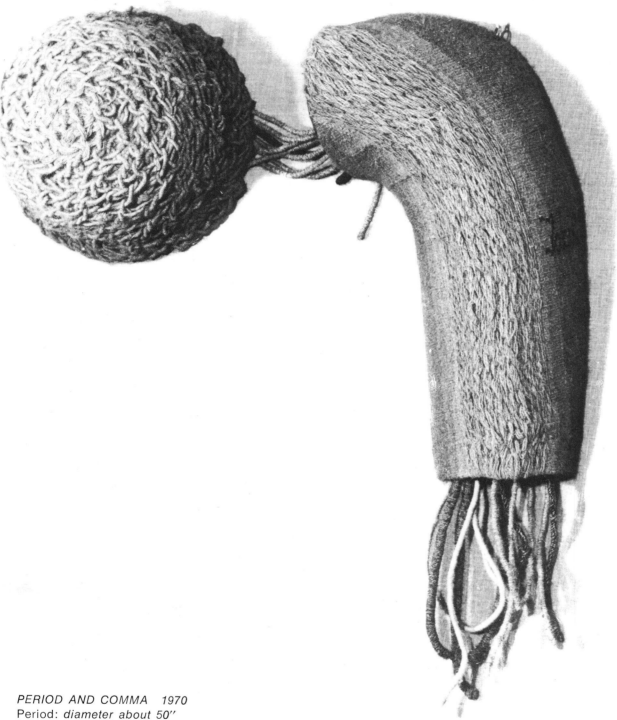

PERIOD AND COMMA   1970
Period: *diameter about 50"*
Comma: *length 100"*
lambswool; red-browns and charcoal grays
Collection: Museo di Arte Moderno, Rome

The comma, woven on the loom, is stretched over a metal armature. The top surface is openly woven to produce a rough, barklike texture while the darker side walls are the traditional rep weave of tapestry.

The period is made up of spirally wrapped and openly looped ropes stretched over a plastic dishpan. These also have gradations of color from dark on the base to light on top. The ropes that connect comma and period are spirally wrapped with yarns of different tonalities. By alteration of scale and dimension and our comprehension of them, these very familiar symbols assume a new formality.

ARMOIR   1971
78" x 48¾" x 21½"
shaped tapestry
heatherspun wool; gray
Collection: The artists
Shown at the Biennale, Lausanne, 1971

Woven flat in one piece on the loom, the convincingly crafted tapestry jackets, superb and almost wearable, are hung on a space frame. Tapestry joinings are used to shade the colors in muted or sharp contrasts. The buttonholes and the trompe-l'oeil details are all exquisitely defined.

jaroszynska

EWA JAROSZYNSKA
Polish, born 1936; resides in Australia

Studied sculpture at Catholic University, Lublin; Lodz School of Fine Arts, specializing in tapestry. Exhibited at Zamek Group Gallery, Lublin, 1958; Writers Club, Warsaw, 1958; The Museum of Modern Art, New York, 1969; Norrkopings Museum, Sweden, 1969; Grabowski Gallery, London, 1970.

Crochet is one of the simplest and earliest techniques for the manipulation of fiber. With one unconventional yarn and a single tool—a hooked needle—Ewa Jaroszynska employs crochet as a new medium for sculptural relief. To do this she has abandoned the tight rosettes and soft filigree character of crochet. Few stitches are used; the few voids are large and meaningful. She retains the concentric movements of crochet but gives these new scale and meaning. By varying structure and density she is able to model with considerable depth and to control the character of her surfaces. These hard, tightly constructed areas are burnished with reflected light. These contrast with the shadowy darks of craters and folded valleys and with areas that are deeply scratched and furrowed.

This single-element technique normally provides pliability, but with the coarse, stiff sisal and hemp, the work emerges unpliant. The rigidity reinforces the construction, defies gravity, and provides body and substance for the compositions. Because of the natural colors and unevenness of structure, the surfaces of Jaroszynska's finished work resemble aged tree-bark, with gnarled burls and discolorations.

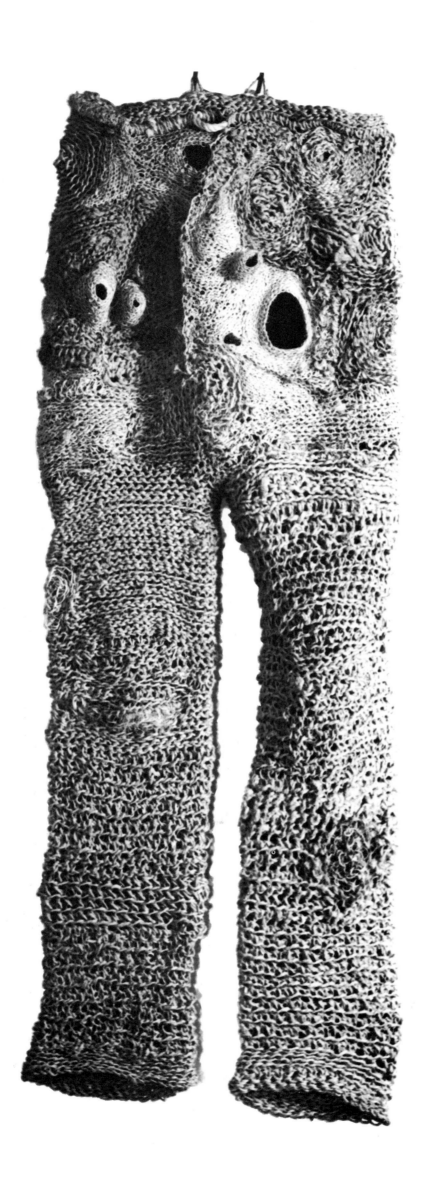

TROUSERS   1969
78" x 27"
crochet
sisal and hemp; natural

Unlike the single thickness of Cocoons II, Trousers
is appropriately tubular. The unmatched variety
of stitch and surface in the pants' legs derives
from their being separately, independently worked.
The tight stitches through the groin, the changes
of texture and color at the hip, and the symbolic
implications of the spiraling craters are composed
with poetic nonchalance. In terms of innovation
and control of technique, the piece is valid. As a
statement about the worn quality and sexuality
of jeans, it is art.

COCOONS II 1967
29½″ x 24⅝″ x 4⅞″ irregular
crochet
sisal and hemp; natural
Collection: The artist

A dominant central form is contained within the asymmetric, rectangular frame. The symbols of dynamic growth are clearly stated and implied. A dominant material and the consistently concentric patterns of the structure balance and unify the several diverse elements.

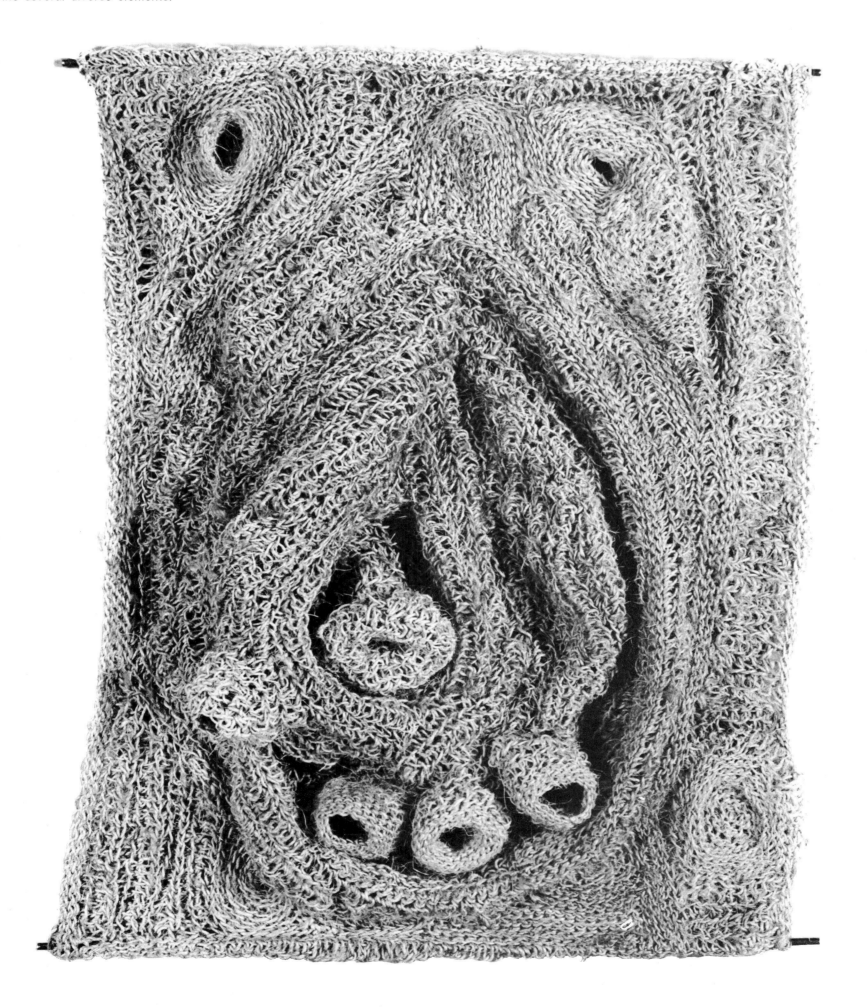

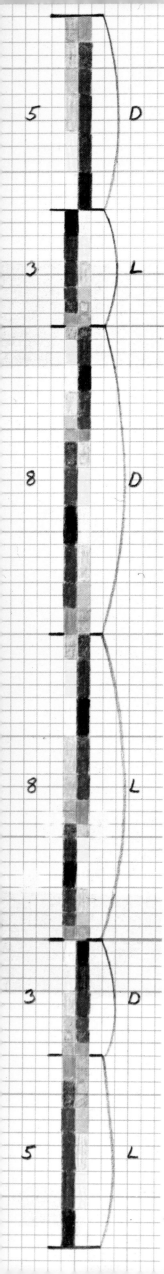

This graph is the working tool with which Landis visualizes his complex color relationships. The plan is for the weft of a cloth similar to Column, 1969. The eight warp colors will multiply the effect of each specification. With this eight-tone system, he will achieve 8 x 8 — 8 or 56 color shades.

In his double cloths, two colors of weft are always weaving simultaneously—these are indicated from left to right. D and L indicate whether, in this warp section, the weft is interlacing through a dark or light warp. 3, 5, and 8 represent the duration between changes of dark and light warp. In the largest, or 8, sections, the light-to-dark tone scale changes position but not warp color, thus giving additional variation.

COLUMN (detail)   1969
10'6" x 14½"
double plain weave
linen; multicolored

Unlike the 1968 Column (p. 206), this piece is similar-faced; that is, front and back are more or less identical. In addition, the pattern breakup of warp and filling stripes is not static, but extremely varied. The color play is balanced between soft shadings of red earth tones in similar values and the sparkle of sharp dark and light contrasts.

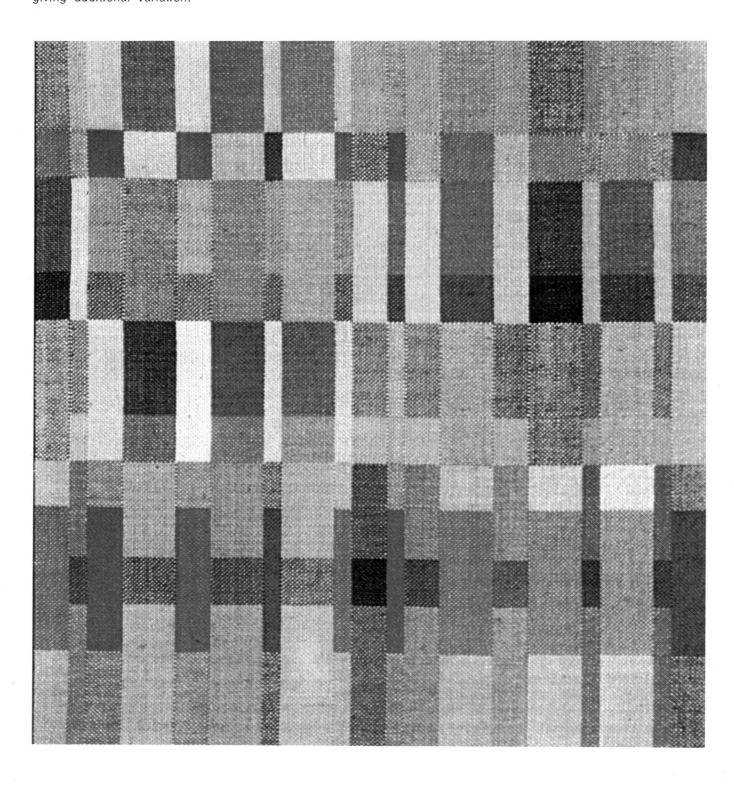

landis

Dick Landis is a loner. His solitary existence in the Arizona mountains is like that of the western plainsman. Direct and independent, neither shy nor impressionable, he is aloof from city ways, unflinching and unaffiiliated. Surrounded only by the hard realities of the Sierra, Landis looks out on worldly commotion with a perspective akin to wisdom. In his detachment, and in being observant and prophetic, he relates to Ed Rossbach and Lenore Tawney. But with Landis the isolation is more severe. So is the chasm between his work and that of others. His singular quest is for systems of tonal patterning, or rather systems of graduated colors and color values. At best these systems (p. 204) are so successful as to produce a mystifying luminosity, and the quiet inevitability found in certain masterworks and much of nature. That his knife-edged abstractions celebrate nature is at first not evident. He explains that "all growth processes, whether in art or biology have interested me. Through photographer Frederick Sommer I came to realize that man had to invent art to understand nature and that perhaps intellect resides in our taste buds. Life is consent to perceiving; there are no puritans."

The medium Landis selected is a balanced double plain weave closely set on the loom. It is consistent with his mode of expression that these cloths are precisely woven and classically finished after weaving. So are their dense surfaces, which are admirable to both weaver and painter. A simple plied linen yarn is used for all this series. This is partly because accepting this technical discipline allows him to concentrate on the tonal systems and partly because he feels "that weaving is best served when materials and means are not excessive in their assertiveness." His concern is how through speculative notation he is able to serve structural possibilities not yet realized.

The austerity of his living and the discipline of his art are of his selection. They serve him well; in seeking a universal expression, he has found a very personal, very beautiful art form.

RICHARD LANDIS
American, born 1931

Studied at Arizona State University; traveled in Europe and Japan; studied weaving with Mary Pendleton and art with photographer Frederick Sommer. Exhibited at Prescott College, Arizona, 1969; Laguna Beach Art Association, California, 1971. Represented in collection of The Museum of Modern Art, New York.

The artist sitting at the door of his cabin in the Sierra Ancha mountains of Arizona.

COLUMN (detail)   1968
68'' x 15½''
dissimilar-faced double plain weave
linen; multicolor
Collection: The Museum of Modern Art, New York

In a classic, nearly symmetrical composition, one
cloth, which Landis calls the matrix, employs the
same color yarn for warp and filling; the other is
striped in both warp and weft so as to create the
greatest number of color variations in the crossings. Although, like musical notes, the eight weft
colors are repeated, their sequence is not. The
sequential variations continue from top to bottom.
That the size and form of the color areas are
similar emphasizes the subtleties of color progression and the luminosity of light tones against
the matrix.

On the reverse side (shown opposite) the stripes
of warp and weft are more in evidence. Color is
softer because only the matrix is pure. All the
other colors are diluted by crossing with it.

muñoz

AURELIA MUÑOZ (de Ventosa)
Spanish, born 1926

Studied at the Escuela Massana de Artes y Arte Applicadas, Barcelona. Awarded scholarship from Juan March Foundation. Exhibited at the Spanish Pavilion, World's Fair, New York, 1964; Biennale, Lausanne, 1965, 1969, 1971; "Experiencias Artísticas Textiles," Madrid, 1969; and in Scotland, Czechoslovakia, France. Represented in collections of the Museos de Arte Contemporáneo, Madrid, Ibiza; Museum Umelecko Prumyslove, Prague, Provinciehuis Noord Brabant, the Netherlands.

Aurelia Muñoz derives inspiration from the great textile and tapestry traditions, particularly those of Spain. For these traditions she has real sympathy, accompanied by a vast fund of knowledge. In Spain and especially in Catalonia, the past is very much available. In Barcelona she finds continuity from Spanish Gothic to Gaudí to the Picasso Museum in a medieval palace.

To her, the use of the past means investigation and interpretation, rather than glorification or a revival in the manner of William Morris. She brings to the present the richness of forsaken techniques found in ancient embroideries, tapestries, and macramé.

Curiously, her earliest work, drawings, prints, and the more recent macramés relate strongly to each other. In between there was a large body of embroidered and patchwork hangings that in their color, surface richness, and subject matter appear to draw more heavily upon the wealth of the past. Although these are both inventive and exquisite, they seem part of another era, perhaps related to the early part of this century.

She has studied the ancient Spanish and Arabic origins of macramé knotting, and is drawn particularly to those Iberian sculptures with ornament fringes of macramé found in Albacete province of Spain. But the structure and the scale of her work speak of our time and particularly of contemporary architecture. Like Grossen and others working in macramé, she mostly employs sisal for her pieces. Unlike theirs, however, her work is fully volumetric. It exists in the round, is solidly, densely built, and often monumental. Most recently, she has worked on models for very large environmental projects (p. 210).

Aurelia Muñoz is deeply and intensely Spanish. A quiet crusader for contemporary expression in her country, she unites in her work and in her teaching the drive of our century with the unity of her heritage.

Aurelia Muñoz with half of Macra I, *1969.*
113" x 70"
macramé
cotton; white

The two wings of this work form a rounded Y. The enormous surface interest derives from the twists and tonalities of the randomly spaced cotton cords—in spite of its subdued monotone. The rhythms are marked by breaks of varying lengths. Behind the Y are the free-hanging vertical cords that are also seen in Macratotem *(p. 211).*

COMET IN CLOSE SPACE   1971
15½'' x 15½'' x 15½'' (model)
macramé
linen and nylon; white
Collection: Museo de Arte Contemporáneo, Ibiza

This monumental piece was designed to be installed in an all-glass room or gallery of 23 to 26
square feet so that the viewer might respond to
the relation of object to defined space. There is
a sure sense of movement in the curved forms
to contrast with the tense rigidity of the supporting cords.

MACRATOTEM   1969
70'' x 31'' x 31''
wrapping and macramé
cotton and sisal cords; copper red
Collection: Museo de Arte Contemporáneo, Madrid

The artist uses her usual materials and a single
technique to create this three-dimensional totem.
The elements of the composition are wrapped
cords, sometimes coiled and sometimes stretched,
and the wrapped frame or armature on which the
coils are suspended. The coils, varied in surface
and weight, are interrupted by the spokes that
support them. The voids offer surprising views
through the totem, revealing the unengaged vertical cords running obliquely through the center
and different views of the apertures opposite.

THREE PERSONAGES   1971
Left to right, height and diameter at base:
68¼″, 33″; 58½″, 27″; 63″, 33″
macramé
sisal; Spanish orange
Collection: The artist
Shown at the Biennale, Lausanne, 1971

The dense construction of the conelike forms gives
stability to these self-supporting pieces. With a
single material and with patterning more regular
than in her other work, the artist expresses individuality with great subtlety and with typical
Spanish enigmatic wit. The center "personage"
has horizontal ribs; the left and right "personages"
are horizontally and vertically ribbed. The closures
of each of these "façades" have their own dis-
tinctive features.

rapoport

DEBRA RAPOPORT
American, born 1945

Studied at Carnegie Institute of Technology, Pittsburgh; University of California, Berkeley. Teaches at University of California, Davis. Exhibited at Biennale, Lausanne, 1971.

For her master's thesis in textiles for the Design Department at the University of California in Berkeley, Debra Rapoport produced the "fibrous raiments" shown here. Her thesis, "Constructed Textiles Related to the Body," written under the guidance of Ed Rossbach, demonstrates a cool, whimsical, yet intellectual attitude toward her work.

As a weaver, she uses traditional techniques, complementing these with commonplace materials (a direct influence of her teacher) such as cotton batting, rags, plastic garbage bags, and sometimes with more elegant fibers. At the center of her concern are the dynamics of the art of fiber in conjunction with surprising materials, stiff and unyielding.

There is a physical reality created in her work that gives meaning to the role she chooses for it. The coverings are not irrelevant to their purpose: they really have to be worn by people to make sense.

Within the uninhibited vigor of the Berkeley campus, Ed Rossbach, her teacher, says: "Rapoport's fabrics appear in special context where rags and patches are the order of the day, and have been refined by both men and women into a kind of affectation and sweetness which is very appealing. Rapoport's fabrics are part of the local scene—although unusually sensitive and refined, not really brutal or harsh or left-handed, but with a peculiar delicacy and elegance. The muted colors, the precise combinations of fibers—all is sensivity."

RUBBER LABYRINTH   1970
weft looping
rubber tubing

Opaque and translucent tubing are combined for
this body covering. The variations in looping occur
through expansion and contraction caused by
body movement.

TRIANGULAR POSITIVE AND NEGATIVE CAPE
1970
shaped weaving
magenta and natural linen, silk, rayon, and wool

*This piece is woven on a triangular loom, piece by
piece, then assembled to cloak the body. Each
triangle has three selvages; the converging warp
ends are bound to form tassels. The artist alternates two different wefts to create a pattern of
deep furrows that resemble corrugated ribs. The
open work is a fine foil for the strongly disciplined
rigid collar from which the garment falls.*

FOOTBAG 1969
wrapping and twining
orange cotton batting, bed pads, toweling,
rags, yarns
Shown at the University Art Museum,
Berkeley, California

*A warm thing to stick your feet into, this object
made with commonplace materials combines
wrapping, twining, and basketry techniques. It is
more symbolic than functional, more anti-form
than form, a piece of funk art influenced no doubt
by the Berkeley scene of the late 1960s.*

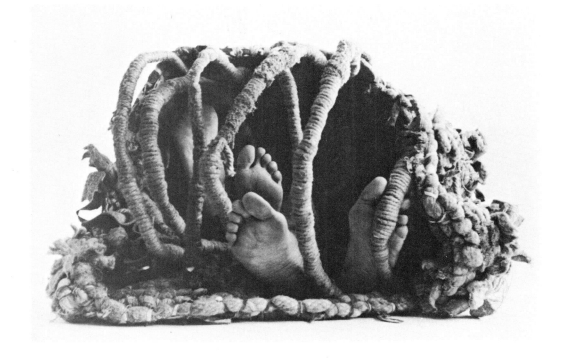

rossbach

ED ROSSBACH
American, born 1914

Studied at University of Washington, Seattle; Columbia University, New York; Cranbrook Academy of Art, Bloomfield Hills, Michigan. Teaches at University of California, Berkeley. Exhibited at Triennale, Milan, 1964; Museum West, San Francisco, 1965; Museum of Contemporary Crafts, New York, 1968; University Art Collections, Arizona State University, Tempe, 1968; The Museum of Modern Art, New York, 1969; Brooklyn Museum. Represented in collections of Women's College, University of North Carolina, Greensboro; California State Fair, Sacramento; University of Indiana, Bloomington; University of Illinois, Urbana; Mansfield State College, Massachusetts; The Johnson Collection; The Museum of Modern Art, New York.

Ed Rossbach, shown opposite at home, photographed by his wife, Katherine Westphal, says, "in the work I like best I seem to be retreating into very personal trifles —domestic artifacts—which I put somewhere in the house and they became part of all the flotsam and jetsam that surround us, a big unmanageable mixture of objects from various times and places. In this private world, a flimsy plastic divider from a package of cookies takes its place alongside a Coptic fragment. . . .

"I wish I could approach the objects and materials of our society with the sort of freshness which I dream that a native from the Brazilian jungle might. I want to experience the delight that I imagine he would find in the shiny plastic, the marvelous transparency and translucency that surround us. I would like to be an acceptance person—accepting—not narrowing what I can respond to, not refining my taste so that I can work only with wool, and then only with hand-spun wool, and then only with vegetable-dyed hand-spun wool. I want to embrace the whole bit, wholeheartedly."

And he does! Rossbach is a timeless man, a thoughtful man, an involved man. His breadth of creativity embraces the whole spectrum of fabrics. Like Thomas Wolfe who wanted to read all the books that had ever been written, Rossbach wants to see all the fabrics that have ever been made and understand their constructions and respond to their expressive qualities.

He has never designed for industry even when it was fashionable to do so; he has never accepted commissions and only rarely has produced useful fabrics of any kind. Monumentality or presence of a finished work has never appealed to him. The center of each piece is inside it, in its concept, in the secret of its technique, in the thought processes or turn of mind required to think out a construction. To him, the center is in his own involvement. "While I like to think big I often enjoy working small. I really regret that so few people are willing to bother with fine elements in handweaving, or with complex, calculated structures, or controlled techniques. Whole areas of fabric experience are denied, or relegated to machines. Much of the magic of fabric, and the satisfaction of creating them, derive only from fine elements precisely controlled."

Rossbach is not a timid man, rather a pathfinder who has explored most of the known techniques, especially the obscure and forgotten ones. In the mid-sixties Rossbach became so intrigued with the archaic technique of bobbin lace that he invested in the traditional pillow and spindles, as well as in countless hours working on the smallest of fabrics. He recognized the technique as the most complex and at the same time the most flexible in the whole fabric range: that warp can become weft, pattern is free, space can be open or dense or firmly filigreed. In *Small White Lace* (p. 226), he is improvising faster with a relatively large vinyl tape. (The loops at the top were, in process, held by pins. At the bottom the tape ends are simply heat-sealed.)

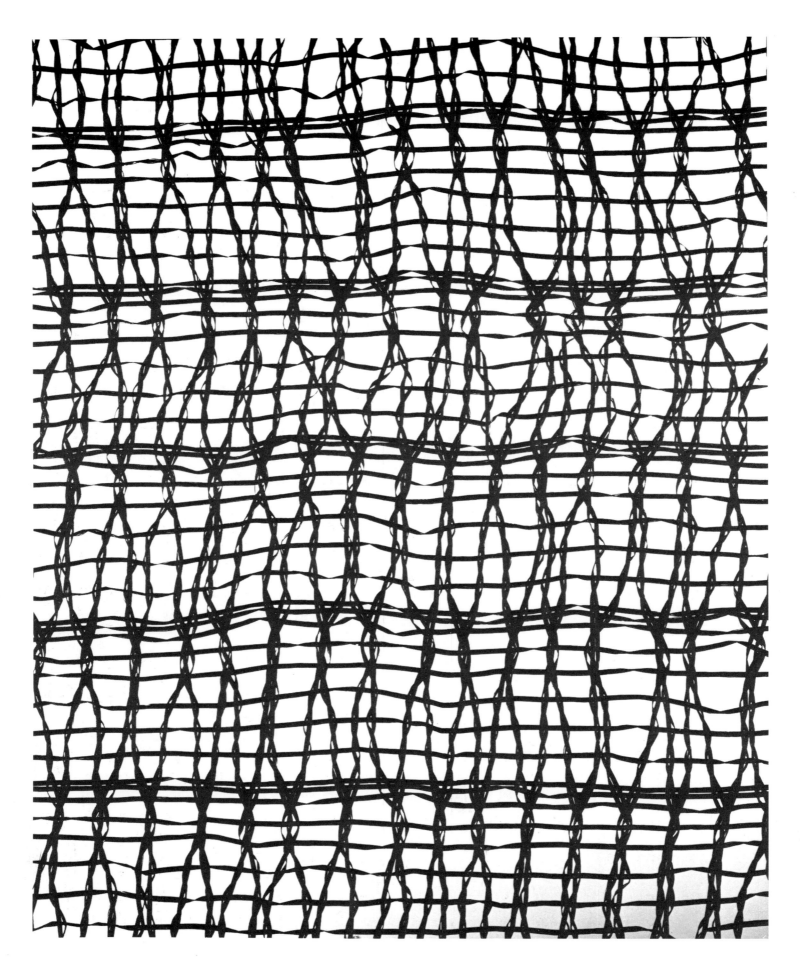

UNTITLED 1951
96" x 40"
warp twining
black rayon straw
Collection: Brooklyn Museum, New York

The flat, paper-like fiber is given dimension by
warp twining, which modulates the form, accen-
tuates the highlights and gives the open filigree
its body. Rossbach is simultaneously exploring the
ancient technique and a then (1951) new material.

UNTITLED 1952
14" x 16"
tatami weave
raffia, cotton and anise stalk; black and natural
Collection: The artist

This study was influenced by the tatami technique
of the Orient. The lively flame pattern is achieved
by the crossing of dark and light raffia wefts. The
paired warps are secured by twisting them around
the rigid stalks.

Although his constructions are often complete works in themselves, they are sometimes more in the nature of *études,* thoughts or meditations directed to the accomplishment of a purpose. "I think that conceptual art which exists only as an idea or a diagram is a nice solution to what to do with projects. But I find that although I often make diagrams and sketches in advance, the work really results quite unpredictably from the doing."

After studying painting, ceramics, and art education, he began his career as a weaver at the Cranbrook Academy of Art. By 1948 he instructed in weaving in the art department at the University of Washington in Seattle, later joining the University of California in Berkeley in the Department of Decorative Art. It is interesting to note that when this department began during the twenties, Dr. Lila O'Neale, an anthropologist, was a faculty member and chairman of the department. She put a strong imprint on the department, and brought to it a concern with analysis and reconstruction of primitive fabrics. This was quite unlike the structural emphasis of the Bauhaus, and quite different in its intentions and goals.

Never separate from his own work and his projects is Rossbach's involvement as a teacher. This has given him financial security and contact with people. ". . . . the wonderful Hippie clothes to be seen everywhere in Berkeley. The visual quality of the Berkeley scene—and teaching in this scene—so absolutely endlessly enchanting and stimulating, such a constant textile experience. . . .

"I don't accept the distinctions between major and minor arts but I don't want to argue about it with anyone. These hierarchies become destructive. So much is destructive in our society. The individual tries to survive with his values as intact as possible. It is not easy. I think that this somewhat accounts for my retreat into the most personal expressions—the most devalued pursuits. . . . when money is the only criterion of value I use old newspaper and throwaway plastic and string. I reconstitute what ceased to be useful—rags and paper cartoons. . . . I find it amusing to value the valueless. . . . I enjoy the soft vulnerable look of the worked newspaper. I want the familiar newspaper to be transformed into a fabric. I dream of plaiting from these newspaper strips . . . (p. 225).

"I suppose, in a way, that many weavers today are trying to function as architects —although such categories as architect, painter, sculptor, seem to have become meaningless . . . in a subtle way a shift is occurring. The architectural spaces provided by architects have not kept pace with the space concepts of sculptors and— although it seems presumptuous to say—of weavers. Although as weavers we are regarded as decorators who decorate the spaces provided by someone else, we are more and more tackling, at least in our thinking, the problems of creating space, and—already it sounds old-fashioned—of controlling and defining space. . . . Now we are concerned more with creating space. The dilemma is that the hand processes in fabrics are so slow, the size becomes so limited, the fabric artist cannot explore his space ideas through the fabrics he is able to construct. . . . a serious tension is resulting in weaving between the artist's concepts and the limitations of the medium as it has traditionally existed. It seems that weavers must either scale down their ideas or they must break through to new means of accomplishing them."

BASKET 1957
14" x 6"
palm, ixtle, and plastic raffia

The strong systemic order of palm fronds has, since earliest times, intrigued the weaver. The ribs and veins supporting a translucent skin have inspired him. Palm fibers such as raffia have been his materials and, in many tropical cultures, the frond itself has been turned into a fan or interwoven into mats and walls of houses.

Here Rossbach has folded the splines of a round palmette into a vase-shaped warp. On this warp he has alternately woven bands of ixtle and plastic ribbon so firmly as to form a dense, hard surface. The palm ribs are expressed in the fluted surface.

CEREMONIAL PLATE WITH APOCALYPTIC FACE 1965
14" at largest diameter
macramé
ixtle; multicolored

A sense of the archaic is preserved in every aspect of this work: in its tight semi-rigid construction, its image, and its uneven circular form. Contributing to the interest of this small piece are the orchestration in colors and the movement provided by the many changes of direction of the wrapping.

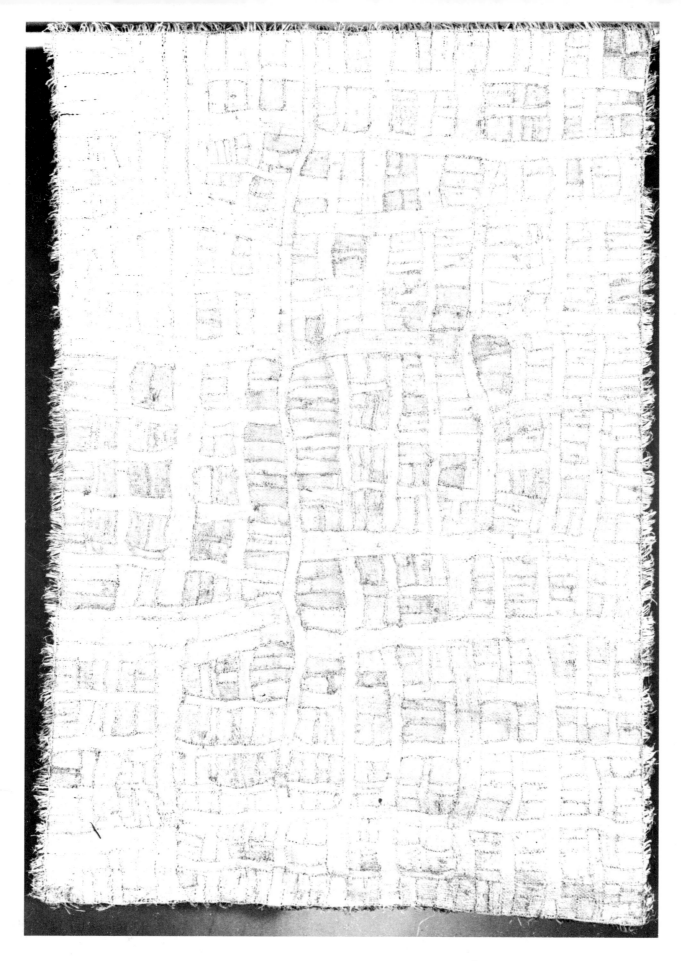

TAPESTRY   1964
71" x 45"
double tapestry
raffia; natural
Collection: The Museum of Modern Art, New York
Shown at the Triennale, Milan, 1964

This work employs the rare scaffold wefting technique of ancient Peru, in which both warp and weft
interlock within the single thickness of the cloth.
Where the Peruvians wove patterns with sharp
color definition, Rossbach, with extreme sophistication, uses no change in color. The subtle pattern
is defined only by the shadow line on the tapestry
join, or it is emphasized by a change in density.

MACRAME   1967
40″ x 30″
ixtle; yellow-green
Collection: University of Indiana, Bloomington

Rossbach's rare use of macramé is singularly successful because he has relied on a single material and on one type of knotting.

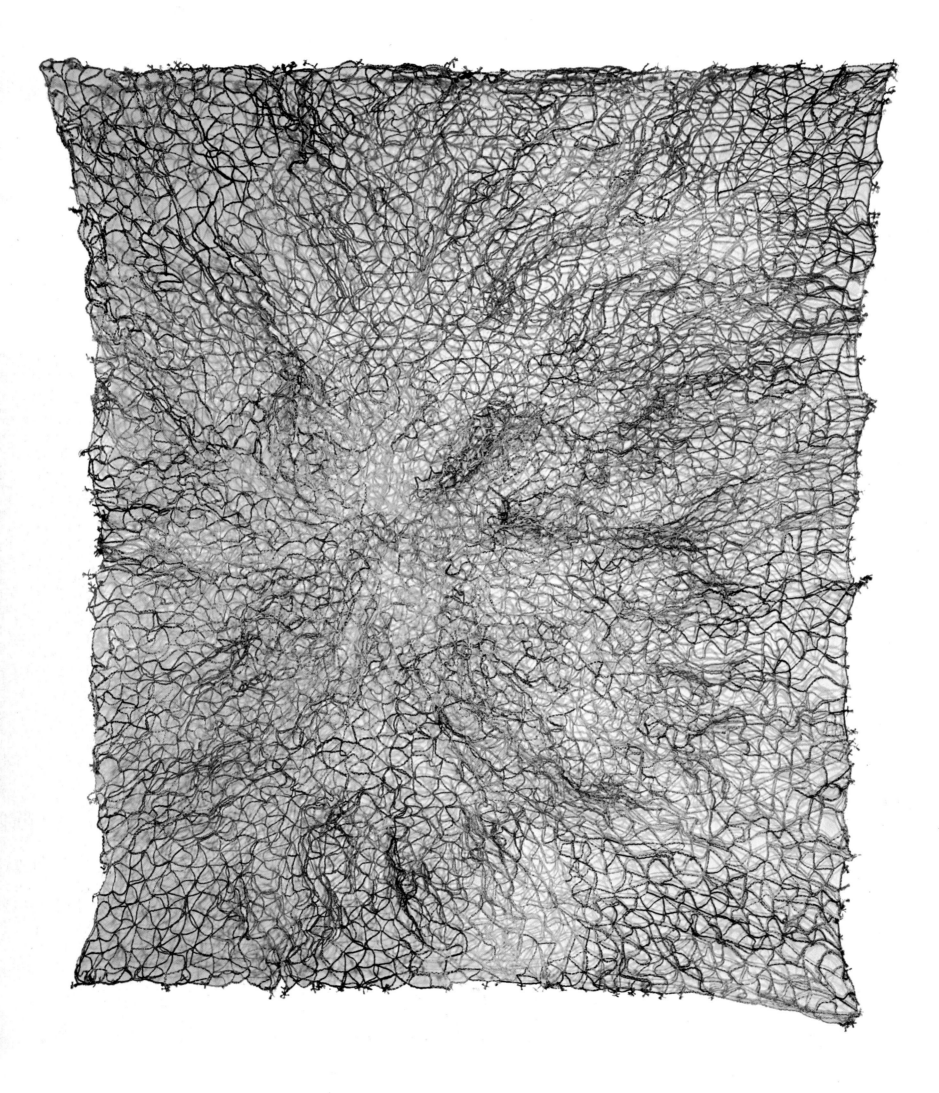

CONSTRUCTED COLOR *1966*
5'11" x 4'9"
braided
synthetic painted raffia; multicolored
Collection: The Museum of Modern Art, New York
Shown in "Wall Hangings,"
The Museum of Modern Art, New York, 1969

*Using a new structural system of braiding in a
filigree pattern, Rossbach achieves illusionistic
qualities transcending deliberately chosen cheap
commercial materials and colors. His early train-
ing as a painter here serves him well.*

**CONSTRUCTION WITH NEWSPAPER
AND PLASTIC** *1968*
30" x 40"
plain weave
*polyethylene film tubing, polyethylene twine,
and newsprint*
Collection: The artist

*In his first experiment with stuffed tubing, a simple
four-selvaged study in a basic weave, Rossbach
departs from his usual reliance upon technique.
He transforms his "throwaway materials" into a
rich aesthetic statement through transparency,
luminosity of surface, drama of scale, and an almost pop use of newsprint.*

WORK IN PROGRESS *1968*
polyethylene tubing stuffed with foam
Collection: The artist

*One of the many "études" using a plastic sleeve
over a bulky material, this piece is woven on a
frame without the use of heddles. To achieve the
four selvages, the warp is wrapped around rods
which are later removed. Temporary scaffolding
is used to maintain weft tension. The visual interest lies in the heavy emphasis on the rectangular pattern in the center of the piece.*

SMALL WHITE LACE 1970
bobbin lace
vinyl tape; white
Collection: The artist

This piece possesses a lively rhythm with an irregular pattern of voids and solids. The thickness of the material gives it substance and body without weight. Construction is limited to a simple plait. The tape ends make a short fringe, and the selvages are ornamented by twisted elements.

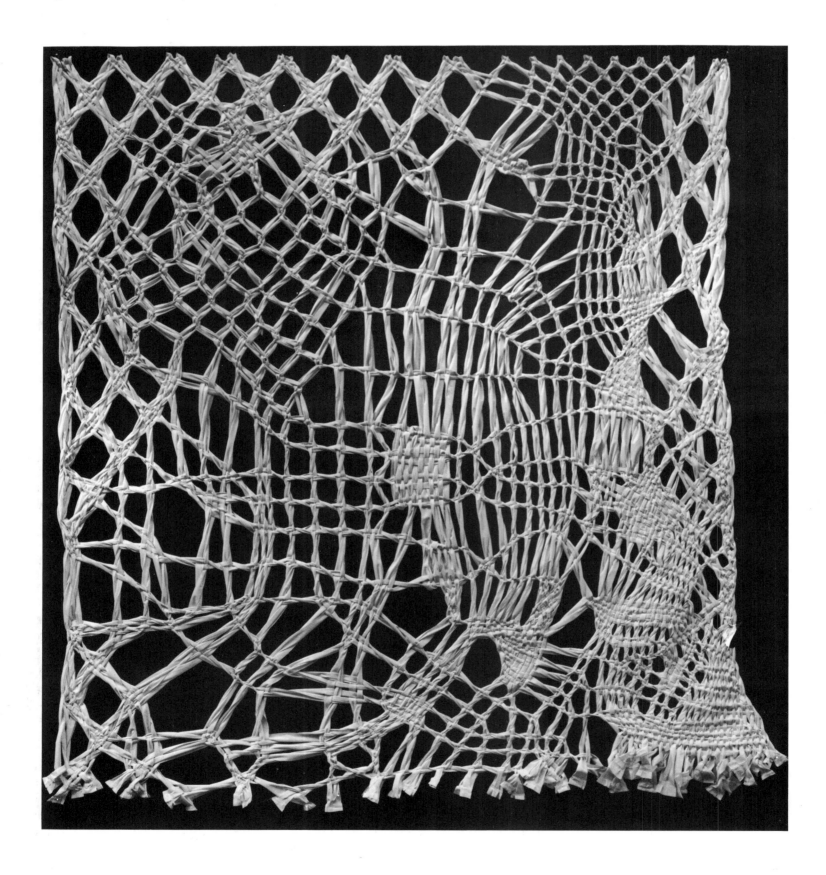

UNTITLED 1971
11" x 14"
needlepoint lace
cotton string; natural
Collection: The artist

Set into a woven frame with eight selvages made of the same yarn, the heavy cotton twine used for the lace technique makes this small, sturdy study an ingenious essay.

UNTITLED 1971
needlepoint lace
cotton string, newsprint; natural
Collection: The artist

About this piece Rossbach says, "I liked the relationship of the lace to the drawing I had made and was supposedly following—it seemed complete so I stopped."

AN IRRELEVANT SOLUTION   1972
11" x 12" x 12"

SOFT CONSTRUCTION   1972
24" x 20" x 17"
plaited newspaper
Collection: The artist

These are related to the earlier "tribe of baskets" (p. 75). Rossbach calls them "interface structures" because of their weightless definition of interior and exterior volumes. He says they "are related to certain architecture of the People of the Reeds on the Euphrates River. There, entire enclosures—

walls, ceilings, floors, furniture, windows—are created out of a single material manipulated in various ways according to the specific requirements of each architectural element."

These baskets of newspaper use the simple technique of plaiting with flexible ribbon-like elements reinforced by the frequent interlacing of plain weave. In traditional basketry such soft structures are further supported by sturdy rims or bases, or vertical supports of bamboo or other more rigid materials. Here this is not the case; rather, the soft cords serve to bind and modify the paper forms and to add the finishing element.

rousseau-vermette

MARIETTE ROUSSEAU-VERMETTE
Canadian, born 1926

Studied at Ecole des Beaux-Arts, Quebec; Oakland College of Arts and Crafts, California; with Dorothy Liebes. Exhibited at Biennale, Lausanne, 1962, 1965, 1967, 1969, 1971; The Museum of Modern Art, New York, 1969; Jack Lenor Larsen Showroom, New York, 1970, New Design Gallery, Vancouver, 1964; Université de Sherbrooke, Quebec, 1965. Represented in collections of National Gallery of Canada, Ottawa; Museum of Contemporary Art, Montreal; Vancouver Art Gallery; Kennedy Center for the Performing Arts, Washington, D.C.; Esso World Headquarters, New York.

Through her art, integrated with architecture, Mariette Rousseau-Vermette wants to bring the calm and beauty of nature into public buildings. She seeks to translate the color of the changing seasons of Canada and the softness of distant mountains into her work. She functions best in closest harmony with the architect, familiarizing herself with the environment in which her work will live. Rousseau-Vermette starts from a sketch made in oil pastel on rough paper. She discusses this with the architect, researches new approaches, and moves on to make a scale model in wool.

Often her pieces are not isolated hangings but more in the nature of soft murals that are massive and monumental. Her non-objective, architectural style and directness of execution are consistent with the spaces for which she designs.

At first she used natural colors of hand-spun lambswool—white, gray, brown, and black. Later she added earth colors and fiery reds. She chose wool because it satisfied the need for permanence and boldness of scale. Her designs are based on strong, orderly geometric areas whose linear gradations are softened by the simple act of brushing the wool. This serves to blur the edges of transition from one color to another while intensifying their brilliance.

In her more recent work she has used strips of Canadian furs in combination with wool. She has also simplified her compositions by omitting the tapestry joinings and with heavy roving introducing broad areas of relief. This produces a pebbled surface in contrast to the brushed areas. These sensual surfaces invite the viewer to share in a tactile experience.

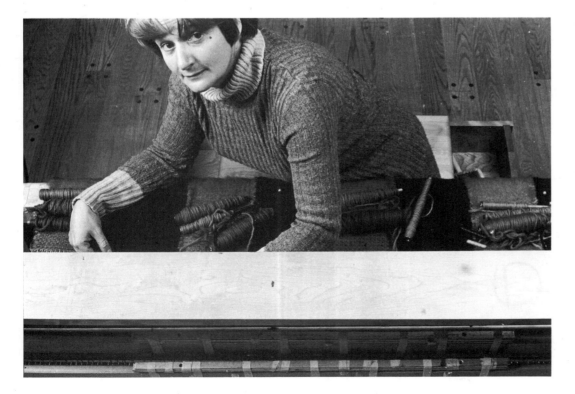

Mariette Rousseau-Vermette in her studio. Without shuttles she weaves on a section of the act curtain for the Eisenhower Theatre of the Kennedy Center for the Performing Arts, Washington, D.C. The vertical bands, which are achieved through tapestry joining, will be brushed.

SPARKS OF GLOWING EMBERS   1966
9'4½" x 6'8¾" turned 90°
tapestry brushed after weaving
wool; reds
Shown at the Biennale, Lausanne, 1967, and in "Wall Hangings," The Museum of Modern Art, New York, 1969

The architectonic pattern is developed by slicing and offsetting a stripe progression. The tapestry join is such that the narrow bands seem superimposed, with an exaggerated shadow line. While softening the color gradations, the brushed surface heightens the clashing intensity and contrasting values.

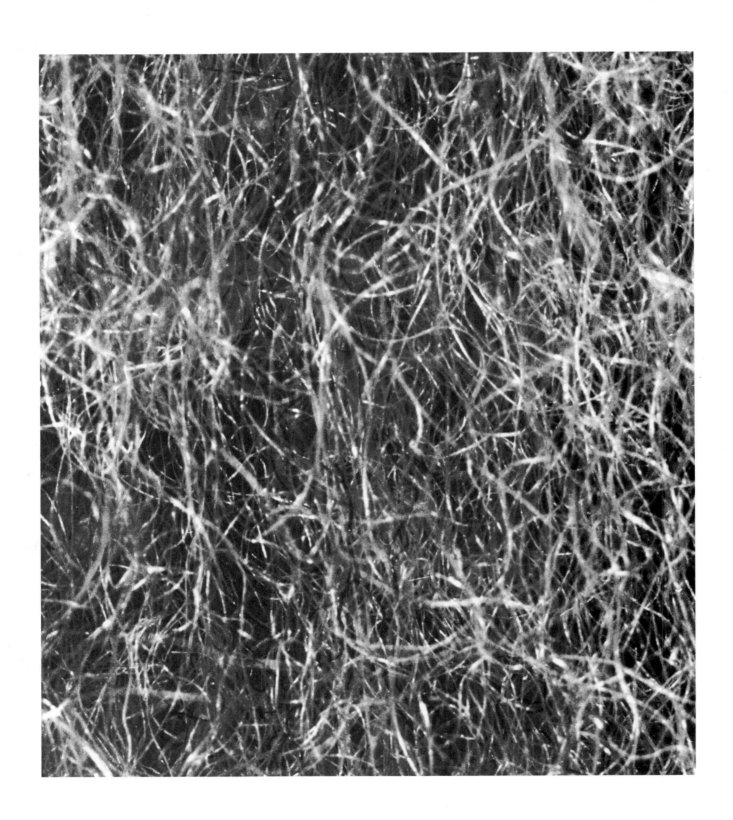

This much enlarged detail is characteristic of the brushed surface in the artist's pieces. The light-refracting properties of unengaged wool fibers become apparent. At the same time, luminosity is enhanced, the color is intensified, and adjoining color areas become softly fused.

DIRECT 1969
20'4'' x 50'10'' turned 90°
tapestry, brushed off the loom
wool; white, blue, and green
Shown at the Biennale, Lausanne, 1971

Woven as a weft stripe, the long mural is a dynamic progression of the softly blended colors of
out-of-doors. The basic simplicity is relieved by a
fine command of proportion, by varying degrees of
contrast, and by the bands woven with wrist-thick
roving to produce a pebbly surface. Through tonal
relationships this relief is beautifully integrated
with the brushed areas.

sadley

WOJCIECH SADLEY
Polish, born 1932

Studied at Fine Arts Academy, Warsaw. Exhibited
at Biennale, Lausanne, 1962, 1965, 1967, 1969,
1971; Bienal, São Paulo, 1966; Festival des Arts
Plastiques de la Côte D'Azur, Antibes, 1966; Gallery 9, London, 1966; Kunsthall, Lund, Sweden,
1967; Hermitage, Leningrad, 1968–70; The Museum of Modern Art, New York, 1969; Stedelijk
Museum, Amsterdam, 1969; in Madrid, Essen,
London, and Stockholm.

Wojciech Sadley belongs to the renowned Warsaw school of weavers. His expression is intensely personal. The paint corner of his Warsaw studio reveals the directness with which he works; here are also the sooty blacks and shrouded spheres that haunt much of his work. Tacked on a wall smudged with spray paint is a sketch and the freshly sprayed, batlike form of *Ikar*, 1966 (58½″ x 97½″). The draped suspension, wildly mixed media, and somberness are characteristic of the pendulous forms in which gravity plays a major role. Usually suspended from two or three points, these forms are executed in hide, fur, filet netting, or cloth, or woven in an assemblage technique of textures and colors that are sometimes macabre and often gloomy. When he works on a loom with less robust materials, he preserves the pendulous forms with threads that seem to pour out of the cloth surface. However surrealist the work may appear, however jarring the juxtaposition of materials, his results are rich, forceful, and commanding of respect.

INFANTKA (detail)   1965
97½″ x 39″ (full piece)
knotted netting
flax, hemp, braided cord, steel;
black and brown

This knotted piece has an arrestingly formal composition, especially in comparison with Ed Rossbach's Constructed Color (p. 224).

The dark colors are only relieved by the reflected light of small bangles of roughly cut steel. In the wiry calligraphy of fine and heavy weights and textures, the lighter vertical elements support the weight of the braided cords.

I WORK ON SERIES OF PROBLEMS —
CONSTRUCTIONAL AND FORMAL

*

APPROACHING EVERY PROBLEM,
I BEGIN BY STUDYING THE RELATIONS
BETWEEN MEANS OF EXPRESSION
AND CONSTRUCTIONAL FACTORS

* *

EVERY SERIE IS SOLVED IN A DIFFE-
RENT WAY VARYING WITH THE
EMOTIONAL AND CONSTRUCTIONAL
PROBLEMS INTERESTING ME.

* * *

I USE EVERY POSSIBLE FORM
OF DEVELOPING MY CONCEPT
BY DRAWING, PAINTING, MODELLING

SADLEY

SLEEPLESS NIGHT   1966
9'10½" x 6'6¾"
tapestry with knotted pile
wool and linen; red and black
Shown at Biennale, Lausanne, 1967, and in
"Wall Hangings," The Museum of Modern Art,
New York, 1969

Still pendulous, but with the soft hanging flow of
perhaps a willow, the lovely colors reveal a more
poetic albeit brooding aspect of Sadley's work.
There is discipline in the "fall" of the cluster and
a wispy quality of the materials.

Installation of one-man exhibition
Zacheta Gallery, Warsaw, 1967

In all Sadley's pieces the pull of gravity is a common denominator, as is the earthy, organic material he uses. The center piece has a woven
tapestry ground with knotted pile like *Sleepless
Night,* but here the ground is completely obliter-
ated and the overflow seems noiseless.

schiele

MOIK SCHIELE
Swiss, born 1938

Studied at Kunstgewerbeschule, Zurich, with Elsi Giaque. Exhibited at Kunstmuseum, St. Gall, 1959; Landesgewerbeamt Baden-Wurttemberg, Stuttgart, 1963; Landesmuseum, Oldenburg, 1964; Kunstverein, Hamburg; The Museum of Modern Art, New York, 1969; Jack Lenor Larsen Showroom, New York, 1970; Biennale, Lausanne, 1969, 1971. Represented in collections of Landesmuseum, Oldenburg; Museum Bellerive, Zurich.

In her studio, Moik Schiele is finishing Raumelement Black, *a three-foot-square column of translucent black bands separately woven and hung at right angles to each other.*

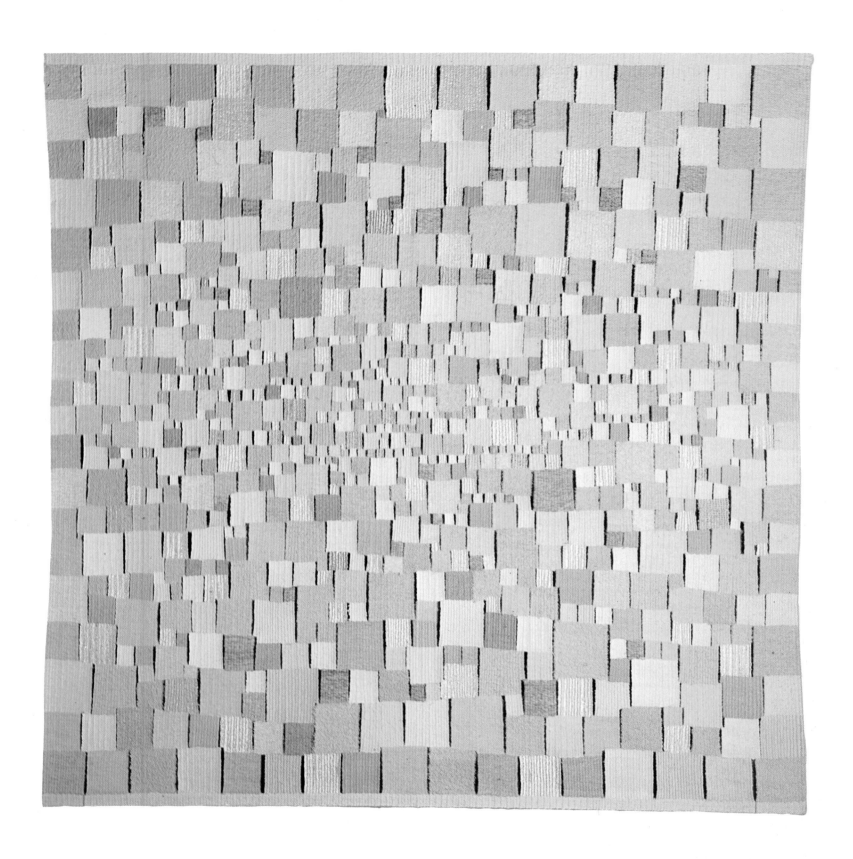

SQUARES   1965
54½" x 54½"
slit tapestry
synthetic and natural fibers;
natural and dyed neutral
Collection: Museum Bellerive, Zurich

The artist has dynamically orchestrated slit size
and length, texture and color so that the most
intricate breakup falls at the center. The surface
texture and light-reflecting qualities of the thirty
weft yarns are modulated for maximum variation.
In a piece which is insistently two-dimensional, a
third dimension is implied by color value and the
see-through quality of the open slits.

Moik Schiele was born and educated in Zurich. She has always lived there. In that her work is clearly ordered, uncompromising, diligent, and without embellishment, it seems the epitome of the Swiss character. One could say that her understated handling of rich materials and her immaculate treatment of color is also Swiss. All this sounds calculating. Not so! Schiele is not, nor is her work. However disciplined, she is obsessive. The intensity with which she pursues a set course is pure emotion. The explanation of her meticulous craftsmanship is that each controlled weft shot is *not* mechanical but impassioned.

At the outset, her concern is the definition of a technical problem expressed in numbers. The design exists in her memory or on a piece of scrap paper written on a sleepless night. Working on the loom, she weaves a section of the work to be executed. She does not produce a miniature; rather she weaves details to be applied on a larger scale, more in the tradition of the architect resolving a detail of fenestration, or mullion and fenestration in combination.

Such solutions, based on mathematics, recall the early drawings of Richard Lippold for his mammoth sculptures, or more recently the work of many conceptual artists whose drawings are complicated mathematical charts. Her solutions also seem related to those expressed in the systemic studies of Richard Landis (p. 204). New materials too fascinate her, since she feels that a weaver who seeks new techniques cannot disregard new materials. Therefore she employs the newest synthetics or combines them with traditional weaving materials (p. 241).

The technical feasibility proven, the warp and wefts are calculated, the color scheme determined, and the materials selected. What remains to be done requires diligent labor and the most exacting craftsmanship. Her expectation of how the finished piece will appear remains unchanged until the last weft thread is woven.

All her pieces are *raumelements* (room elements) not to be hung on the wall, but away from it; or as architectural elements conceived in space, blending harmoniously in contemporary architecture with light and air as essential elements.

Consistent in her work is a preoccupation with solid and void, and more particularly the many ramifications of slit-tapestry technique. An alternate form is the square-sectioned "columns," as shown on p. 240. Repeatedly, she concentrates pattern in the center of her compositions, and most often she works within a narrow range of luminous, light neutral colors. Her favorite alternates are dead black or reflective aluminum yarns.

BLUE OPALESCENT TAPESTRY 1972
47" x 47"
slit tapestry
synthetic raffia; blue

This piece is one of a long series in which color is the principal concern. Within an exact module of sawtooth diamonds, reminiscent of the small shingles on old Swiss farm houses, or the sequined scales of an exotic reptile, Schiele builds an illusionary image. Color is so subtly graduated that in some lights the image all but disappears. In others, it glows with a strange luminosity.

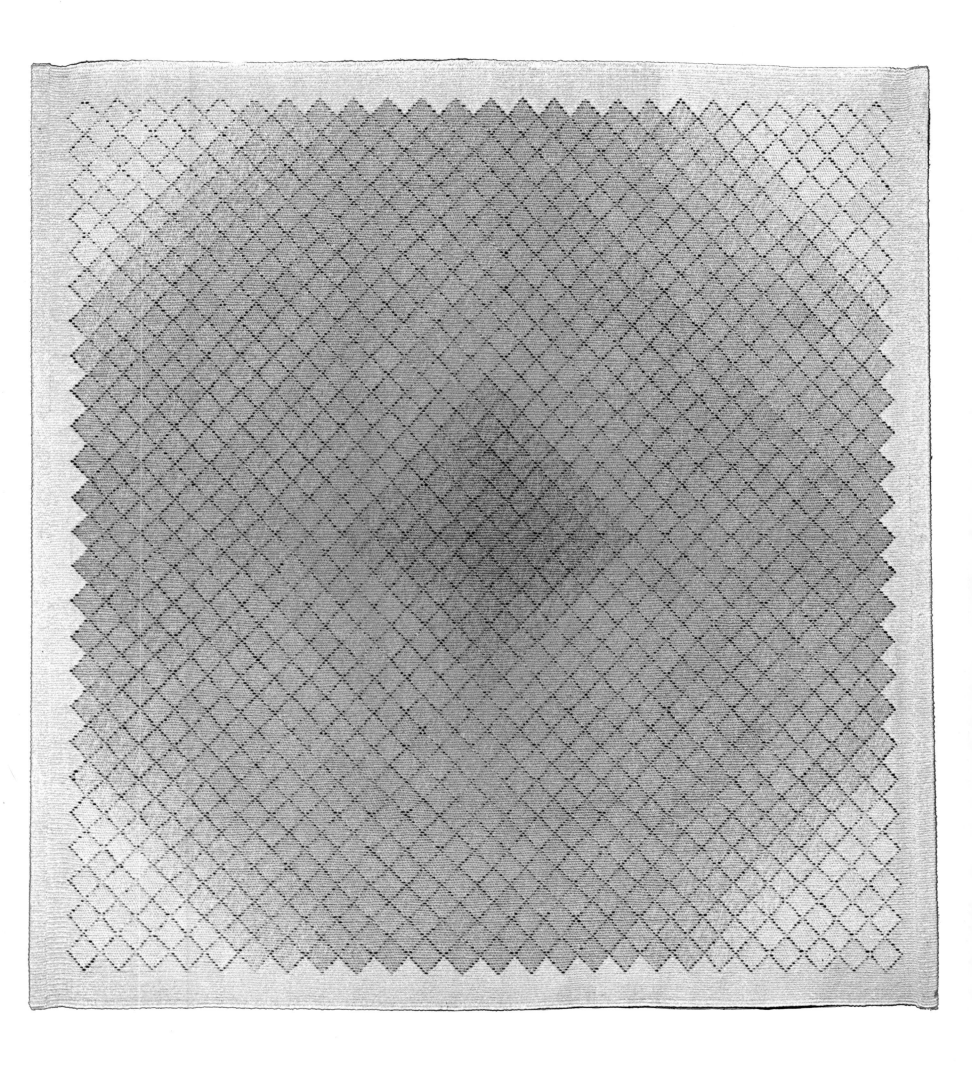

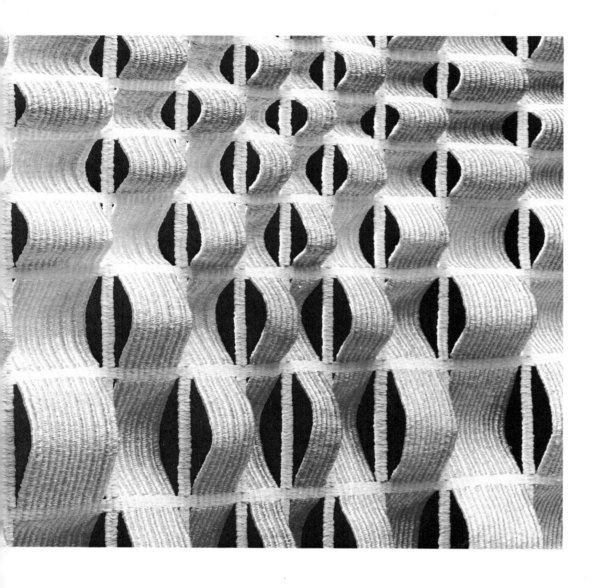

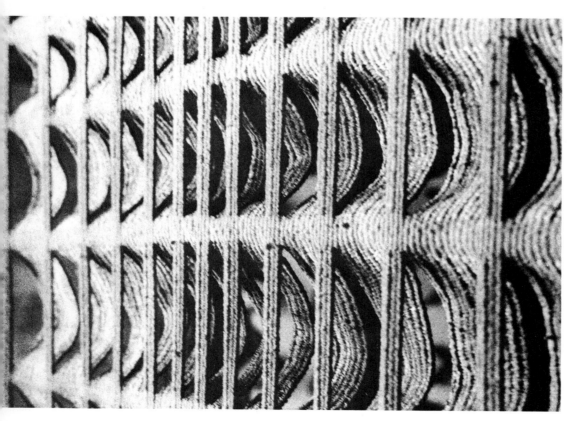

RAUMELEMENT, YELLOW 1969
117″ x 78″ x 9¾″ (in six parts, each 3¼′ square)
slit tapestry, with tension differential
viscose straw; gold
Shown at the Biennale, Lausanne, 1969

Working within the slit-tapestry technique, with a single color and material, and an extremely formalized plan, the artist has realized an important innovation.

The depth, which is most apparent in the detail (above), was achieved with two sets of warps independently beamed so that the curving bands are twice as long as the verticals. The man-made straw produces a cloth sufficiently rigid to support the concave and convex forms, with a sharp precision consistent with the design.

The section (left) shows the same piece transformed by pushing all of the long bands to the same concave form. At the far left one sees the metal frame covered in a tubular woven sleeve of the same material.

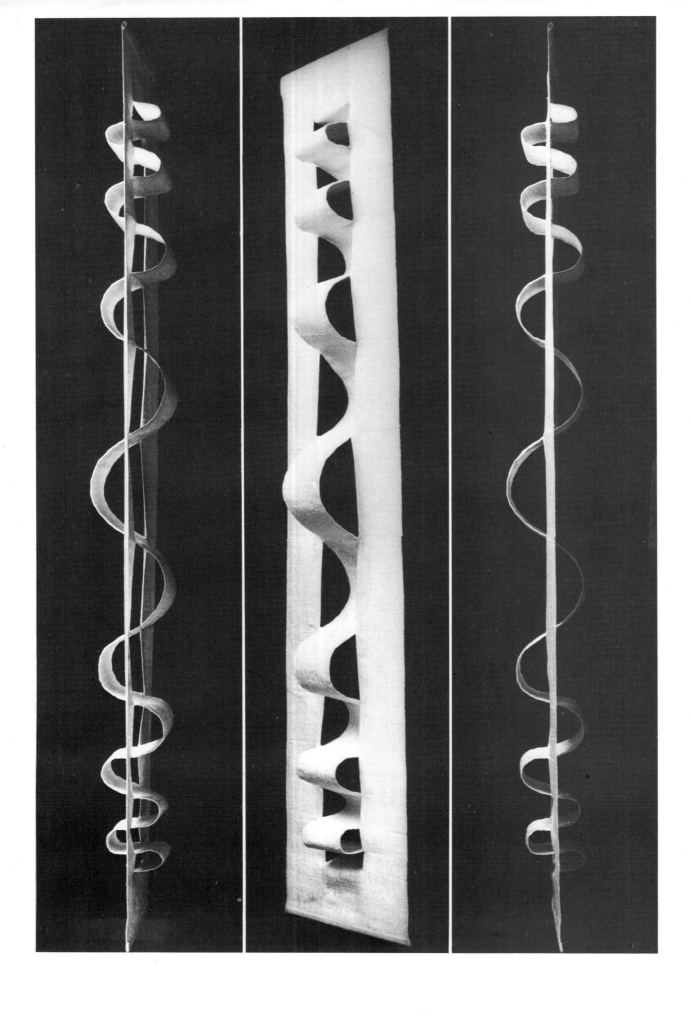

WHITE WAVE   1970
9'4'' x 21'' x 20''
slit tapestry with tension differential
synthetic multifilament; white
Shown at the Biennale, Lausanne, 1971

Photographed here from three different perspectives, this is a further development of the double-beam technique combined with the tapestry slit.

Here all else has been subordinated to the exploitation of the sinuous curve: so that the front to back dimension might be maximized, the curved band is elongated to three times the panel length. In this refinement the wefts common to both curving and flat elements are minimal. The immaculately white, silky, luminous material enhances the formal severity of the piece and dramatizes the soft modeling of the curves.

scholten

HERMAN SCHOLTEN
Dutch, born 1932

Studied at Rijksakademier van Beeldende Kunsten, Amsterdam. Teaches at Akademie voor Industriele Vormgeving, Eindhoven; Koninklijk Academie voor Kunst en Vormgeving, s'Hertogenbosch. Exhibited at Stedelijk Museum, Amsterdam, 1959, 1963, 1964, 1966, 1967; Biennale, Lausanne, 1965, 1967, 1969, 1971; The Museum of Modern Art, New York, 1969. Represented in collections of Dutch Government; Stedelijk Museum, Amsterdam; Dreyfus Fund Collection, New York; Ruth Kaufmann Gallery, New York.

Outside the Scholtens' Gerrit Rietveld house at Bambrugge, the Netherlands
On the wall is Up and Down, *1970*
70" x 70"
shaped tapestry
wool and flax; brilliant yellows
Collection: Stedelijk Museum, Amsterdam

Diagram of construction is shown on p. 257

Scholten's work is characterized by a manly strength. The great reliefs have presence and monumentality in the sense of Egyptian sculpture; that is, with restraint and without exuberance. They are static, self-contained, and while not aggressive, they are certainly unflinching. His words explain a man moralistic and forthright, who conceptualizes objectively and executes cleanly. The essence of his structure is here described—but not the *un*cool virility that is embodied in his work.

"My tapestries express themselves. They do not render anything else and do not represent anything. I make no tents or coats, neither is my tapestry fetishistic. And I do not derive themes or motifs from folk art. My tapestries are woven structures, forms, and colors put together and related to one another in such a way that they render as closely as possible the emotional value that I wish to express.

"I try not to be obtrusive as regards my personal emotions but I try to present my tapestry in a clear, plain form but nevertheless to the point and well-balanced. I think my work is typically Dutch."

By nature adverse to frivolity and extravagance, he warns against the decorative approach and the sensual effect. "Yarns and woven surfaces have a natural charm deriving from their color and texture and natural fall. The danger arises—and in my opinion we see instances of it all too often—when the delicate sensual properties of the material are exploited beyond sobriety. Too easily a woven material can become mere glamour."

The formidable scale is appropriate to his structured reliefs and to the public spaces in which most of the works hang. So is his meticulous craftsmanship and concern with permanence. Although his style has a natural appeal to architects, Scholten prefers not to accept commissions for specific spaces but to work abstractly and uninvolved, concerned only with the essential relationships within the piece.

An acceptable decorative effect, he feels, is the inherent contrast between the rigidity of building elements and the softness of the woven piece: "I do not wish to create a tapestry which is decorative in itself, but with a possible decorative function in regard to its surrounding. In this case it must agree with the proportions, rhythms, and color of the surroundings."

The continuity of Scholten's work is in his search for the essence—or essences—of weaving. He feels that a fabric is preeminently a structure. "The way in which the threads are connected and the choice of material determine the aspect of the structure. When expressing my plastic intentions, I make the most of this structure or combination of structures, each of which can evoke a sensibility."

BLACK SPOTTED   1969
62½" x 70"
shaped tapestry
wool and sisal; white, black, brown, and gray
Collection: Polytechnic Fashion School,
Amsterdam

Like The Knot, this piece is assembled from four
shaped bands. Because the two vertical bands
hang free, the viewer is made more aware of their
interlacing action.

THE KNOT (2)   1967
78" x 117" turned 90°
tapestry
wool, sisal, flax; white, black, red, and yellow
Collection: Department of Culture, Rijswijk, the
Netherlands

This construction relies upon the interwoven join-
ing of many bands. Like other Scholten pieces, its
execution required planning and precision.

First the five vertical and four horizontal bands
were woven on a conventional tapestry loom. The
shaping is accomplished by improvising with the
"wedges" of temporary weft, shaded dark in Fig-
ure 1. When off the loom, these are removed and
the warp ends pulled tight, as in Figure 2, to
effect a segmented curve.

The piece is woven "on its side"; the top and
bottom "frame" were set up as two narrow warps
spaced on either side of a wide loom. During the
process of weaving the warp ends of the five
vertical bands were woven into the web to produce
an integrated join. Another pair of warps was set
up for the right and left frame. Then the unfinished
tapestry was turned 90° so that the warp ends
from the upper and lower frame and from the
horizontal bands could—as wefts—be joined to
the side frames.

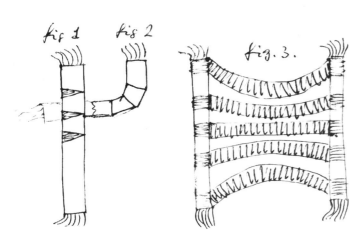

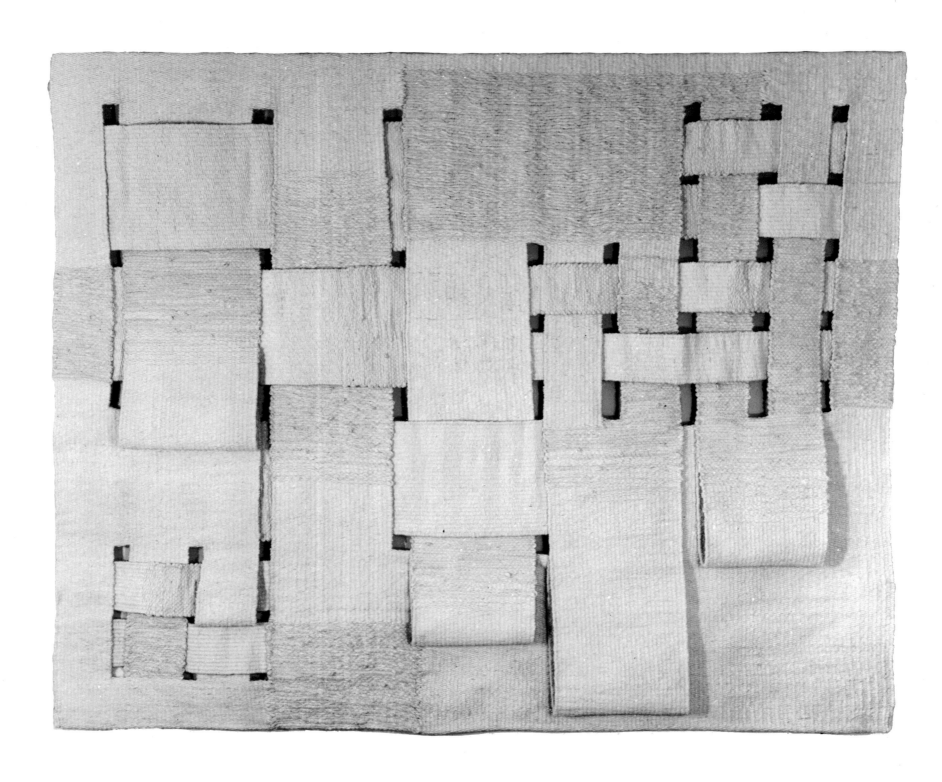

THE MIRROR   1966
7'5'' x 8'
tapestry, reconstructed after weaving
undyed wool and hemp; white
Collection: The Dutch State Collection, The Hague
Shown in "Wall Hangings,"
The Museum of Modern Art, New-York, 1969

The monumental form, with large kilim slits, is
supplemented with the separately woven horizontal bands which are sometimes interlaced, sometimes stitched. The freehanging folds are stuffed
to maintain the third dimension. The composition
is given emphasis by the contrast of rough and
smooth yarn.

The concept or motif of a piece invariably derives from structure, sometimes from intertwined bands or bands that form loops (p. 252) or woven material in layers (p. 256). *Up and Down* (p. 247) is the essence of plain weave increased in scale a thousand times so that the interlaced yarns become broad woven bands.

"I make tiny sketches of my ideas; I have piles of these sketches. But because weaving is such a labor-intensive occupation, and because I make my tapestry alone, I can, to my regret, work out only a small part of my ideas.

"Before I start working out a tapestry, I make an exact, colored paper model in scale. I take care that the composition is good, and while designing it I never fail to remember that it is to be a woven material. The original idea must remain central; as soon as one deviates from it and adds elements foreign to this starting point, one treads the wrong road.

"Textile materials are my basic elements and very often my source of inspiration too. Every kind of material has its own characteristics and naturally I like to make use of its various properties and possibilities. Properly speaking, I have no special preference for any distinct material; I do not discriminate. I use every one of them alternately or in combination: wool, linen, cotton, synthetic yarns, sisal, manila, plastics, and copper."

His color is fresh, crisp, and pure. Rooted in the checkerboard floors of Vermeer and the sunflowers of Van Gogh, its total effect is often the lightness and brilliance of abstract expressionism. The sunny cadmium yellows and oranges are even sensual in that the warm and cool yellows have been heightened by contrasting textures and the highlight and shadow of woven relief. This is particularly true in recent works that use exaggerated shading to heighten the apparent depth.

As a color, white is dominant. Sometimes the white reliefs are *all* white, chalk white, relieved only by integral contrasts in materials and by highlight and shadow. Other times colors are woven into white grounds (or in the case of the linen series, into natural linen) in the manner of Mondrian and Van Doesburg.

Scholten bears a strong relationship to the de Stijl movement of the 1920s, for in addition to his color usage, he works with the same clarity, and with the emphasized horizontals and verticals. The containment within an unframed rectangle is the same; so is the emptiness of his white spaces. In fact, few weavers since Gunta Stölzl-Stadler and Anni Albers seem plastically so connected with a major art movement.

Scholten agrees that this is so: he was from 1952 to 1958 associated with de Stijl publicist Michel Seuphor. His house-studio is by de Stijl architect Gerrit Rietveld; he lives with one painting—a Mondrian. The deliberate austerity of the environment is de Stijl. But here the afterglow fades. Herman Scholten lives now, two generations later, and he is a craftsman, too organic for the de Stijl movement and without its intellectual predilections.

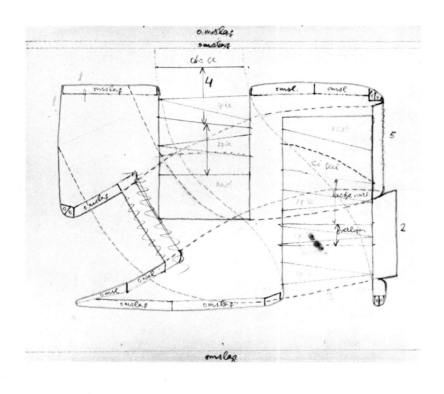

YELLOW BRAID   1969
82″ x 101½″
tapestry
wool, hemp, sisal, plastic; yellows
Collection: Dreyfus Fund Collection, New York
Shown at the Biennale, Lausanne, 1969

Maintaining the rectangular form, this deceptively simple major work is a culmination of Scholten's method of shaping and interlacing. His plan for joining the bands reveals the complex structure.

Within the discipline of the frame, the free and open composition of undulating planes moving freely creates varied and beautiful voids. Here texture goes beyond structural emphasis to an exuberance that ornaments the entire surface. Skillful modulation of a single color allows extravagance of texture pattern without reducing the cohesion of the design.

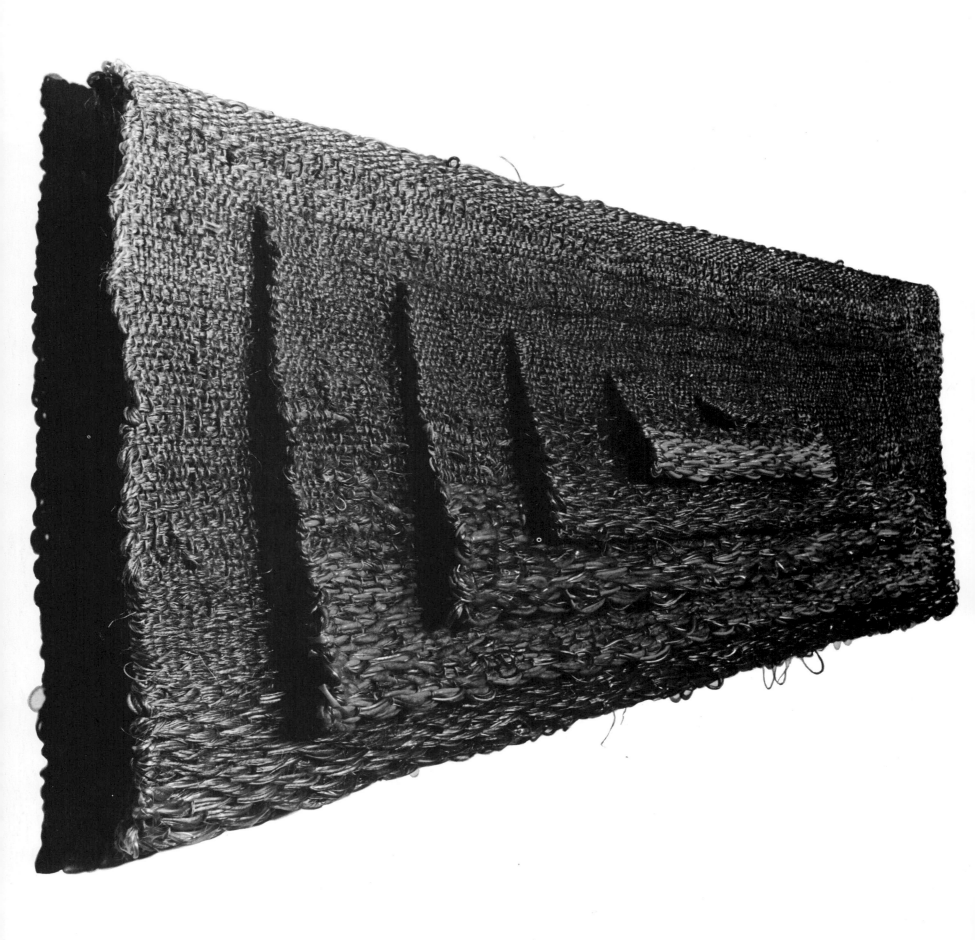

week kalender

SIX YELLOW LAYERS   1970
86" x 2¼"
tapestry
wool, manila, hemp, and plastic; yellow and ochre
Collection: H. Vos-Strümphler, Loenersloot,
the Netherlands

Scholten explores and itemizes the possibilities
within a technique as can be seen in the sketch
(above). Then he selects the one that he most
wants to weave.

Each layer is woven separately, and joined to the
others, by darning the warp ends into the layer
behind. In each of the layers, he gains weight
and emphasis by using a coarser construction
consistent with the graduating scale of material
and color.

The preliminary drawing at right illustrates the
construction used in Up and Down (p. 247) in
which scaffold wefts become the warp of the horizontal bands. As shown in the drawing, this piece
was constructed of three woven parts, with the
horizontal bands sewn to the verticals.

sekimachi

KAY SEKIMACHI
American, born 1926

Studied painting and design at California College of Arts and Crafts, and later, at the same school, weaving under Trude Guermonprez; at Haystack Mountain School, under Jack Lenor Larsen. Teaches in Berkeley and San Francisco. Exhibited in "Fabrics International," 1960; "Modern American Wall Hangings," Victoria and Albert Museum, London; "Threads of History," American Federation of Arts Traveling Exhibit; The Museum of Modern Art, New York, 1969; "Deliberate Entanglements," UCLA, 1971. Represented in Thiel Collection, Oakland Art Museum; St. Paul Art Center Collection of American Crafts, St. Paul, Minnesota; John Magnani Memorial Collection, San Francisco State College; Permanent Collection, Illinois State University, Normal, Illinois; The Johnson Collection; Dreyfus Fund Collection, New York.

Kay Sekimachi is very much the product of California's Nisei subculture and the intellectual-creative climate of the Bay Area. Like Rossbach, Guermonprez, and Asawa, she has developed her own style, without precedent and without successors. Her persistent researches in a single technique and her faithfulness to one wiry material bring her closest to San Francisco pioneer Ruth Asawa (see p. 30). With her, too, she shares the use of an organic symmetry and soil-resisting monofilament.

In the early 1960s, about simultaneously with Dominic Di Mare (p. 49), she developed a technique for weaving multiple layers, which off the loom would become fully dimensional. Unlike his shaggy, often feathered, zoomorphic fetishes, hers are purely conceived in an immaculate material. Her spatial structures are all layered meshes of woven monofilament, convoluting to form an arresting cumulative image. The fiberless, smooth yarn surface is consistent with the precision of the woven mesh and with the spirited regular spring of the vaults. Her material and technique allow lightweight, easily hung volumetric forms that, because of their airy transparency, ingratiate the space around them. Her material is sufficiently durable, fadeproof, and dustfree as to seem permanent.

In her Berkeley, California, studio, Kay Sekimachi ties transparent monofilament to the warp stick of her eight-harness loom.

SHIRATAKE III 1965
50" x 12" x 15"
multiple-layered cloth
nylon monofilament; clear
Collection: Elena Anger, Stockholm

This relatively small, simple piece most clearly reveals the Sekimachi technique. On the loom, the four layers are woven taut and flat. At the top, just below the wispy warp ends, all of the warp is engaged in single plain weave; from a woven-in Lucite reinforcing rod, the cloth first divides into two layers, then four. Then, on an alternating plane, the four warps pass through each other so that the front-most is eventually in the back. At this point, the four cloths reduce to two, which terminate in a bead-studded mane of warp ends.

The wavelike dimensions derive from foreshortening caused by the monofilament guy wire at each side.

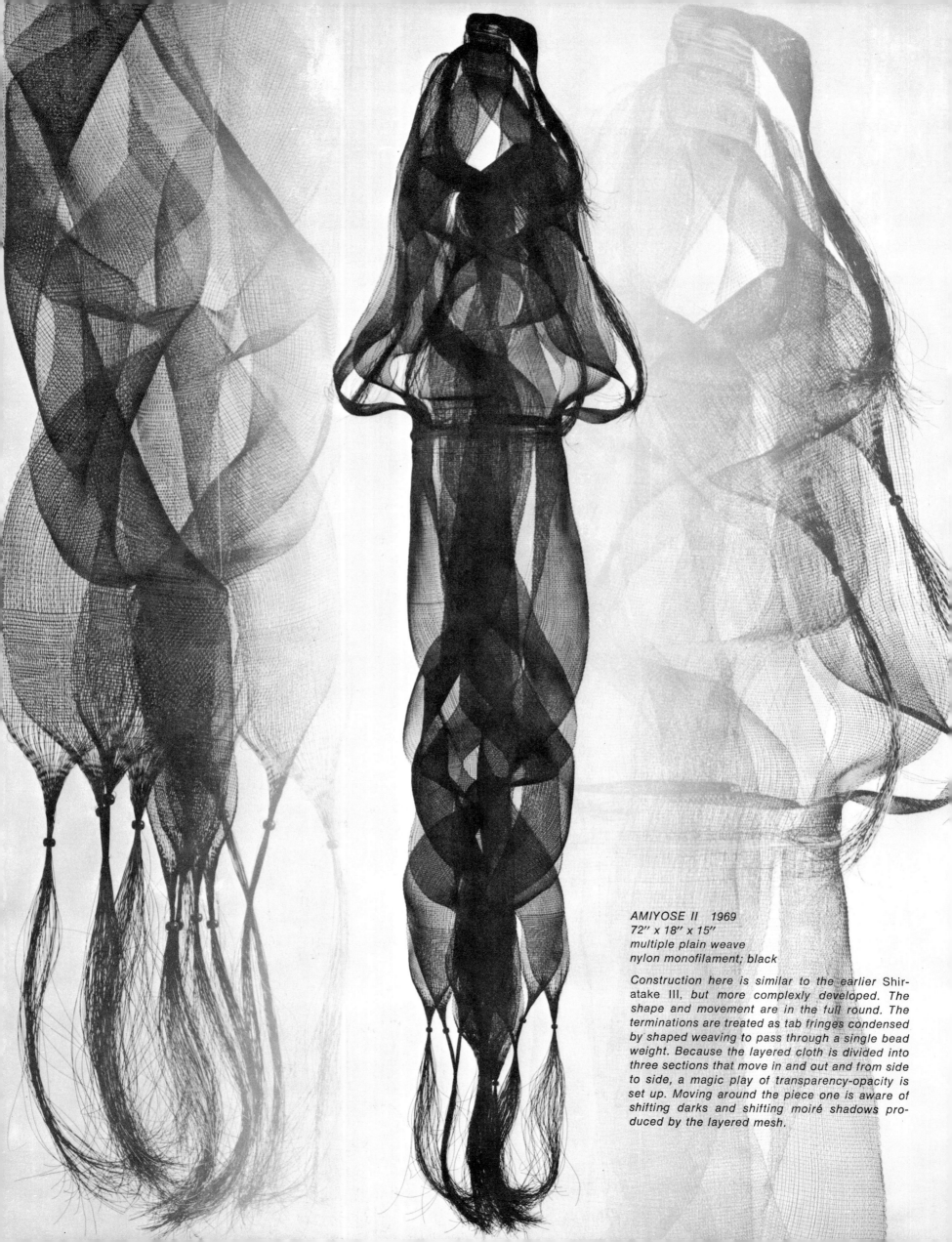

AMIYOSE II   1969
72" x 18" x 15"
multiple plain weave
nylon monofilament; black

Construction here is similar to the earlier Shiratake III, but more complexly developed. The
shape and movement are in the full round. The
terminations are treated as tab fringes condensed
by shaped weaving to pass through a single bead
weight. Because the layered cloth is divided into
three sections that move in and out and from side
to side, a magic play of transparency-opacity is
set up. Moving around the piece one is aware of
shifting darks and shifting moiré shadows produced by the layered mesh.

smith

SHERRI SMITH
American, born 1943

Studied at Stanford University, Palo Alto, California; Cranbrook Academy of Art, Bloomfield Hills, Michigan. Was a textile designer with Boris Kroll Fabrics, New York, and Dorothy Liebes, New York. Awarded Young Americans Fellowship Grant, American Crafts Council, 1970. Teaches in Colorado Springs. Exhibited at The Museum of Modern Art, New York, 1969; "Young Americans," Museum of Contemporary Crafts, New York, 1969; Katonah Gallery, 1970; one-man show at Colorado Springs Fine Arts Center, 1970; Biennale, Lausanne, 1971.

In her poetic explorations of conventional weaves with ordinary yarns, Sherri Smith is representative of the talent incubating in the new weavers who are experimenting in loom-controlled techniques. For several years she has probed the potentials of waffle weave, searching for the outer limits of the construction once it is freed from workaday considerations of economy and performance. She wove first with heavy yarns openly spaced to achieve scale and depth. More recently she has sought effects that are fully three-dimensional and often environmental.

Her use of waffle weave permits her to weave flatly but with a third-dimensional form inherent in the structure. When the pieces are removed from the loom, warp tension relaxes, and gravity pulls so that a lush mass of yarns unfolds like a blossom or parachute. This is particularly true of *Caryatids* (p. 263) and *Stalactites* (p. 262) in which the cloth is stretched horizontally so that, like distended bellows, the cellular structural frames fall earthward. When several layers are stitched together, like the six-decker sandwich of *Stalactites,* the depth is cumulative and great height is possible.

True to her constructions, Sherri Smith is preoccupied with aesthetic and fantasy potentials. Hers are the midsummer-night's webs that dreams are made of. They are fairy stuff, diaphanous, inherently elegant, and as ephemeral as milkweed. While it is true that these pieces can be collapsed and transported, they are, by their nature, fragile. She admits, "I would like all my work to be durable, able to be felt and handled and soil resisting. I don't always succeed in these goals . . . if there appears an option for astonishing beauty I seem willing to sacrifice any or all of them."

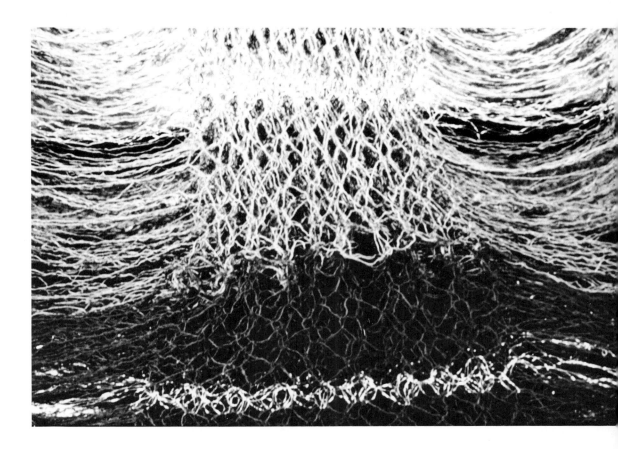

STALACTITES 1972
108" x 8' x 8'
waffle weave, layered
mohair, piece-dyed; gray, red, orange

Many square pieces are woven on a sixteen-harness loom, then piece-dyed in six shades. These varicolored layers are then joined by sewing the top of one layer to the bottom of the next. When the layered construction is hung from the ceiling, the bottoms of each cellular unit "fall out" to cause the enormous elongation. Because the piece is shown here in profile, rather than frontally, what was the thin selvage becomes the major surface, and the waffle-weave pattern is only visible from top and bottom. Gravity has attenuated the columns so their profiles have become concave; the spaces between become vaulted caverns.

CARYATIDS (detail) 1971
8' x 8' x 4' (detail about 24" x 30")
waffle weave, layered
mohair and metallic gimp, piece-dyed; browns

The construction here is like that of Stalactites— six layers stiched together, then dropped from a horizontal plane. The detail shows part of four layers that shade from the top, white, gray, brown, and beige. The long floats of yarn are the warp, left unwoven between the woven sections.

WHITE LACE (detail) 1971
5' x 3'
waffle weave
wool and mohair; natural color

For a series of long, narrow woven panels, Sherri Smith has broken the essential premise of waffle weaves: the balanced symmetry of using the same yarn and spacing for warp and weft. Here the fine warp is too openly spaced to hold firmly the softer, heavier weft. As a result, the weft yarns are pushed first up, then down, to form shell-like cups of luminous fiber.

The decorative selvage that is so consistent with the whole is an inevitable outgrowth of turning the weft on the same diagonal progression, which in waffle weave mirrors itself to form a diamond pattern.

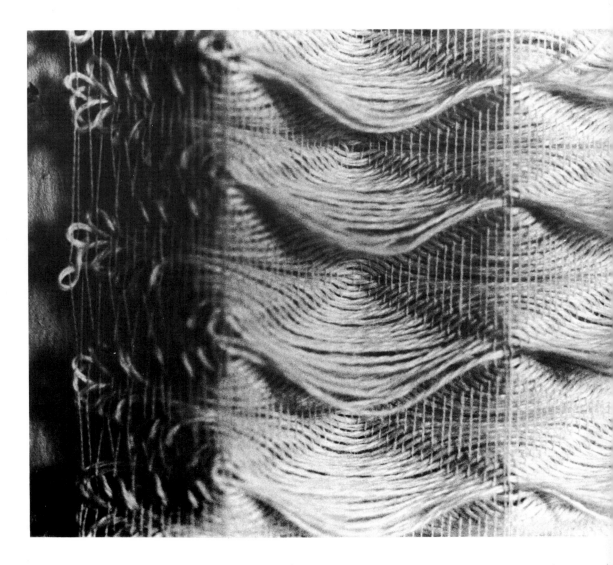

CHEVRON   1971
5'4" x 3'
waffle weave
worsted and mohair; natural color
Collection: John Andrikopoulos

In a high relief, the long floats of warp and weft
are so precisely built up as to bring about the
sharply chiseled planes. The precision that produces the contrasts of highlight and shadow belies
the lightweight softness of the material. A complex weave plan on a twenty-four-harness loom
permits the extended pattern repeat.

LENORE TAWNEY
American, born 1925

Studied at University of Illinois, Champaign-Urbana; Institute of Design, Chicago (weaving with Marli Ehrman); sculpture with Archipenko; tapestry with Marta Taipale, Finland. Exhibited in "Good Design," The Museum of Modern Art, New York, 1955; at Art Institute of Chicago, 1956; World's Fair, Brussels, 1958; Staten Island Museum, New York, 1962; Columbia University, New York, 1963; "Woven Forms," Museum of Contemporary Crafts, New York, 1963; Kunstgewerbemuseum, Zurich, 1964; The Museum of Modern Art, New York, 1969. Represented in collections of Museum Bellerive, Zurich; Museum of Contemporary Crafts, New York; The Museum of Modern Art, New York; Chicago Public Library; Cooper-Hewitt Museum, New York; Riverside Church, New York; and private collections.

tawney

SHADOW RIVER   1957
3'6" x 3' turned 90°
plain weave with discontinuous wefting;
laminated between plastic and glass panels
linen, silk, wool, nylon; natural and dark neutrals
Collection: The artist

*This piece is prophetic of Tawney's work after
1960 in that it is an abstraction, is neutral in color,
and indicates her later interest in stability and
permanence. In this experiment, she is concerned
with protecting a frail web—and if protected, its
fragility could be carried to even further extremes,
as in the unengaged warp here. Both weft and
warp are eccentric. The fusing was accomplished
by enclosing the piece in thin plastic film that
would melt sufficiently to become the bonding
agent, then sandwiching it between glass panels
and kiln-firing at 275°F.*

Of all the artists who have been the inspiration for the next generation of weavers, Lenore Tawney is the presence around whom they have rallied. Since the fifties her deep involvement has brought responsive accolades from critics and fellow artists. Physically ethereal and diminutive, she is strong aesthetically and emotionally. Her importance in the development of the Art Fabric is discussed in the Introduction.

When in 1953 she left her native Midwest, she moved from a Chicago townhouse to an expansive sail loft on New York's South Street waterfront, surrounded by painters Jack Youngerman, Robert Indiana, Agnes Martin. Her work unfolded quickly and surely, as did her technique and personal expressiveness. First the tapestries opened up. Pattern areas became more sheer. Warps were no longer a single linen yarn to be covered but mixed combinations of soft, colored wools. The warps were more and more exposed, so that the silhouette of yarn suspended became in itself a strong compositional element. Transparency counted; so did an enormous palette of yarn types and colors.

Content was important, even though rendered with increasing abstraction (p. 46). In 1957, a commission for a tapestry was offered by the Interchurch Center of Riverside Church, New York. Tawney refused the pressure of a commission, but said she would weave a piece that might be suitable. If they liked it when finished, they would have the option to purchase. They did. *Nativity* was completed in 1958. Achieving it gave her the confidence to attempt other large works, including *Triune,* 1961' (p. 270).

She had by this time mastered and personalized the tapestry technique, freely floating bundles of close-hued yarns over the surface in order to build masses with the soft singing iridescence of bird wings.

At this time, she was subconsciously aware of the strong, hard forms around her —the winches and paraphernalia of a sail loft, the great iron spikes, the precision of old brass stencils (which she gave to Bob Indiana), the stark reality of river patterns and her own newly structured metaphysical reality. Then too there was her growing collection of works of art by her friends—hard-edge, strong works by Youngerman, Voulkos, Egret, and the abstractions of Agnes Martin. She worked precisely with a ruling pen on a series of small drawings, or diagramatic illuminations that seemed to have no relation to her weaving, but perhaps to her spiritual core. Preparation for her one-man show at the Staten Island Museum in 1962 strengthened her productivity, but rather than building complacency it left her restless and searching. Success and acclaim did not appease her inner drive; it fanned it. A change was brewing. And then she bolted, veering sharply away from the past, foregoing all the heady color and sensuous materials and sensitive drawing she had lived with for ten years.

She considered working off the loom and in three dimension, but so much freedom seemed foreign to her reticent nature. She dipped into the possibilities of double cloth but abandoned them. Instead she made the decision to strip herself bare of infatuations with color, yarn surfaces, and subject matter. She cleared her studio of all the hoarded yarns that had filled baskets, racks, and bowls. To her order, five strands of linen were specially cable-plied and polished satin-smooth into a yarn that was round in section. This yarn was sufficiently dense and hard that it would not change shape when tightly packed into the weft, and was smooth enough to allow the warp to be closely crammed together in the reed to produce a sub-

BIRD-NEST-EGG   1960
36" x 45"
tapestry in two layers
linen, silk, wool, feathers; naturals and pastels
Collection: Win Anderson, New York

At the end of her shore-bird series Tawney wove this tapestry of two transparent layers. With a two-inch space between the layers and an even wider space between them and the wall, the piece was designed to include in the image its own shadow. The detail explains the manner of her unjoined discontinuous wefting, the eccentricity of her weaving, and the insertion of feathers to reinforce both image and the nuance of color and materials.

From the middle 1950s a tender, tenuous quality appeared in Tawney's work, particularly in a long series of shore birds. Like the paintings and wash drawings of Morris Graves, these pieces were bathed with an almost mystical luminosity. She was handling subject matter with the same delicacy and tenderness with which she selected and placed her fragile wefts. Other elements, usually bird feathers, were woven into those webs. In the detail (below) the fierce grasping talons of a predator are expressed in the painted tips of large goose quills.

The two details (right) illustrate an unprecedented degree of contrast between a transparent web of wiry linen and densely woven areas of luminous silk. Where called for by the subject or by the yarn character, the wefts are floated over the web so as to develop a densely textured color fusion. To suit these expressions her once flower-bright palette has softened and lightened.

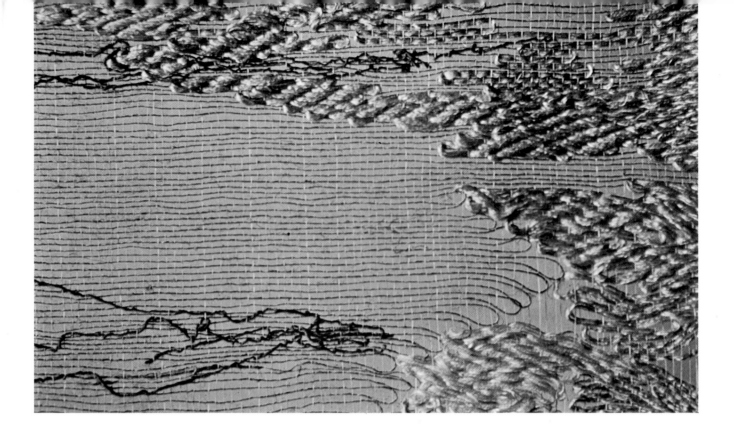

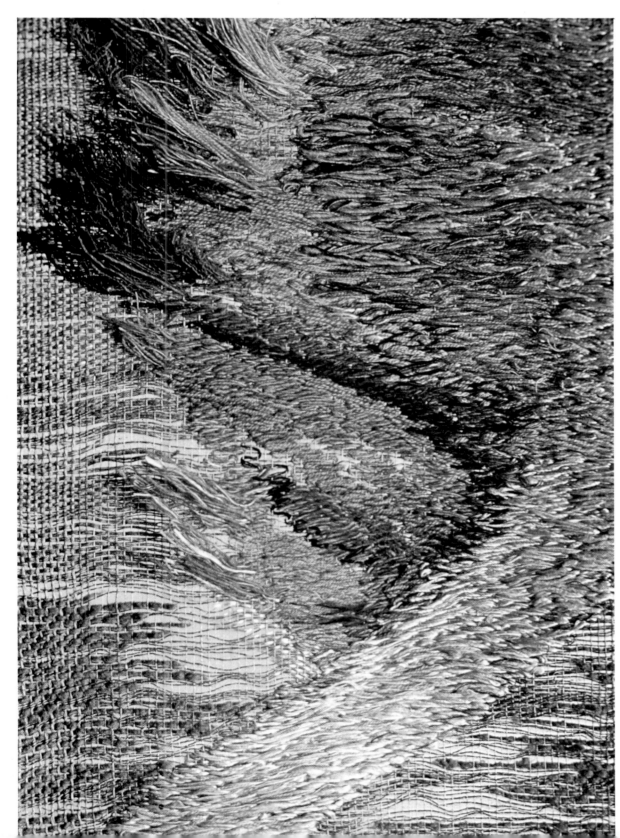

TRIUNE   1961
9′ x 9′
tapestry with discontinuous brocade
linen, wool and silk; blue, purple, white
Collection: The artist

Of the monumental tapestries, Triune was the last
and most successful in its handling of a simple,
strong form. The symbolism is abstract and pow-
erful. The free-flowing gradations of full-blooded
blues and purples contrast sharply and surely
with the white silk "cross." The heavily built up
areas have heft and weight consistent with the
large square format. By American standards, especially at the time, the scale was enormous. Because Tawney's standard flat warp handloom was
only relatively wide, two panels 54″ wide by 108″
long needed to be joined to achieve the 9′ x 9′
dimension. Tawney's own method of blending
colors through hatching long weft floats is readily
visible in the detail (right).

stantial, horizontally ribbed surface. This structural texture together with the weight of the woven cloth gave convincing substance to the emerging work. The yarn was also thick enough to permit the weaving to progress quickly.

She ordered the linen in natural and black and a few primary colors. Because she progressed fastest and surest in natural or black, or natural *and* black, the colors were only later and occasionally used.

At this time, Tawney embarked on another series of innovations in technique. She pursued a study of Peruvian gauze weave and invented a new reed. She studied Jacquard weaving but came away more fascinated with the beauty of the Jacquard loom than its pattern-making abilities. Most important was her development of new techniques for shaped weaving, which made possible a whole range of personal expressions new to her and to fabric. Although the first attempts were clumsy, they possessed a crude strength and fresh concept. First she halved her warp, shaping each part simultaneously but separately. Then she separated her warp into more parts, combining this technique with shaped weaving and using rigid dowels or rods to maintain the width. She had then invented a technique and a style to express organic upward growth. Craftsmanship and technique were so resolved that she could, at will, orchestrate form to express her spiritual growth and aspiration. In all, it was a synthesis of hand, mind, and spirit and it worked—wonderfully.

She worked obsessively. Her narrow pieces grew taller, to twelve, fourteen, eighteen, and even twenty-seven feet high. Sometimes, so as to maintain dimension, their form required strategically placed stays that were woven into the web (p. 272). Always the raw warp ends required a fitting termination. From her study of pre-Columbian art Tawney felt that finish might be the most detailed, most labored part. One typical result was knotted top knots (pp. 273, 278). At other times she attempted embellishments such as soft rolled gold (p. 274). And frequently she used feathers (p. 268).

Her neighbor, painter Agnes Martin, named the series *The King, The Queen, The Bride, The River, The Fountain, The Veil, The Arc,* and so on. These identifications were important to Lenore Tawney. So were the pieces: when not on exhibition they were kept hanging in her studio. There followed a series in finer linen yarns. The color was still natural but a honeyed tan rather than pewter white. Because the profile of the finer single ply yarn was somewhat irregular, smaller pieces resulted, less dense and more delicate. Rather than grill-like filigrees they became veils, often triangular in form, such as *The Egyptian* (p. 277). At about the same time she developed in the heavy cabled linen a series of small convex "shields" lavishly embellished with goose quills.

Tawney was traveling, and searching, in remote parts of the west, to South America, India, and Japan. When uprooted, her expression was reduced to miniscule collages: symbolic, personal, and full of her discovery of pebbles or feathers as small as a match head. Rare papers and antique scripts without meaning but meaningful fascinated her. These techniques were later extended to the larger collages and boxes which she exhibited at the Benson and Willard Galleries in Bridgehampton and New York.

She has woven precious miniatures such as that on p. 279; she is experimenting with environmental works: cubicles, sculptural facades, conceptual systems. These have not yet been executed. This is not a default but an incubation. Tawney is patient; to her, creativity and quiescence are aspects of the same phenomenon.

THE RIVER   1961
13' x 22½''
double wefted, slit tapestry
linen; black
Collection: The Museum of Modern Art, New York
Shown at the Triennale, Milan, 1964

Although relatively early, The River *is the undisputed masterpiece of Tawney's major black-and-white period. Both proportion and the relation of weight and material to technique and color are immaculate. Basically* The River *and the works that followed it grew out of the combination of three techniques. This combination is one of her own invention. The first technique is slit tapestry, which (although ancient and although frequently used by such practitioners as Schiele and Amaral) was undeveloped when Tawney adapted it. Second was her device of double wefting or inserting a weft from each selvage. This process, especially in her heavy, smoothly polished cabled linen, ensured the flawless selvage so necessary to her new medium (detail). The double weft also exaggerated the horizontal rib. Third was Tawney's invention of a new reed or comb that allowed her to execute a perfectly controlled shaped weaving by spreading her warp or constructing it into a narrower width. In* The River, *she does both. She also splits the width into nine, then ten, twenty, and forty sections. Finally, at the top, each warp end counts as a section. The stays stabilize the various widths. The final wefts are a floss of several yarns twisted and twined in pairs. The detail of the top illustrates Tawney's mature resolution of warp finish (compare this with* Thaw, p. 46). *Above the wooden collar, the warp ends are neatly braided and tied.*

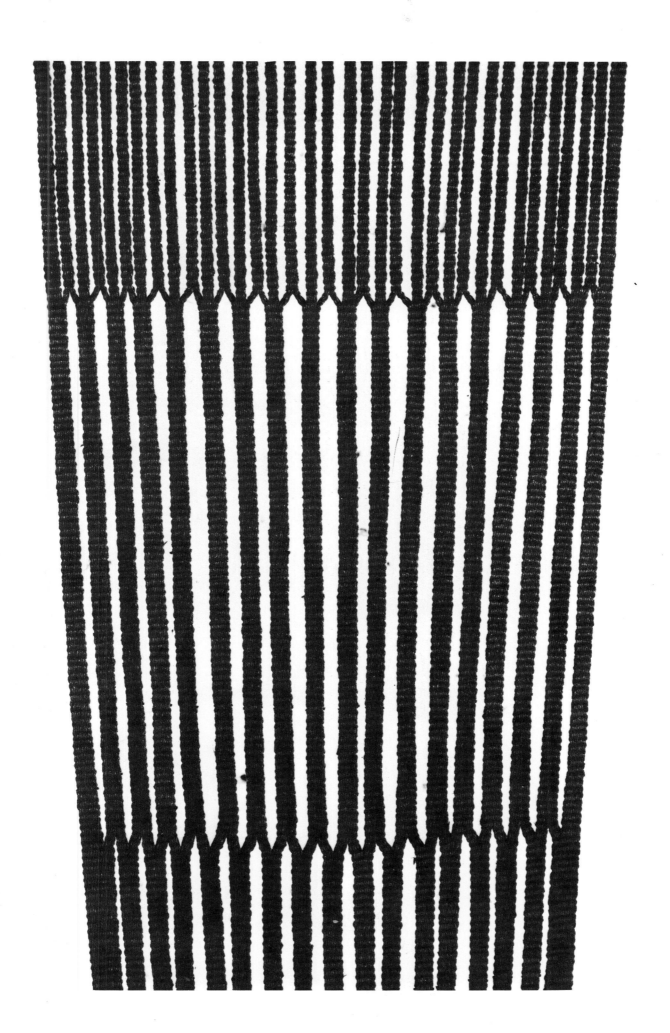

274

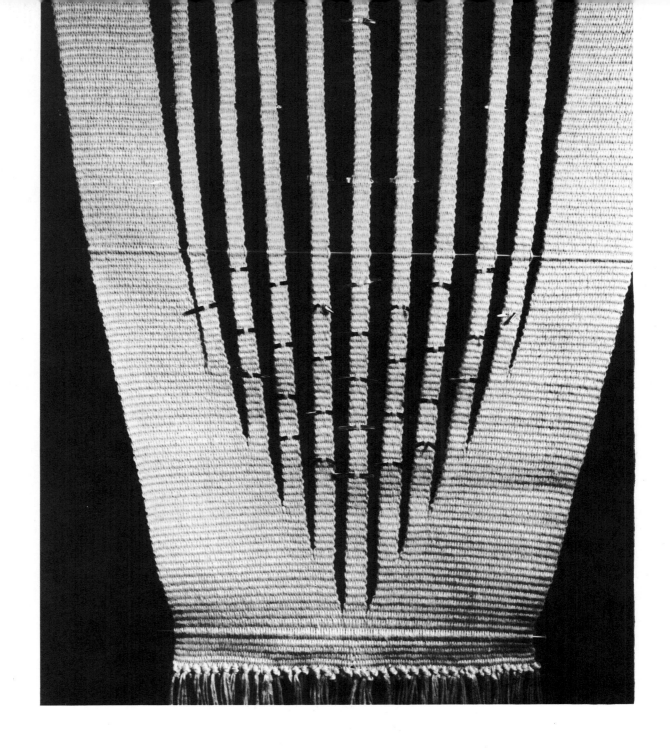

THE PATH   1962
11' x 4'
plain weave, double-wefted and shaped
cable-ply linen; natural color
Collection: The artist

This work is typical of several pieces in which
Tawney achieves cruciform shapes by weaving in
two widths, then cutting the warp ends of the
narrower sections. The full-width arms are supported top and bottom by rods woven through a
plain-weave shed. The center slit is laced with
strips of twenty-four-karat gold. The warp ends
are knotted or braided.

THE FLAME (detail)   1962
9' x 18''
slit tapestry, double-wefted and shaped
polished cable-ply linen, polished steel;
natural and gray
Collection: Museum Bellerive, Zurich

A refinement of those techniques used for The
River (p. 272) are at work in this piece—the warp
bands branch in succession so as to form a doubly
concave interior form. In an alternating pattern
the bands are ornamented with small strips of
polished steel. Note the two horizontal stays of
fine metal rod.

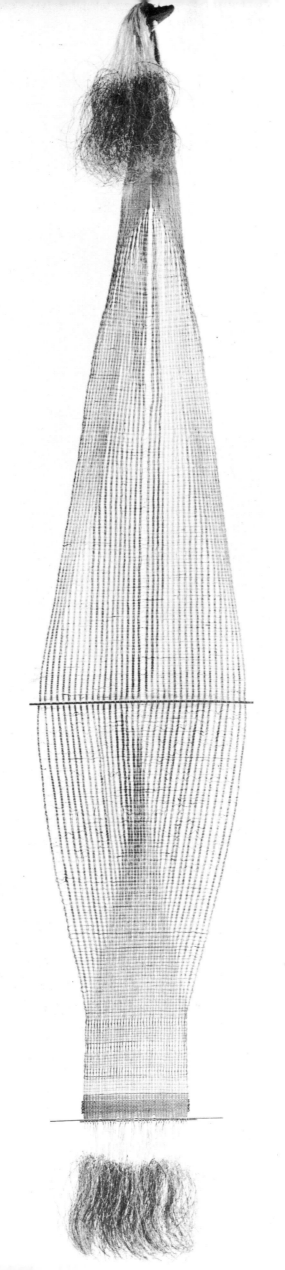

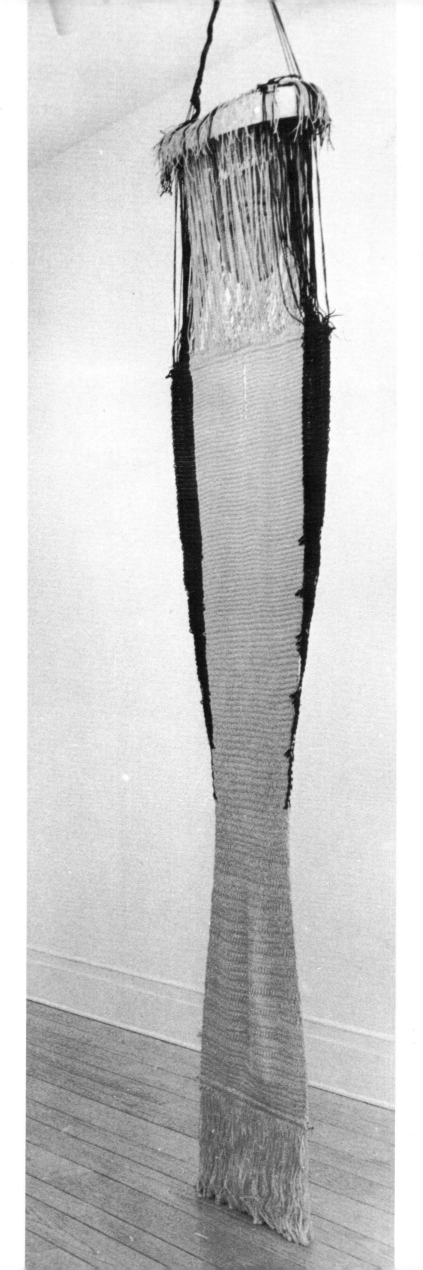

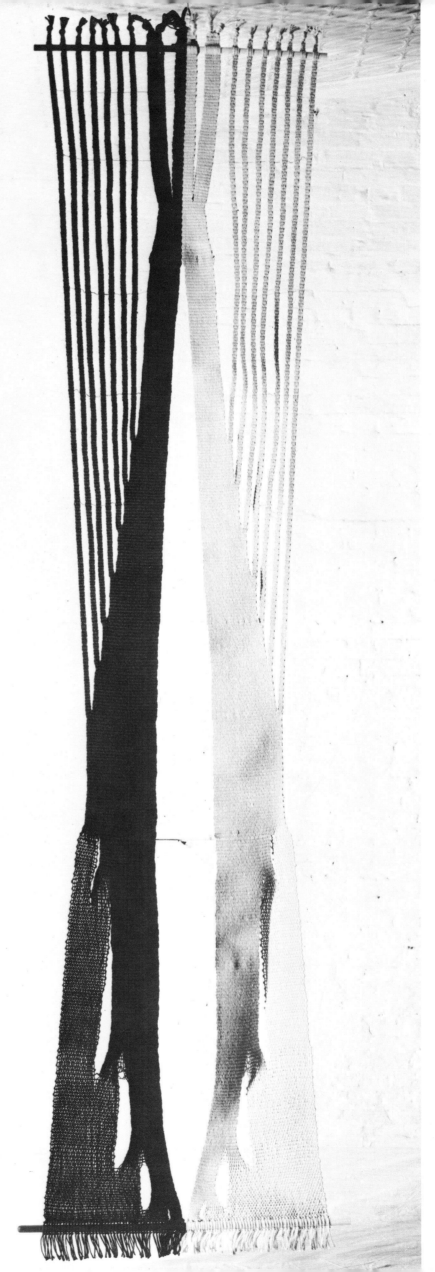

THE EGYPTIAN   1964
9' x 16"
plain weave and gauze weave
wet-spun linen; natural gray
Collection: Mrs. John Hauberg, Seattle

Although this piece is similar in technique to The
Flame, *by working with a very fine wet-spun linen
Tawney has achieved a quite different expression.
Perhaps that expression is best described by her
names for similar pieces in the same yarn:*
Whisper, The Veil, *or* The Fountain.

Unlike The Flame, *here warp sections branch from
a central band of dense plain weave so as to form
in positive an elongated triangle. The succession
of regrouping at the top is more like* The Flame.
*In order to secure the fine yarns Tawney has em-
ployed the twisted warp technique of Peruvian
gauze weave. The bronze bar at center is slightly
curved. The bottom rod is straight; below it and
at the top the warp ends are finished by tying
on additional lengths of a darker linen.*

*In the detail (overleaf) one can trace the final
progressions of the shaped weaving. The wooden
collar is ancient Egyptian.*

PHAROAH   1965–67
12' x 20"
tapestry, double-wefted and shaped
cable-plied polished linen; natural gray and black
Collection: The artist

*Here Tawney is using her shaped technique to
achieve a representational form—a sarcophagus.
The top center has a tiny split; the black sections
are formed by black warp and weft.*

*The Egyptian funeral mask is of the Ptolemaic
period. Above it is a carved wood form covered
in gesso.*

THE KING I   1962
12' x 30"
plain weave, double-wefted and shaped
cable-plied polished linen; natural gray and black.
Collection: The artist

*Here the warp is divided into equal black and
natural sections. Contrasts in the weight of the
bands add a further element of symbolism and
power. The top is finished with tab fringes. The
lower outside edges are made translucent by the
omission of double wefting.*

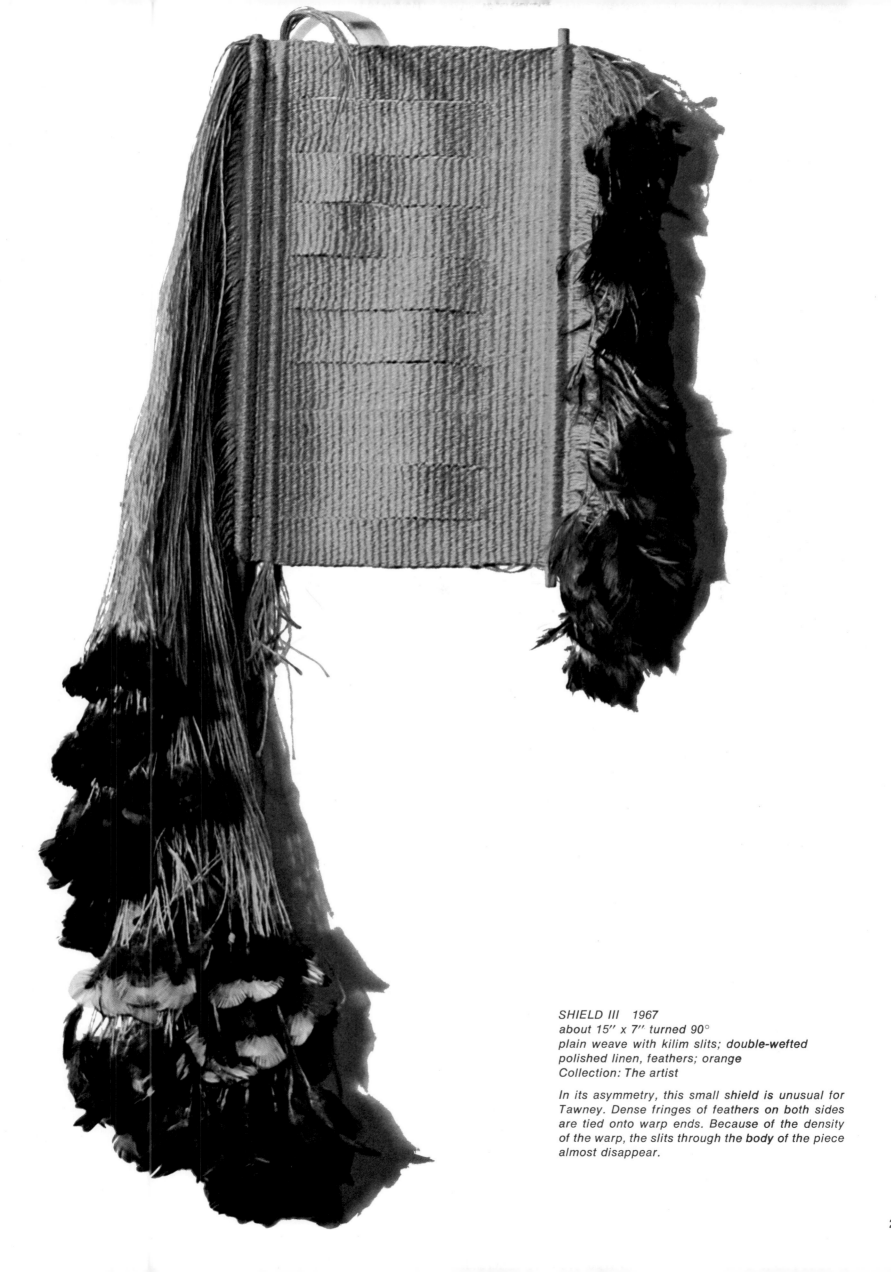

SHIELD III 1967
about 15" x 7" turned 90°
plain weave with kilim slits; double-wefted
polished linen, feathers; orange
Collection: The artist

In its asymmetry, this small shield is unusual for
Tawney. Dense fringes of feathers on both sides
are tied onto warp ends. Because of the density
of the warp, the slits through the body of the piece
almost disappear.

weitzman

SUSAN WEITZMAN
American, born 1933

Studied at Smith College, Northampton, Massachusetts; studied painting at Art Students League, New York; weaving at Fashion Institute of Technology, New York; tapestry techniques with Alice Adams. Exhibited at Manhattanville College, Purchase, New York, 1965; Greenhouse Gallery, Little Rock, Arkansas, 1966; Museum of Contemporary Crafts, New York, 1966; The Museum of Modern Art, New York, 1969; Biennale, Lausanne, 1969; one-man show at Jack Lenor Larsen Showroom, New York, 1970. Represented in collections of The Museum of Modern Art, New York; The Johnson Collection; Dreyfus Fund Collection, New York; J. Walter Thompson Co., New York.

Although she is neither prolific nor steady in output, Susan Weitzman has developed a unique style along two simultaneous paths. In her earliest work she was both figurative and representational and worked in a large format. But the confines of her studio led her into making miniatures and into simplification of composition. In a series of small works she exploits yarn differential qualities and color contrast to achieve small gems of strong impact (p. 282).

In *The Kiss* (p. 283), produced only a short time later, Weitzman invented a means of creating an image by controlled twisting of vertical elements. This seems to have led her to the next step.

When Weitzman had been spinning for some time, her innovation in the use of spinning with a differential of twist was a spontaneous moment of discovery. She saw in the extremes of the twist differential the image-making possibilities of her yarn. As she controlled the thin and thick areas of each strand of yarn, she used the natural variety of color of the ungraded fleece for its particular place in the whole. Her first experiment with this discovery (p. 284) was originally destined to have a pattern-spun weft as well. But when she saw the completeness of the unfettered warp, she abandoned the convention of a weft.

Although the artist says that the circle is not a consciously chosen symbol, it has been an insistent image in her work of the last decade. She has subordinated all design elements to this strong statement. Perhaps both the pure circle and softly glowing color of her recent work are unconscious reactions and responses to eastern religions with which she is involved.

The early influence of Lenore Tawney briefly manifested itself in the use of feathers and fetishes. This direct influence did not last very long. But Tawney's guidance and support have remained a deep spiritual force, best exemplified, perhaps, in *Homage to Lenore Tawney* (p. 285).

Susan Weitzman, in front of the incomplete Homage to Lenore Tawney, *carding the ungraded fleece.*

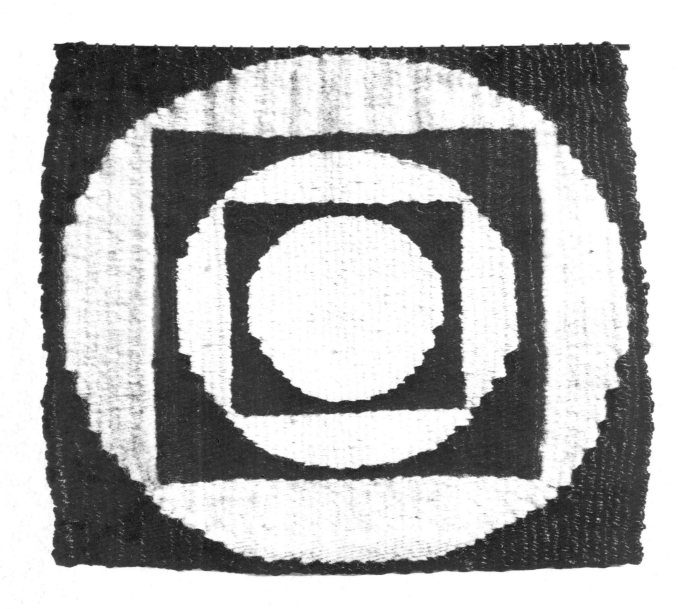

SQUARE TAPESTRY #1   1966
about 6" square
linen, silk, rayon, wool; black and white
Collection: The artist

The structure of densely interlaced tapestry is here emphasized by exploiting the character of four different yarns in two colors. Yarn texture and construction pattern are seemingly magnified because of the small scale of the piece, shown here actual size.

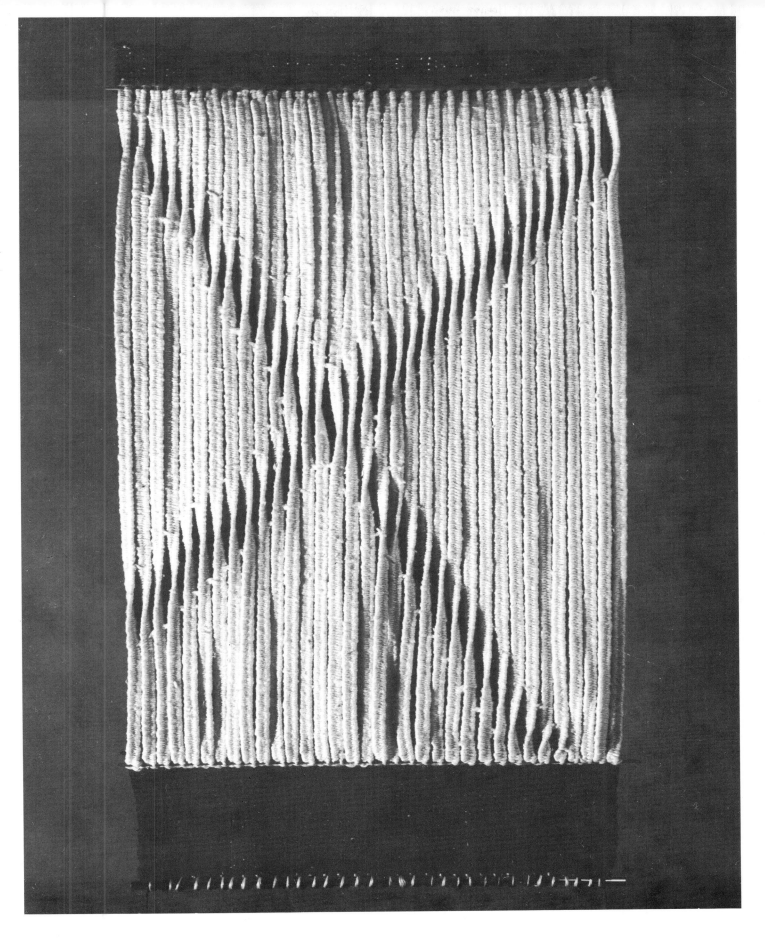

KISS   1967–68
20'' x 11½'' x 1¼''
double woven with slit tapestry
linen; black and white

A black linen base cloth supports the white composition, framing it top and bottom and accentu-
ating the silhouette of the diagonal image. The
extremely long tapestry slits are broken only when
joined by a diagonal progression of single weft
shots. These joins control the position of the twist.
Surface character and the impact of the image
are heightened by the solidity of the projecting
woven bands. Their rigidity dramatizes the illu-
sive X.

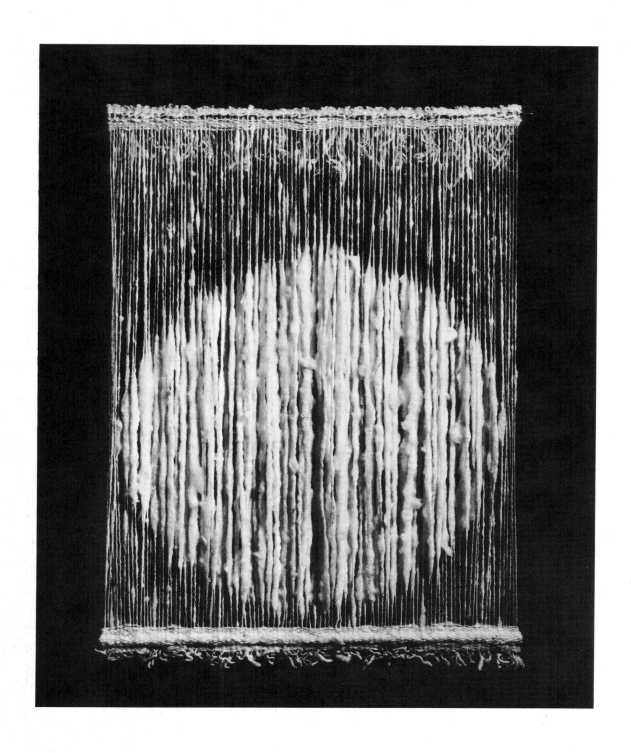

TAPESTRY FOR FRANCES LYNN   1967
32⅜″ x 22⅜″
hand-spun wool; natural
Collection: The Museum of Modern Art, New York
Shown in "Wall Hangings,"
The Museum of Modern Art, New York, 1969

This first of the artist's work with hand-spun unfettered warp is accomplished with the most extreme differential of twist. The high contrast between the densely opaque image and the wispy
ground makes for a compelling composition. The
natural color of the fleece lends warmth to the
pale lunar light creating the circle. The warp ends
of this piece terminate in a woven band at top and
bottom, a device which she abandoned in her
later work, Homage to Lenore Tawney.

HOMAGE TO LENORE TAWNEY   1968
7′ square
hand-spun wool; natural
Collection: The artist
Shown in "Wall Hangings,"
The Museum of Modern Art, New York, 1969,
and at the Biennale, Lausanne, 1971

Two layers of exposed warp with differential of
twist combine to produce an almost hallucinatory
image. The areas of heavy yarn reverse in the two
layers. A luminous depth is added by the mysterious space between the layers, by the projected
shadow, and by the soft profile and changing
diameters in the unfettered warp. Although it is
much larger in scale than Tapestry for Frances
Lynn, there is less contrast in the differential of
twist. The one shaded color is used with a sure
hand, each strand chosen for its subtle shadings
and placed for its particular contribution to the
total composition.

HUM 1969
about 30'' square
hand-spun linen; natural
Collection: Dreyfus Fund Collection, New York

Like Homage to Lenore Tawney, *this is a two lay-*
ered piece in which the image is developed by a
differential of twist. It differs, however, in that its
horizontal and vertical layers shift on center from
over to under, producing a line of demarcation
between the horizontal and the vertical yarns. Each
strand of the wiry linen is separately wrapped and
tied over a Lucite frame.

zeisler

CLAIRE ZEISLER
American, born 1903

Studied at Columbia University, New York; Institute of Design, Chicago. Exhibited at Chicago Public Library, 1960; Renaissance Society, University of Chicago, 1961; Art Institute of Chicago, 1964; Richard Feigen Galleries, Chicago and New York, 1968; Stedelijk Museum, Amsterdam, 1969; Northern Illinois University, DeKalb, 1970; group shows: "Woven Forms," Museum of Contemporary Crafts, New York, 1962, "Collectors Show," 1965; "Sculptures in Fiber," 1971; Kunstgewerbemuseum, Zurich, 1963; Indianapolis Museum, Indiana, 1968; Kranert Museum, Urbana, Illinois, 1969; Ravinia Festival, Highland Park, Illinois, 1969; Ruth Kaufmann Gallery, New York, 1971; Biennale, Lausanne, 1971; Denver Art Museum, Colorado, 1971; "Deliberate Entanglements," UCLA, 1971. Represented in collections of the First National Bank, Chicago; First National Bank, Brussels; Dreyfus Fund Collection, New York; Wisconsin Art Center, Milwaukee; Art Institute of Chicago; University of Wisconsin, Madison; Stedelijk Museum, Amsterdam; Museum Bellerive, Zurich.

Claire Zeisler holding a pom-pom yarn ball, one of twenty-five that when placed together form a floor sculpture. The balls, ranging in size from 8″ to 30″ in diameter, are multicolored.

It is natural to consider Claire Zeisler as belonging to the flourishing "concept and process" school of art. Her work illustrates pure intention of purpose along with a maturity of style and technique. More than most weavers working in three dimensions, she is a sculptor with a developed sense of the full round. At best her work possesses weight and dignity and a commanding presence.

Her recent work is not woven; rather it employs macramé and wrapping to create regal sculptured forms with dramatic contrasts of hard, tightly controlled wrapping, and free-flowing unfettered ropes. The characteristic "fall" of heavy materials provides gravitational movement, slow and deliberate.

The earlier small works that were shown in "Woven Forms" and at the Kunstgewerbemuseum, Zurich, in 1963 were double weave, stuffed to form pillows. These were suspended in a filigree web like spiders' packets. They were executed on a conventional loom in soft, fine yarns. To the extent that they were highly personal statements, sometimes surréal and even macabre, these works broke with tradition.

In the early 1970s, as a change of pace from the monumental forms, Zeisler has returned to the diminutive fantasies; sometimes these are in the miniscule scale of jewelry, often they are "sketches" in a variety of single-element techniques.

In her home, she is surrounded by a collection of baskets and artifacts from primitive cultures. It would seem that their simplicity and directness of form reinforce these same qualities in her work. At the same time her pieces demonstrate the sophistication of her era and of her own vision.

Experiments in jute and wool on a wall of the Zeisler studio, about 1970.

These small sketches, tightly knotted and loosely fringed, are studies made prior to larger works. Mostly they pertain to resisting and complying with the pull of gravity. In its contrast of open vaults and dense spill of material, the four-layered piece at left is especially successful.

SYMBOLIC PONCHO   1971
35" x 29"
*unfinished jute wrapped with wool; natural, red,
and green*

HANGING UNITS   1971
5½' high
*unfinished jute wrapped with wool; red, blue,
and green*

Symbolic Poncho *is extraordinary for its convincing force with a minimum of means. The plied jute cords are simply knotted over a bar. At the "throat," the ascot tie amplifies the knot. So does the knotting of the brilliant sleeve caps. Here, the cords are spiral wrapped. Under the wrapping, a spring-steel wire spirals downward, arresting the fall. Important to the whole is the rapport of yarn and armature (which is also the base).*

Although relatively simplistic, Hanging Units *shares the directness and authority of Symbolic Poncho. A stouter spring wire is wrapped with three cords to effect a distended coil. Against a rich dark red, the blue and green of equal intensity vibrate with a jeweled brilliance.*

PREVIEW   1969
6½' x 5' x 4'
knotting and wrapping
jute; red

An imposing, dramatic structure, with a romantic-expressionist facade, the three-dimensional treatment of this work begins with a firmly knotted mesh centered within the symmetrical organic arch. The yarns from the ends of the knotting tightly and precisely wrap a core of yarns to form the arch that gives shape and support to the work. At the back of the piece two metal strips keep it flat against the wall.

Glossary of Terms Used

BOBBIN LACE — A lace based on plaiting in which, for individual control, each end is wound on a weighted bobbin; synonymous with pillow lace.

BROCADE — A woven cloth in which a supplementary element is introduced onto the two-element ground; brocades may be in the filling or the warp or may be discontinuous.

CABLE PLY YARN — A firm, round yarn usually of eight or more strands twisted together.

COUCHING — An embroidery technique in which one element is laid over the cloth, then stitched to it by another, usually finer, element.

DISCONTINUOUS BROCADE — A free weaving technique in which the brocade yarn does not run from selvage to selvage but is laid-in according to the requirements of a figure or motif.

DOUBLE CLOTH — A four-element weaving technique using two sets of warp and two sets of weft, producing two interwoven cloths, one over the other.

ECCENTRIC — Term applied to woven elements deviating from the horizontal-vertical definition of textiles.

ELEMENT — In the construction of fabric, a component or set of components: knitting is a typical single-element technique; most weaving is two-element; pile fabrics and brocade are three-element; double cloth is four-element, etc.

ENDS — See *Warp.*

FABRIC — A pliable plane of any material or technique. Most fabrics are constructed of fibrous yarns.

FILLING — In weaving, the crosswise element which interlaces at right angles with the warp; synonymous with weft and woof (archaic).

FILLING-FACED — Term applied to cloth in which the filling picks predominate over the warp ends; the filling may conceal the warp completely.

FLOSS — A yarn in which the several strands or plies are not twisted together but lie loose and parallel.

FREE WEAVING — Weaving in which pattern is not controlled by the loom but through manipulation by the weaver, usually with a discontinuous weft; examples are tapestry, soumak, and knotted pile.

GAUZE — A loosely woven cloth often stabilized by twisting the warp or wrapping with the weft.

GIMP — A yarn in which one strand is spirally wrapped around a core of yarn or yarns.

GOBELIN — From the famous French tapestry center of Gobelin: conventional tapestry joinings in which wefts of adjacent areas are looped around each other.

HARNESS — In the loom, a frame from which are suspended the heddles, through which the warp yarns are threaded.

HEDDLE — In the loom, one of a set of cords or wires, suspended from a harness, with heddle eyes through which warp ends are threaded.

HIGH WARP *(haute lisse)* — A tapestry loom in which the warp yarns are vertical so that the beat-up is downward.

INTERLACE — To engage the filling yarns with the warp ends to make a web or woven cloth.

KILIM — A flat, woven rug, cover, or hanging, originally oriental and often reversible. Often kilims employ a tapestry joining of unsewn slits, sometimes called kilim slits.

LAID-IN — See *Discontinuous Brocade.*

LENO — A technique for woven fabric in which pairs of warp ends are twisted between each insertion of weft.

LOW WARP *(basse lisse)* — A tapestry loom in which the warp yarns are horizontal so that the beat-up is forward, toward the weaver.

MULTIPLE HARNESS — A loom with six or more harnesses; a cloth woven on a loom with multiple harnesses, such as an eight-harness twill, satin, damask, or figured double cloth.

PLAITING — A fabric technique employing two elements which are interlaced over and under in the manner of braiding or plain weaving. Often both elements run on the diagonal.

PICK — A single shot of weft.

RYA — The Finnish designation for a woven rug with a long, hand-knotted pile.

SCAFFOLD WEFTING — An obscure, difficult technique used in few cultures other than pre-Columbian Peru. Literally, a supplementary weft is used as a frame or scaffold to wind a small warp on. When this warp is interlaced with weft, the scaffold is removed.

SELVAGE (literally, self-edge) — In a woven cloth, the warpwise edges at which the weft wraps around the outermost warps as it re-enters the web. The selvages prevent unraveling. A few hand-woven cloths, especially those woven on a frame or backstrap loom, have horizontal selvages as well, and so are four-selvaged.

SETT (also set) — Usually refers to the disposition of the warp ends in the dents of the reed, determining the density of the cloth. Cloth sett includes the closeness of the weft as well.

SHAPED WEAVING — Cloth in which the selvages are not parallel but angled or curved, usually achieved by relaxing warp tension and pulling in on the weft yarn.

SHED — The space between sets of warp ends made by the raising or lowering of harnesses, so that the filling can be passed through.

SINGLE-ELEMENT — Fabric constructions based on a single component or set of components; typical are knitting, crochet, knotting, and braiding.

SOUMAK — A technique of wrapping wefts around two or more warp ends to produce a surface similar to chain stitch.

TAPESTRY — Any of several free weaving techniques for joining (or separating) wefts that are horizontally adjacent. In slit tapestry the separation is made by consistently turning the wefts around adjacent warp ends so as to produce a vertical slit. A tapestry is a fabric woven with tapestry joinings.

TEXTILE — A fabric woven with two or more sets of elements.

TURNED 90° — Term applied to a finished piece hung with the warp not vertical as woven, but horizontal.

TWINING — A construction older than weaving which is based on twisting pairs of elements. Weft twining involves a warp plus pairs of wefts. Warp twining may have a weft or be single-element (sprang).

WARP — The lengthwise or vertical element in woven cloth which is threaded into the loom. The warp is composed of many yarns individually called "ends."

WARP-FACE — Cloth in which the warp or vertical element dominates over the weft.

WEB — The woven cloth on the loom resulting from the interlacing of warp and weft.

WEFT — Horizontal or crosswise element(s) in woven cloth; also called filling (see also *Pick*).

WRAPPING — Refers to spiral winding, in which one yarn element is wound around another element or core.

Bibliography of Works Consulted or Cited

Books

ALBERS, ANNI. *On Designing.* New Haven, Conn.: Pellango Press, 1959.
———. *On Weaving.* Middletown, Connecticut: Wesleyan University Press, 1965.
Art Nouveau. Edited by Mildred Constantine and Peter Selz. New York: The Museum of Modern Art, 1959.
Bauhaus 1919-1928. Edited by Herbert Bayer. New York: The Museum of Modern Art, 1938.
BELJON, J. J. *Waarjekijkt Erotiek.* Amsterdam, 1967.
BEUTLICH, TADEK. *The Technique of Woven Tapestry.* New York: Watson Guptill, 1971.
CASSOU, JEAN, EMIL LANGUI, AND NIKOLAUS PEVSNER. *Gateway to the 20th Century.* New York: McGraw-Hill, 1962.
EMERY, IRENE. *The Primary Structures of Fabrics, An Illustrated Classification.* Washington, D.C.: The Textile Museum, 1966.
D'HARCOURT, RAOUL. *Textiles of Ancient Peru and Their Techniques.* Edited by Grace G. Denny and Carolyn Osborne; translated by Sadie Brown. Seattle: University of Washington Press, 1962.
PEVSNER, NIKOLAUS. *Pioneers of Modern Design.* New York: The Museum of Modern Art, 1949.
WEIBEL, ADELE COULIN. *Two Thousand Years of Textiles.* New York: Pantheon Books, 1952.
WINGLER, HANS M. *The Bauhaus.* Cambridge, Massachusetts, and London, England: MIT PRESS, 1969.

Catalogs and Periodicals

de AMARAL, OLGA — MUROS TEJIDOS Y ARMADURAS. Catalog of the exhibition at the Museo de Arte Moderno. Bogotá, 1972.
BIENNALE INTERNATIONALE DE LA TAPISSERIE. Catalog of the exhibitions. Lausanne, 1962, 1965, 1967, 1969, 1971.
CRAFT HORIZONS. New York, November-December 1953, March-April 1969, October 1971.
DELIBERATE ENTANGLEMENTS. Catalog of the exhibition at the UCLA Art Galleries. University of California, Los Angeles, 1971.
FABRICS INTERNATIONAL. An exhibition catalog reprinted from *Craft Horizons,* New York, September-October 1961.
ROSE, BARBARA. "Crafts Ain't What They Used To Be," *New York Magazine,* March 6, 1972.
PERSPECTIEF IN TEXTIEL. Catalog of the exhibition at the Stedelijk Museum. Amsterdam, 1969.
TEXTILES U.S.A. Catalog of the exhibition at The Museum of Modern Art. New York, 1956.
THREADS OF HISTORY. Catalog of the exhibition at the American Federation of Arts. New York, 1966.
WALL HANGINGS. Catalog of the exhibition at The Museum of Modern Art. New York, 1969.

Photo Credits

AVILA, Adam   Pasadena, California   95
BEZZOLA, Leonard   Zurich, Switzerland   13, 159, 163, 164
BOEKHOFF, Jan   Amsterdam, Holland   152
BOESCH, Ferdinand   New York   73, 74, 75, 76, 77, 84, 85, 183, 272, 282
BRAUT, Snimila Marija   Zagreb, Yugoslavia   133, 134
CALVET FOTO   Barcelona, Spain   210, 211, 212, 213
CONNAISSANCE DES ARTS   Paris, France   189
CORPUS, Chris   New York   281
COOPER-HEWITT MUSEUM   New York   35
CRAFT HORIZONS   New York   221
CRANE, Tom   New York   14, 109, 110, 171
CROZE, Harvey   Bloomfield Hills, Michigan   28
CUGINI, Thomas   Zurich, Switzerland   161
DI LIBERTO, Richard   New York   286
DOVYDENES, Jonas   Chicago, Illinois   287, 289, 290, 291
DABAC, Toso   Zagreb, Yugoslavia   130, 131, 134, 135
DUSARD, Jay   Prescott, Arizona   205
EMLEN, Gay   Stony Brook, New York   112, 113
FORBERG, Charles   New York   43
FOTO STUDIO LEMAIRE   Amsterdam, Holland   154
GASPARINI, Paolo   Caracas, Venezuela   73
GRAPHIC HOUSE, Inc.   New York   40
GROSS, Richard   Los Angeles   221
HANSON, Bob   New York   75, 170, 228, 229
HARRIS, Ned   New York   21, 174
HASSEL, Paul A.   San Francisco, California   30
HAUSHERR, Rosmarie   New York   165
HOLZMAN, Marek   Warsaw, Poland   86, 201, 202, 203
HOUSEZ, David   Paris, France   2, 185, 188, 192, 193
INTERNATIONAL TEXTILES STUDIOS   Amsterdam, Holland   96, 97
IMSAND, Marcel   Lausanne, Switzerland   132
KNAPP, Tamara   So. Acworth, New Hampshire   61
KUNSTGEWERBE MUSEUM   Basel, Switzerland   19
LAGIOS, Demetre   San Francisco, California   71, 214, 215
LANDIS, Jerry   Phoenix, Arizona   204, 206, 207
LEWANDOWSKA, Emanuela   Warsaw, Poland   137, 234
LIDINGÖ, K. Bernhard   36
LÜTHI, Ursula   Zurich, Switzerland   70
MAKOWSKI, Z.   Warsaw, Poland   147, 148, 149, 151
MANOR STUDIOS   Hassocks, England   119
MATES, Robert   50
MEYER, Vincent   Paris, France   177
MORAL, Angeles   Barcelona, Spain   209
MICHELON, J.   Paris, France   184
MOUNT, Elizabeth   225
MUSEUM OF CONTEMPORARY CRAFTS   New York   51, 85, 231, 237
MUSEUM OF MODERN ART   New York   12, 18, 22, 23, 72, 176
NELSON, O.   New York   169
NORDAHL, Jan   Södertälje, Sweden   87, 90, 91, 92, 93, 94
OTTO, Jindrich   Prague, Czechoslovakia   55
PALMER, Phil   San Francisco, California   33
PELGROM, Hans   Amsterdam, Holland   247
PIETINEN, Aarne   34
PITTMAN, Don   San Francisco, California   259
PORTILLO   Madrid, Spain   59
PRICE, Clayton J.   48, 265
RIBOUD, Marc   Paris, France   190, 191
RIES, Stan   New York   65, 168, 224, 279
ROY, Ruth   Zurich, Switzerland   240
SEELY, Charles   Dedham, England   52
STEDELJK MUSEUM   Amsterdam, Holland   56, 57, 58
STERN, Faith   New York   172
STOPCZYK, Barbara   Warsaw, Poland   88
STONE & STECCATI   San Francisco, California   258, 260
SWEDEN HOUSE   Stockholm, Sweden   53
TADIC, K   Zagreb, Yugoslavia   129
VON WAGENINGEN, Ton   Amsterdam, Holland   249, 250, 252, 256, 257
WESTPHAL, Katherine   Berkeley, California   217
WILCZEK, Lech   Warsaw, Poland   54, 76, 77, 79, 82, 83, 84, 144, 145, 150, 235, 238, 239
WITLIN, Diane   Bogotá, Colombia   98, 99, 105
ZAMONSKI, Stanley   108

The authors acknowledge with thanks the use of photographs taken by the artists themselves.